Realistic
MARKETING
Strategy

Main Authors:

DINH TRAN NGOC HUY, MBA
SYLWIA Gwoździewicz, Dr.
PHAM VAN TUAN, Dr.
NGUYEN DINH TRUNG, Dr.
PHAM MINH DAT, Dr.
Nguyen Trong Diep LLD

Dinh Tran Ngoc Huy

WORKBOOK PRESS LLC
187 E Warm Springs Rd,
Suite B285, Las Vegas, NV 89119, USA

Website: https://workbookpress.com/
Hotline: 1-888-818-4856
Email: admin@workbookpress.com

Ordering Information:
Quantity sales. Special discounts are available on quantity purchases by corporations, associations, and others.
For details, contact the publisher at the address above.

ISBN-13:   978-1-954753-47-1 (Paperback Version)
                        (Digital Version)

REV. DATE: 06/23/2022

Realistic Marketing Strategy in Governance And Responses To Competitor Risks

Cases in Banking -Investment -Finance -Commerce -Tourism - Airlines -Hotels -Hardware -Medicine -Agriculture - Manufacturing -Electric & Water -Gas & Oil and Other Industries

After Global Economic Crisis (Part I)

Main Authors:
DINH TRAN NGOC HUY, MBA
SYLWIA Gwoździewicz, Dr.
PHAM VAN TUAN, Dr.
NGUYEN DINH TRUNG, Dr.
PHAM MINH DAT, Dr.

Co-Authors:
ESRA Sipahi Dongul, Dr.
PHAN ANH, Dr.
LE NGOC THANG, Dr.
TRAN THI THANH NGA, Dr.
LE THI THANH HUONG, Dr.
DO THU HUONG, Ms.
TRAN THI BICH HANG, Dr.
LE HUONG HOA, Dr.
DO THI SANG, Ms.
NGUYEN THI HANG, Dr.
NGUYEN THI PHUONG THANH, Ms
NGUYEN THUY DUNG, Ms.
NGUYEN THI HONG NHUNG, MBA
NGUYEN THU THUY, Dr.
LE NGOC NUONG, Dr.
LE THI MAI LIEN, Dr.
LE THI HAN, Ms.
LE THU HA, Dr.
PHAM THI HONG NHUNG, Ms.
NGUYEN THI PHUNG, MBA
NGUYEN THI PHUONG HONG, Dr.
NGUYEN THI THANH PHUONG, Dr.
NGUYEN THI PHUONG THAO, PhD
LE THI VIET NGA, Dr.
LE VU LINH TOAN, Master
PHAM TUAN ANH, Dr.
TA VAN THANH, Dr.
HOANG THANH HANH, Dr.
NGUYEN TIEN DUNG, Dr.
HOANG VAN LONG, Dr.
NGUYEN THU HIEN, Ms.
VU THI THU HA, Ms.
LE QUANG HIEU, Dr.
TRUONG DINH TRANG, Master
VU VIET TIEN, Master
NGUYEN VIET DUNG, Master
NGUYEN TRONG DIEP, LLD
DINH THIEN PHUC, Mr.
DINH TRAN NGOC HIEN, BSc.

About the book

So far, there are new trend in marketing in a challenging world in industry 4.0 and covid 19 effects. Hence the ideas of writing a consulting marketing book has shown up in our plan 1 year ago. Also, after publishing some corporate governance books, we realize the need to publish a marketing book in governance, which means that the theories and concepts in this book will be make our corporations and governance system and leadership stronger to encounter with risks from competitors and environment.

The book is organized into three (3) main parts:, Part I is divided into 5 Chapters And Part III consists of 5 chapters:

Part I: Theories, Practices and Perspectives in Marketing in Banking and Other Industries: Commerce-Investment-Finance-Tourism-Airlines-Hotels-Manufacturing-Hardware-Medicine-Agriculture-Electric & Water-Gas & Oil and Other **Industries**

Chapter 1: New Marketing theories and concepts in a changing world

Examples of Marketing models

(written by Dinh Tran Ngoc Huy, Tran Thi Bich Hang, Tran Thi Thanh Nga, Do Thi Sang, Bui Thi Suu, Nguyen Thi Hoa, Pham Van Tuan, Phan Anh, Pham Minh Dat, Nguyen Trong DIep, Truong DInh Trang, Vu Viet TIen, Nguyen Viet Dung)

Chapter 2: What risks affecting marketing responses from competitors

External and Global Macroeconomic Factors Affecting Marketing

(written by Dinh Tran Ngoc Huy, Nguyen Thu Thuy, Le Ngoc Nuong, Le Huong Hoa, Le Thi Mai Lien, Pham Van Tuan, Pham Minh Dat, Phan Anh, Hoang Thanh Hanh, Vu Thi Thu Ha, Dinh Tran Ngoc Hien, Nguyen Trong DIep, Vu Viet TIen, Nguyen Thi

Phuong Thao)

Chapter 3: Action Leadership in Marketing in Banking and Other Industries

Marketing in global leading firms in Various industries Further Analysis on Relation between Marketing and Leadership

(written by Dinh Tran Ngoc Huy, Esra Sipahi, Bui Thi Suu, Tran Thi Thanh Nga, Le Thi Viet Nga, Nguyen Thi Hoa, Pham Van Tuan, Pham Minh Dat, Nguyen Tien Dung, Le Thu Ha, Le Thi Mai Lien, Vu Trung Dung, Nguyen Thi Phuong Thao)

Chapter 4: Common Techniques and Tools for Marketing

The Role of Digital Technology, and IT in Marketing

(written by Dinh Tran Ngoc Huy, Tran Thi Thanh Nga, Le Thi Viet Nga, Nguyen Thi Thanh Phuong, Tran Bich Hang, Nguyen Thi Phuong Hong, Pham Van Tuan, Pham Minh Dat, Nguyen Tien Dung, Vu Trung Dung)

Chapter 5: SWOT Analysis and Conclusion Part I (written by Dinh Tran Ngoc Huy, Nguyen Thi Thanh Phuong, Le Thi Viet Nga, Le Thi Han, Pham Thi Hong Nhung, Phan Anh, Hoang Thanh Hanh, Nguyen Thi Phuong Hong, Nguyen Tien Dung)

Part II: Eleven (11) Case Studies in marketing in Banking and Various Industries: Investment-Finance-Commerce-Tourism-Airlines-Hotels-Manufacturing-Hardware-Medicine-Agriculture-Electric & Water-Gas & Oil and Other **Industries** (written by Dinh Tran Ngoc Huy)

Part III: Recommendations for Marketing in Banking and Other Industries: Investment-Finance-Commerce-Tourism-Airlines-Hotels-Manufacturing-Hardware-Medicine-Agriculture-Electric & Water-Gas

& Oil and Other **Industries**

Chapter 1 - Marketing principles and standards (written by Dinh Tran Ngoc Huy, Pham Minh Dat, Pham Van Tuan, Nguyen Thi Phuong Thanh, Nguyen Thuy Dung, Do Thu Huong, Phan Anh, Le Ngoc Thang, Dinh Tran Ngoc Hien, Truong Dinh Trang, Nguyen Viet Dung)

Chapter 2 - Recommendations for Improving Marketing in Various Industries (written by Main Author Dinh Tran Ngoc Huy, Dr Esra Sipahi, Do Thu Huong, Le Thi Thanh Huong, Pham Van Tuan and Dinh Tran Ngoc Hien)

Chapter 3- Lessons from The US, European And Asia in Marketing (written by Dinh Tran Ngoc Huy, Dr Esra Sipahi, Le Thi Thanh Huong, Nguyen Dinh Trung, Le Quang Hieu, Truong DInh TRan, Nguyen Viet Dung)

Chapter 4- E-commerce, IT and Digital Technology Suggestions to Improve Marketing (written by Dinh Tran Ngoc Huy, Nguyen Thi Phuong Thanh, Nguyen Thi Hang, Dr Esra Sipahi, Nguyen Thuy Dung, Le Quang Hieu)

Conclusion

Generally, typical following people is directly involved and relevant in this book:

CEO - CMO – CRO - Board of Directors –Executives – Non Executives - Independent Directors – Supervisory Board – Supervisory Management – Senior Administrators – Officers - Management Team – Management Board - Corporate Secretary – Compliance Officer – Marketing division - Sale division- Front office - Shareholders – Stakeholders – Employee – Company as a whole entity – Consultant and Business Compliance Officer.

The book uses some contents of same author's papers "**Management**

Issues of Tea Planting and Tea Crops in Vietnam in the Concept of Sustainable Agricultural Development – and Recommendations on Marketing 4P" which have been published in SSCI/SCIE Journal : **Tobacco Regulatory Science, Vol.7(6-1), 2021,** etc…

In this edition, the book has implemented new changes such as: Adding Appendix for a reference on marketing framework. And it also includes a short analysis on marketing principles and recommendation in part 3. Last but not least, it suggests three (3) implementation forms for marketing management activity in companies which operate and encounter with business risks, i.e business risks that are rising from their competitors.

Brief Description of Its Application

Basically the book has ten (10) immediate uses or application: 1) case studies or reference material for teaching and studying at undergraduate and Master or MBA levels or postgraduate research implications, as well as reference book and source for PhD students; 2) reading material and reference for business officers at all levels with an attention on management team, corporate leaders and directors; 3) policy and macroeconomic framework, standards, principles and guidelines for government and non-government, academic and non-academic institutions and people, or any person who is interested this continuing subjects in relation to changes in the social economic market conditions; and 4) reference material for corporate leaders, management, specialists and analysts in developing products or services or growing employee and others to serve better and wider needs of company, clients and public; 5) English reading book for economic relevant people and those who want to explore their knowledge in economics, business, management and leadership; and 6) consulting book for business, officers and training material for academic, lecturers and business people and experts; and 7) reference sources for scholars and researchers in Economics, business, management, leadership and risk and other relating fields; and 8) giving topics for discussion in seminars, conferences and round table and 9) this book as your friend during free time or vacation; and lastly 10) a gift book to the person you like. Last but not least, it may be used to train board of directors and management in various organizations.

For the purpose of case studies discussion, below are, but not limited to, among recommended case questions for appropriate Professors to use in case write-ups, class discussion, presentation, analytical paper, homework or group meeting. Moreover, trainers around the world can use this consulting book as reference for learners.

Abstract

Marketing in our new concept will have connection to firm leadership and therefore it will play a vital role to reduce failures in corporate governance system and esp, contribution to risk management system in enterprises after the global crisis and compounding impacts from Covid 19 and China-Trump commerce war.

In response to strategies of competitors, each company has to find out suitable marketing strategy. It will depend on sizes of competitors big or medium or small, then our firm will design competitive marketing plans. Big companies such as Walmart, HSBC or Alibaba even local banks or companies will identify their close competitors to deliver marketing, advertising and sale solutions to protect market share.

To some extent, marketing concepts are quite close to leadership perspectives in the company. Good leadership will require better marketing tools, models and plans. And vice versa, effective marketing and advertising channels will ensure market positioning of firms.

For global as well as local businesses, analyzing main factors that affect their marketing strategies to response to risks from competitors and to increase customer satisfaction is meaningful. Moreover, the linkage between marketing strategy efficiency and leadership position in a firm also needed to be discuss. Last but not least, specialists and researchers from manufacturing, commerce and services industries may present various viewpoints on marketing plans to respond to firm competitors.

This book plays a role both as a consulting book to use in marketing management in many kinds of business, government agencies, and as a teaching book for Professors and students (last year undergraduates and graduates/MBA/PhD). It will provide many case studies and case questions in Vietnam, and instructions for case discussion in class as well. In future, its ambition is to develop many more money international case studies for readers and students.

The concepts, theories and practices of marketing shown in the title for part one of this book: **Theories, Practices and Perspectives in Marketing in Banking and Other Industries:** Investment-Finance -Commerce-Tourism-Airlines-Hotels-   Manufacturing-Hardware-Medicine-Agriculture-Electric & Water-Gas & Oil and Other **Industries**, then, its following Case Studies and Recommendations are presented in next parts.

Although the book is suitable for developing countries, esp. It uses cases from Vietnam and US market, its theories, standards and principles can be applied for various relating organizations in other countries and markets, in the context of compounding impacts from Covid 19 and China-US commerce war.

Also, though this book is written for banks and other industries including tourism, airlines and hotels, medicine, real estate and retail, manufacturing, technology and renewable energy firms, most of other companies and government-related bodies can also see implications for their policies and practices in this version. This is another goal of this book presence.

To contribute to build a better marketing policies in Viet nam and emerging markets context, esp. the above industries, we divide the book into three (3) sessions in which session two (2) presents our case studies on marketing in specific industries, then suggestions and general principles will be recommended in session three.

About the Main Author

Mr. Dinh Tran Ngoc Huy born in 1980, currently a PhD candidate with about 450 articles published in prestigous Intl. Journals (ISI, Scopus,…), in Finance and Management field. He teaches many courses: English (Cambridge), Corporate Finance, Leadership, Risk management, Commercial Bank, Principles of Banking, Business Communication, etc…He also held an MBA in Intl. Management from Graduate School of International Management, International U of Japan from 2005-2007 with full ADB scholarship. He used to be an exchange MBA student at Arhus business school, Denmark and at Tuck school of business, Dartmouth College, USA, in 2006. In previous years, 1998-2002, he got a Bachelor of Economics from Banking University in Ho Chi Minh city where he received partial tuition scholarship. In 2007, He and his colleagues have presentation at Urasa Conference, Japan(www.iuj.ac.jp/platform/pdf/s7-2.pdf). In 2010, he received full IT scholarship at SKT Telecom IT training centre, Viet Nam and full Master scholarship for MSc in International Banking and Finance from Lingnan University, Hong Kong. From 2010 to 2012, he is a member of Royal Journal in the UK. He also served as Guest editor for Springer, Elsevier in recent year.

Among his papers is "Should SA Tour, a Singapore travel company, uses external financing to expand MICE business in China and Singapore markets", accepted at the 1st International Conference on Business and Management placed in Turkey. Another paper "A Set of Limited Asian Pacific Corporate Governance standards After Financial Crisis" is accepted for the 36th Annual Economic & Business Historical Society Conference in Columbus, Ohio, USA in Jan 2011 and at the Advances in Business-Related Scientific Research Conference 2011, Italy. Next paper "Corporate Restructuring Under Holding Company Structure – NTT Case" with his IUJ's group is accepted for presentation at International Conference on Social Science and Humanity – ICSSH 2011, Singapore. His recent paper series of "Corporate governance standards" are posted on various e-journals such as: Corporate Finance:

Governance, Corporate Control & Organization eJournal, International Corporate Finance eJournal, IO: Firm Structure, Purpose, Organization & Contracting eJournal, Organizations & Markets: The Firm as a Nexus of Contracts (Boundaries of the Firm) eJournal and Cognitive Social Science eJournal.

While his study is in overseas, mostly his jobs are in Viet Nam. He used to work for several companies such as: BIDV (Bank for Investment and Development of Viet Nam), Citibank-Viet Nam, and Saigon Commercial Bank-Viet Nam where he worked in Risk and ISO department. Besides, he used to be Visiting Finance lecturer at University of Economics, Hung Vuong, IT and Van Lang University, Ho Chi Minh city. He took several trips to Itochu Group, Japan and Deutsche Bank AG, Japan in 2007. In 2008, he received an ISO 9001:2008 Lead Auditor Certificate from GIC, UK, as well as a SMEs Management Assessment Certificate from Asian Productivity Org, Japan. Before 2005, he held a Certificate for Modern Banking training by Professor Vilanova, Toulouse University, France.

In April 2011, his paper is accepted both the 1st Intl Conference on Business and Management, Turkey and at the 36th Economic and Historical Business Society Conference, Ohio, USA. And his first publication is the book title "The Backbone of Corporate Governance Standards Around The World : Case Studies and Analysis, First Edition" in Jan 2011.

Visit his personal information at: www.dinhslife.blogspot.com / www.dinhtranngochuy.com and welcome any email to dtnhuy2010@gmail.com. One of his ambitions is developing the book into more detailed chapters by cooperating with many experienced graduate lecturers and Professors.

2nd Co-Main Author

Dr. Sylwia Gwozdziewicz is an experienced senior lecturer and has been teaching in the field of Cyber technology, Cyber criminal, Cyber security policy in organizations, etc. in Poland. She is Editor In Chief of several reputable International Journals and published some Polish and international books.

She has been teaching at 4 universities in Poland. She is in charge of contents relevant to cyber security and risk management in this book

Roles:

Assistant Professor, Faculty of Administration and National Security, The Jacob of Paradies University in Gorzow Wielkopolski / Poland

President, International Institute of Innovation «Science-Education-Development» in Warsaw/ Poland

Email: sylwiagwozdziewicz@gmail.com

3rd Co-Author

Dr. Esra Sipahi graduated from Istanbul Gelisim University business administration doctorate program. Her areas of expertise are data analysis, management and organization, and emotional analysis. She is currently working in the Ministry of National Education, Privacy Office.

Dr. Esra SİPAHİ is a SEO Specialist. Within her studies, she had an opportunity to develop her knowledge about these SEO areas. Also she is an a editor an academic journal. https://issjournal.com

4th Co-Main Author

Dr Pham Van Tuan currently working as Vice Dean (Marketing Faculty) at National Economics University (NEU) Hanoi Vietnam. He has published many articles in reputable international journals.He did Consulting for some domestic and foreign companies on building distribution channels, business activities, administration, ... Main research directions: B2B and B2C consumer behavior, distribution channel management, Digital Marketing Specialized consulting in pharmaceutical and medical fields; Paper reviewer for Elsevier.

5th Co- Main Author

Dr Nguyen Dinh Trung currently working at National Economics University (NEU) Vietnam. He has published many articles in reputable international journals.

Email: trungnd@neu.edu.vn

6th Co-Main Author

Dr. Pham Minh Dat, currently the Sectretary of Editorial Office of the Journal of Trade Science - Thuongmai University, Hanoi, Vietnam. He has published many articles in reputable international journals

His favorite research areas include: Business Administration, Risk Management, Marketing Managemant and International Trade.

Thuongmai University

Email: minhdat@tmu.edu.vn

7th Co-Author

Ms. Do Thi Sang, teaching at Kindergarten in Dist 7 , HCM city Vietnam. She is an experienced kid instructor and a close friend of Main author Dinh Tran Ngoc Huy.

Email: dothi0639@gmail.com

8th Co-Author

Ms Nguyen Thi Phuong Thanh, Master degree in Electronics Engineering, currently working at Thai Nguyen University of Information Technology and Communications, Thai Nguyen, Vietnam. Her specialized area is Computer electronics, handling computer problems, network, data transmission system, technical solutions for computers, designing electronic circuits using microprocessors or microcontrollers, etc.

9th Co-Author

Ms Le Ngoc Nuong, PhD, currently working at Faculty of Management - Economic Law, University of Economics and Business Administration (TUEBA), Thai Nguyen University Vietnam.

She has published book chapters in Finance and articles in reputable International journals.

10th Co-Author

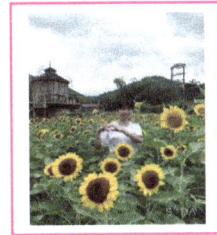

Ms. Nguyen Thu Thuy, PhD, currently working at Facuty of Economics, University of Economics and Business Administration (TUEBA), Thai Nguyen University (TNU) Vietnam. She has published many articles in reputable national and international journals.

11th Co-Author

Ms Nguyen Thuy Dung, Master, currently working at University of Information Technology and Communications, Thai Nguyen, Vietnam

Email: ntdung.cndt@ictu.edu.vn

12nd Co-Author

Dr Nguyen Thi Phuong Hong, currently working at University of Economics Ho Chi Minh city, Vietnam. She has published many articles in reputable national and international journals.

Email: hongntp@ueh.edu.vn

13rd Co-Author

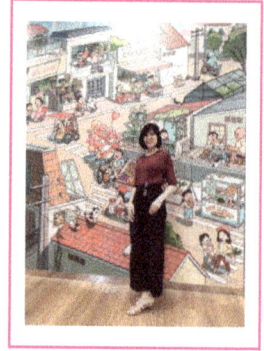

Ms Le Thi Han, Master, currently working at Banking University of Ho Chi Minh city, Vietnam. She has published books and articles in reputable journals.

Email: hanlt@buh.edu.vn

14th Co-Author

Ms Pham Thi Hong Nhung, Master, PhD candidate at Banking University of HCM city, currently working at Ho Chi Minh College of Economics, Vietnam. She has published books and articles in reputable journals.

15th Co-Author

Dr. Ta Van Thanh, currently working at University of Finance-Marketing (UFM), Vietnam. He has published many articles in reputable international journals

Email:tvthanh@ufm.edu.vn

16th Co-Author

Dr. Pham Tuan Anh, currently working at Thuongmai University Vietnam. He has published many books and articles in reputable international journals.

Head
Department of Financial Management
Thuongmai University

Email: phamtuananh@tmu.edu.vn

17th Co- Main Author

Dr. Hoang Thanh Hanh, currently working at Academy of Finance, Vietnam. He has published many articles in reputable international journals. His research interests are finance, accounting, economics.

Email: hoangthanhhanh@hvtc.edu.vn

18th Co-Author

Dr. Phan Anh - Manager of Scientific division, Banking Academy, Hanoi Vietnam. He has published many articles in reputable international journals

Research fields: Banking and Finance

Email: : phananh@hvnh.edu.vn

19th Co-Author

Dr. Le Ngoc Thang - currently working as lecturer at Law Faculty, Banking Academy, Hanoi Vietnam. He has published many articles in reputable international journals

Research fields: Law, Banking

Email: thangln@hvnh.edu.vn

20th Co-Author

Dr. Le Thi Viet Nga - Lecturer at Thuongmai University, Hanoi Vietnam. She has published many articles in reputable international journals

Research fields: International business

Email: : vietngale@tmu.edu.vn

21ˢᵗ *Co-Author*

Dr. Nguyen Thi Hang

Faculty of Economic Information Systems

University of Information and Communication Technology, Thai Nguyen, Vietnam

E-mail: nthang@ictu.edu.vn or nthang100483@gmail.com

22ⁿᵈ *Co-Author*

Dr. Le Thi Mai Lien

She current working as teacher/lecturer at Cat Linh Secondary School, Dong Da, Hanoi. She has published many good articles in Scopus Journals.

F-mail: mailienk19@gmail.com

23ʳᵈ *Co-Author*

Dr. Le Huong Hoa

She currently working as lecturer at Faculty of Foreign Languages and Informatics, The People's Police University, Vietnam

She has published many good articles in Scopus Journals.

E-mail: hoahuongle@yahoo.com

24th Co-Author

MBA. Nguyen Thi Hong Nhung

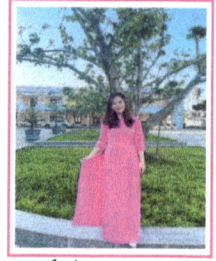

She has been working as lecturer at University of Finance and Accountancy, Vietnam. She published many good articles in Scopus Journals.

E-mail: nguyenthihongnhung@tckt.edu.vn

25th Co-Author

MBA. Nguyen Thi Phung

She has been working as lecturer at University of Finance and Accountancy, Vietnam. She has published many good articles in Scopus Journals.

E-mail: nguyenthiphung@tckt.edu.vn

26th Co-Author

Dr. Nguyen Tien Dung - Lecturer at Hanoi University of Science and Technology (HUST), Vietnam. He has published many articles in reputable international journals

Research fields: Banking, Management, Marketing

Email: : dung.nguyentien3@hust.edu.vn

27th Co-Author

Dr Tran Thi Thanh Nga currently working at University of Finance-Marketing, HCMC Vietnam. She has published many articles in reputable international journals.

Email: thanhngatcnh@gmail.com

28th Co-Author

Ms. Nguyen Thu Hien, currently working at Faculty of Information Technology, University of Economics - Technology for Industries. Her areas: handling computer problems, computer network, data transmission system, etc…

Email: nthien@uneti.edu.vn

29th Co-Author

Mr Dinh Thien Phuc, he is the son of main author Dinh Tran Ngoc Huy.

He is currently living with his family at Binh Tan dist, HCM city Vietnam.

30th Co-Author

Mrs Do Thu Huong, currently working at Dai Nam University, Vietnam. She has published many articles in reputable international journals.

Email: huongdt@dainam.edu.vn

31st Co-Author

Mrs Tran Thi Bich Hang, currently working at Thuongmai University, Hanoi Vietnam. She has published many articles in reputable international journals.

Email: tranbichhang@tmu.edu.vn

32nd Co-Author

Mrs Nguyen Thi Thanh Phuong, currently working at Thuongmai University, Hanoi Vietnam. She has published many articles in reputable international journals.

Email: phuong.nt@tmu.edu.vn

33rd Co-Author

Mrs Le Thi Thanh Huong, currently working as Vice Rector at Dai Nam University, Hanoi Vietnam. She has published many articles in reputable international journals.

Email: lethanhhuong@dainam.edu.vn

34th Co-Author

PhD Hoang Van Long, currently working at University of Law in HCM city. Vietnam. He has published many articles in reputable international journals.

Email: hvlong@hcmlaw.edu.vn

35th Co-Author

Ms. Le Thu Ha, Doctor of Public Management , currently working at TNU - University of Economics and Business Administration

Email: lethuha.cva@gmail.com

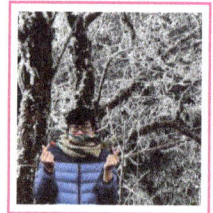

36th Co-Author

Master. Trung-Hieu Le, currently working at Dai Nam University , Vietnam. He has published many articles in reputable international journals.

Email: hieult@dainam.edu.vn

37th Co-Author

MBA Vo Kim Nhan, teaching at Tien Giang University, majoring in Business Administration and International Business, is a full-time PhD student at the University of Economics Ho Chi Minh City. She studied science and teaching in the field of international business, tourism management, research econometric tools in economics such as PLS-SEM, SPSS, AMOS.

Email: vokimnhan@gmail.com

38th Co-Author

Mrs Le Thi Mai Huong currently work at HCMC University of Technology and Education, Ho Chi Minh City, Viet Nam.

She has published good articles in reputable journals.

Email: maihuongbd@gmail.com

39th Co-Author

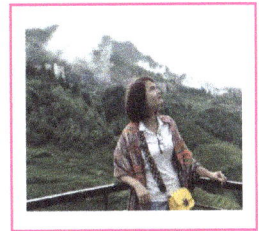

Ms Ly Thu Trang, Master, currently working at University of Information Technology and Communications, Thai Nguyen Vietnam.

Email: tranglt@ictu.edu.vn

40th Co-Author

Ms. Vu Thi Thu Ha

She current working at Postgraduate Faculty, Banking University HCM city Vietnam. She has published many good articles and conference proceedings.

E-mail: havtt@buh.edu.vn

41st Co-Author

Mr Nguyen Viet Dung, Master, currently working as lecturer at PTIT University, Hanoi Vietnam. He has published many articles in reputable journals.

Email: dungnv@ptit.edu.vn

42nd Co-Author

Mr Le Quang Hieu, PhD currently working as lecturer/Faculty head at Hong Duc University, Thanh Hoa Vietnam. He has published many articles in reputable journals.

Email: lequanghieu@hdu.edu.vn

43rd Co-Author

Mr Truong Dinh Trang, Master, currently working as lecturer at PTIT University Hanoi Vietnam. He has published many articles in reputable journals.

Email: truongtrang.dig@gmail.com

44th Co-Author

Mr Vu Viet Tien, Master, currently working as lecturer at PTIT University Hanoi Vietnam. He has published many articles in reputable journals.

Email: tienvu@ptit.edu.vn

45th Co-Author

Mr Nguyen Trong Diep, LLD, currently working as lecturer at School of Law, Vietnam National University Hanoi Vietnam. He has published many articles in reputable journals.

Email: dieptrongnguyenvnu@gmail.com

46th Co-Author

Ms Nguyen Thi Phuong Thao, PhD, currently working as lecturer at DaLat University, Lam Dong Vietnam. She has published many articles in reputable journals.

Email: thaonguyendhdl@gmail.com

47th Co-Author

Ms Le Vu Linh Toan, Master, currently working as lecturer at Van Lang University, HCM city Vietnam. She has published many articles in reputable journals.

Email: toan.lvl@vlu.edu.vn

48th Co-Author

Ms Bui Thi Suu, Master, currently working as lecturer at Tay Bac University, Son La Vietnam. She has published many articles in reputable journals.

Email: buithisuu@utb.edu.vn

49th Co-Author

Mr Dinh Tran Ngoc Hien born in 1986, used to be an Apprentice at P&G Vietnam (2010) and living in Ho Chi Minh city at the present time, is the experienced Sale Manager for Qubetrix Singapore Co., who is the co-author of the book "Modern International Corporate Governance Principles and Models After Global Economic Crisis". He graduated from Technical University Ho Chi Minh city, with his thesis " Smart House Solution".

Acknowledgement

After our eight (8) previous books (on Action Leadership, Risk management, Realistic Financial management, Macroeconomics, Global Modern corporate governance principles and models) have been published in Singapore, UK, US and distributed worldwide via www. amazon.com, eBay, Walmart, etc. this is an opportunity to look at new marketing concepts in banking and other industries.

One of this book's scopes is to provide CEOs, CMOs, CFO, CRO, CTO, marketing and sale team, and business consultants of relevant companies with proper marketing management matters.

I would like to take this opportunity to express my warm thanks to Dr. Yea-Mow Chen and Dr. Yu Hai-Chin at Chung Yuan Christian University for class lectures, Dr. Borucki at Temple University, also my ex-Corporate Governance sensei, Dr. Shingo Takahashi, sensei Jay and sensei Xing at International University of Japan. My warm and special thanks for Prof. Howell, Prof. French, Prof. Karin, Prof Ella and all other Professors at Amos Tuck school of business and Arhus business school during MBA exchange program. Also my sincere thanks are for Jade, Jenny Tucker, Darcey, Brittany W. and the editorial office, for their helpful work during my research. And this is also my chance to send special thanks to my ex-Executives, Mr. Tran Van Vinh at BIDV-HCM City, Mr. Le Dang Xu at COFICO – HCM city, Ex-GD. Pham Anh Dung, Nguyen The Linh and his colleagues at SCB-HCM city, as well as Mr. Nguyen Ba Vuong, Dinh Ngoc Son, Nguyen Quoc Sy and colleagues at WTB- HCM city, Viet Nam. I also would like to express warm thanks to the help of Dr. Nguyen Van Ha, Dr. Ngo Huong, Dr. Ho Dieu, Dr. Nguyen Thi Nhung, Dr.Nguyen Ngoc Thach, Dr. Bui Dieu Anh, Dr. Le Dinh Hac and my Lecturers at Banking Universities – HCM city, as well as SKT Telecom Viet Nam Board.

Lastly, thank you very much with special emotion for my family, mother Tran Thi Manh and father Dinh Van Tai, my grandmothers Mrs Man and Mrs Ut, uncles, aunts and relatives, my niece Samiel Dan Thu, my son Dinh Thien Phuc, my colleagues, officers, and brother Dinh Tran Ngoc

Hien in assisting convenient conditions for this edition. And we would like, also, to show great thanks to our uncle, business consultant Tran Huy Phuoc, for their strong support this publication as well as Dr.Esra Sipahi, Dr.Sylwia G. and editorial office , for their in-need help.

Introduction

Further researches in marketing will indicate that New and Realistic Marketing Perspectives in Banks, Commerce, Manufacturing and Other sectors After The Global Economic Crisis is one of crucial factors making better and stronger Modern Corporate Governance.

Not paying attention enough to marketing our firms will lose clients and profits. That's why New Marketing Perspectives and Concepts becomes one of vital issues of corporate governance.

Its Theories and Practices, Standards and principles might be applied in other industries and economic sectors to help better business performance and lasting client relationship.

CEO, CMO, CFO, and Board and Chair and Management need to own knowledge of Marketing, in their specific field as well as in general. For senior management, they need to know marketing in business operation as well as in strategy levels.

This book is not just about theories and history, but it is about practical and as a kind of consulting marketing book for all those who could read, interested in Marketing, understand and use it in their field in many sectors, for academic and business.

Reading concepts about marketing, case studies is practical, and coming to conclusions and recommendations is subjective ideas of authors, while readers can suggest their own recommendations with our implications.

Thanks very much everyone for giving comment on it!

CONTENTS

About the book

Brief Description of Its Application

About the author

Acknowledgement

Abstract

Part I: Theories, Practices and Perspectives in Marketing in Banking and Other Industries: Investment-Finance-Commerce-Tourism-Airlines-Hotels-Manufacturing-Hardware-Medicine -Agriculture-Electric & Water -Gas & Oil and Other **Industries**

Chapter 1: New Marketing theories and concepts in a changing world

1. New Marketing theories and concepts in a changing world
2. Types of Marketing
3. Examples of Marketing models
4. Factors influencing marketing activities

Chapter 2: What risks affecting marketing responses from competitors

5. What risks affecting marketing responses from competitors
6. External and Global Macroeconomic Factors Affecting Marketing
7. The Compounding Impacts of Covid 19 and China-Trump Commerce War

Chapter 3: **Action Leadership in Marketing in Banking and Other Industries**

8. Roles of Marketing in Banking

9. Marketing responding to competitors in Manufacturing, Commerce vs. Services fields

10. Marketing in global leading firms in Various industries

11. Extra Analysis of Strengths and Weaknesses in Vietnam Manufacturing, Technology and Renewable Energy Sectors

12. Further Analysis on Relation between Marketing and Leadership

Chapter 4: **Common Techniques and Tools for Marketing**

13. Common Techniques and Tools for Marketing

14. Several key indices, measurements and KPIs in marketing management activities of firms

15. The Role of Digital Technology, and IT in Marketing

16. Benefits Vs. Cost of Effective Marketing Strategy

CONTENTS *(cont.)*

Abstract

Marketing strategy in corporate governance is rising as one of hottest issues since global crisis 2007-2009, esp. After corporate scandals and failures as well as much effects from covid 19 pandemic. The financial crisis in 1997-1999 and 2007-2009 and the recent covid 19 epidemic has cut global supply chain and lead to failures in corporate governance system and created more challenges for marketing activities in enterprises.

This book plays a role both as a consulting marketing book to use in many kinds of business and as a teaching book for Professors and students (last year undergraduates and graduates/MBA/PhD). It will provide many case studies and case questions in Vietnam, and instructions for case discussion in class as well. In future, its ambition is developing more many international case studies for readers and students. And this is a kind of revisiting marketing strategy in new perspectives and concepts of corporate governance, risk management, standards, principles, implementation forms as well as marketing strategy control and PDCA marketing applied.

The recent marketing trend is affected by and shown in the title for part one of this book: Theories, Practices and Perspectives in Marketing in Banking and Other Industries, then, its following Case Studies and Practices are presented in next parts.

Although the book is suitable for developing countries, esp. It uses cases from Vietnam market, its theories and principles can be applied for various organizations in other countries and markets.

Also, though this book is written for banks and financial service, commerce, manufacturing and tourism firms, most of other companies can also see implications for their policies and practices in this version. This is another goal of this book presence.

To contribute to build a better marketing strategy and activities in Viet nam enterprises, esp. Banks and financial service firms, we divide the book into three (3) sessions in which session two (2) presents our findings on Vietnam banks and financial service industry and other sectors and general principles will be recommended in session three.

Part One

Theories, Practices and Perspectives in Marketing in Banking and Other Industries: Investment-Finance-Commerce-Tourism-Airlines-Hotels-Manufacturing-Hardware -Medicine-Agriculture-Electric & Water -Gas & Oil and Other **Industries**

The contents are presented in the following order:

Chapter One

New Marketing theories and concepts in a changing world

Chapter Two

What risks affecting marketing responses from competitors

Chapter Three

Action Leadership in Marketing in Banking and Other Industries

Chapter Four

Common Techniques and Tools for Marketing

Chapter Five

SWOT Analysis and Conclusion Part I

Chapter One

New Marketing theories and concepts in a changing world

1. New Marketing theories and concepts in a changing world

In an active world today, marketing has activities to deal with risks rising from competitors of our firms which under this pressure our market share can be shortened. Therefore, marketing not only created a desire or demand in clients but also it will help to enhance brand of our firms or products/services and maintain clients relationship through a process of linking with customer services and satisfying their demand. In our definition, marketing activities can take place before-during-and after sale activities and it will enable to boost sales as well as help corporate governance and leadership stronger (so this is also our new conceptual point).

Marketing conceptual theories in developed countries and impacts on businesses:

First, Marketing refers to activities a company undertakes to promote the buying or selling of a product or service. Marketing includes advertising, selling, and delivering products to consumers or other businesses. Some marketing is done by affiliates on behalf of a company (source: investopedia.com, access date 8/1/2022)

Second, Marketing is the process of exploring, creating, and delivering value to meet the needs of a target market in terms of goods and services;potentially including selection of a target audience; selection of certain attributes or themes to emphasize in advertising; operation of advertising campaigns; attendance at trade shows and public events; design of products and packaging attractive to buyers; defining the terms of sale, such as price, discounts, warranty, and return policy; product placement in media or with people believed to influence the buying habits of others; agreements with retailers, wholesale distributors, or resellers; and attempts to create awareness of, loyalty to, and positive feelings about a brand. Marketing is typically done by the seller, typically a retailer or manufacturer. Sometimes tasks are contracted to a dedicated marketing firm or advertising agency. More rarely, a trade association or government agency (such as the Agricultural Marketing Service) advertises on behalf of an entire industry or locality, often a specific type of food, food from a specific area, or a city or region as a tourism destination. (source: wikipedia.org, access date 8/1/2022).

And third, as defined by the American Marketing Association (AMA) as «the activity, set of institutions, and processes for creating, communicating, delivering, and exchanging offerings that have value for customers, clients, partners, and society at large».Then the 2008 definition with the AMA's 1935 version: "Marketing is the performance of business activities that direct the flow of goods, and services from producers to consumers". The newer definition highlights the increased prominence of other stakeholders in the new conception of marketing.

As Contreras and Ramos (2015) mentioned: one of the definitions provided by a CEO was: "I have always defined marketing as brand management plus sales" (Webster et al., 2005, p. 36). These senior officers also noted that marketing has moved from the advertising and merchandising divisions to be part of the sales and service divisions; in fact, some marketing executives tended to equate marketing with sales.

Investopedia defines marketing strategy: A marketing strategy refers to a business's overall game plan for reaching prospective consumers and turning them into customers of their products or services. A marketing strategy contains the company's value proposition, key brand messaging, data on target customer demographics, and other high-level elements. A thorough marketing strategy covers «the four Ps" of marketing—product, price, place, and promotion.

In fact in traditional business people know that 4P meanings are vital for firm survival. Beside, they can choose a kind of marketing strategy such as:

Undifferentiated marketing strategy: Businesses consider all consumers in the market as the target market. Not paying attention to market segments

Differentiated Marketing Strategy: A company selects several segments as its target market. There is market segmentation and potential competitor analysis.

Concentrated marketing strategy: Enterprises choose only the best segment as the target market this is single market - targeted, while niche marketing strategy may focus on multiple target markets/ clients.

We see in the below figure our marketing concept from competition approach, in our views, this affects better corporate governance system: The below figure also shows marketing will interact with customer service to serve target clients and keep customer relationship.

Beside, it also define marketing from competitor risk point of view, and may different from other traditional definitions of marketing.

The channels can be either online or offline.

Moreover, why we put in the fig: Promotion and advertising in separate places? Promotion will be a superset concept that consist of direct marketing, personal selling, advertising and PR and may include forms such as coupons, discount, trial offers, free distribution, and services that value added, while advertising is a subset with means such as TVs, radio, billboards, pamphlets, poster, magazines, etc.

Figure 1 - What is Marketing

(source: made by authors)

2. Types of Marketing

Marketing can be categorized into: internet marketing, social media marketing (Facebook, Zalo, Instagram, Twitter, Linkedn, TikTok, Snapchat, etc.), Email marketing, or Print marketing, Content marketing and Influencing marketing. So here we do not define again traditional marketing types for example B2B or B2C and we imply that readers need to know about these.

Among them, Internet marketing is a good channel esp. during covid 19 pandemic as it will help us to sell products and services from long distances (at home, at coffee shop, or any places with internet, etc.). Nowadays with search engine tools and google, clients will get interested in our products/services.

And whereas content marketing will be conducted under various flexible forms of publishing contents and advertisements (blog, web, TV, newspapers, magazines, slides, discussion papers, other channels…), influencing marketing will use influencers or figures - those who are famous and have power on audiences. These marketing types can help us to express products/services light to potential clients.

3. Examples of Marketing models

First model: Marketing 4P: for instance, we see in most of banking/ finance or tourism/airlines/hotels or commerce/retail/computer and other sectors, expressed in below table:

Table 1- Model 4P

Price	Product
- We can decide pricing based on client psychology or cost-based pricing or competitor-based pricing	- We can compare substitutes (products) to fulfill market demand
Place	Promotion
- We choose online of offline channels	- Advertising, public relations and sponsorship

(source: author add analysis)

Then it is developed into 7Ps model by adding:

- **Process**: The operations behind the business, such as product delivery, customer service, research and development, etc.

- **Physical evidence**: The product experience and what this looks like (offline and online stores, staff experience, customer experience, packaging, etc.)

- **People:** staff involved

Second model: Marketing will connect to product life cycle (PLC) in below figure:

Figure 2 - PLC

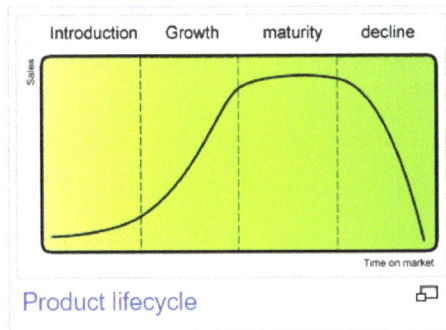

Product lifecycle

Whereas more advertising made in initial phase, more communication and marketing activities take place during growth and maturity to maintain and boost sales and during decline phase, we need to maintain good relationship with our clients in order to prepare new product development.

Third model: Forrester 4Is model

Figure 3- Forrester model with 4 components

INVOLVEMENT	INTERACTION	INTIMACY	INFLUENCE
What To Track			
• Site visits • Time spent • Pages viewed • Search keywords • Navigation paths • Site logins	• Contributed comments to blogs • Quantity/frequency of written reviews, blog comments, forum discussions, and UGC	• Sentiment tracking on third-party sites (blogs, reviews, forums, etc.) • Sentiment tracking of internal customer contributions • Opinions expressed in customer service calls	• Net Promoter (NP) score • Product/service satisfaction ratings • Brand affinity • Content forwarded to friends • Posts on high-profile blogs
How To Track			
• Web analytics	• eCommerce platforms • Social media platforms	• Brand monitoring • Customer service calls • Surveys	• Brand monitoring • Customer service calls • Surveys

(source: Forrester research, Inc.

Note: **Intimacy** *delves into the emotions behind the interaction and* *includes sentiment tracking and customer service calls or surveys to understand behavior better)*

So the values of marketing strategy is to build and enhance our brand loyalty.

Beside, a marketing campaign which is effective will consist of many actions: online video, advertisement, radio, postcard, outdoor advertising, partner relation, etc. Successful marketing campaigns we can see examples of Facebook, Linkekln, Google, Coca Cola, Huyndai, Honda, etc. And another successful example is Gucci a famous fashion brand - they used Wechat as effective tool to advertise and enter Chinese market. Last but not least, Procter & Gamble has used stories of Mum behind Olympic athletes and their success to win audience hearts.

Finally, marketing plays a vital role in promoting export-import. Ejramie t al (2016) stated The results of study signify that the marketing potentials affect on competitive advantage of the importer company and at the same time marketing capability impacts on performance of importation company while competitive advantage might affect on performance of importation companies.

4. Factors influencing marketing activities

First, that is the business environment: PEST (political-economic-social-technological) these factors. Economic situation and income of the market or population will affect our pricing strategies. Also, the loyalty of clients (might change) also affect our marketing strategy and making decision to deliver our products/services to new markets.

Second, it is the competition environment and competitor factor. Our firms need differentiate strategies in delivering products and services to the market to win market shares, compared to other bigger competitors.

Third, this is the client psychology during buying or selling products and services. When clients feel they are in real need of our products, with proper communication, then they will buy our products. The art of marketing is lying on communication with clients to make them feel good and trust our products.

Fourth is the leadership and corporate governance factors. Leaders can give opinions or comments on marketing, pricing, new products, promotion plans.

Fifth factor is the senior marketing manager or CMO experiences. Throughout their years of practice and works, these seniors will understand values of marketing strategies and can put into actions their marketing plans at the right time to attract clients.

Six factor will be market research because without it, marketing will have no direction to go. A detailed market research can disclose which market segment is attractive for our firms to attack and spend more resources.

Seven factor is advertising campaign. A good advertising program in proper channel will attract more clients in need.

Eight factor is public relations. In fact, with stronger network with public, we can deliver more messages about our products/services and our social responsibility programs will drive or affect public trust.

Chapter Two

What risks affecting marketing responses from competitors

5. What risks affecting marketing responses from competitors

Firstly, this is risks from substitutes for our products/services. This is a kind of marketing risk that can put a threat on companies business results, profits and market share. Newly established competitors will make difficulties for our companies and it is hard for us to increase price or reduce costs.

Secondly, The size of competitors might affect to some extent, to our business risks. Bigger size of competitors will put competitive threats on professional, business environment, data privacy and security, professional staff, etc. Smaller size of competitor will crate more convenient channels in delivering products, for ex.

Thirdly, the slower our firm responds to competitor risk, the worse it harms our profits. This is risk of business results and opportunities lost.

Fourthly, pricing risk happens when our prices are not competitive than competitors and clients may compare the better.

Last but not least, we consider a concept of perceived risk of clients, which is risk perception of clients about consequences after buying products. It can be reduced in import-export when foreign countries or importers need source of goods.

Figure 4- Perceive risk

Performance	Will the product or service perform to expectations?
Financial	Is the product or service worth the price charged?
Opportunity/time	Will there be associated opportunity costs if the product or service fails?
Safety	Is the product or service safe to use? Does it pose a threat to the health or the environment?
Social	How will the product or service be perceived in a social context?
Psychological	Does it fit the personality and values of the customer?

(source: Martin Roll, 2006)

Theories related to competition analysis

First of all, we need to identify competitors and substitutes, their business or marketing targets in markets.

To make assessment on our competitors we need to analyze their capabilities in management, organization, human resource, in entering markets, 5-force models of Porter, barriers to enter such as scale-technology, production and finance and in new product research. Even their public and social relation also needed to assess.

Then from their strengths and weaknesses and marketing characteristics, our firm can have suitable responses to enter and expand markets.

Understanding our competitors and substitutes will help our firms to identify gap in the markets, catch the markets and set up suitable better strategies to expand markets. Moreover, from this, we can make suggestions on our firm ability to create market trend.

Additionally, there is positive impact on competitive advantage of our firms from competitors' threats and risks that put more pressure on improving marketing strategies and plans as well as product development.

Moreover, competitor risk is a component of marketing intelligence. Marketing intelligence is the systematic collection and analysis of publicly available information about consumers, competitors, and developments in the marketplace (Kotler & Armstrong, 2013).

Last but not least, it will help us to know potential dangers from competitors in order to give out risk management strategies in marketing for proper prevention actions. In order to know that, our firm need to analyze current capabilities of competitors and their ability to reach future targets and their influence within the industry.

There are 2 possibilities of our firms after analyzing competitors: first we can give new marketing strategies and new responses, second or firm can modify existing marketing strategies for better.

For example, Vinaphone in Vietnam market will face risks from their competitors such as Viettel and Mobifone, Vietnamobile, etc. Which might lead to reduction in market share. Therefore, Vinaphone need to improve customer services, add more values to products, offer various products, expand rural markets, many payment methods, shorten network stucking time, etc.

Hence, we see competitor risk analysis and risk management are necessary in marketing strategy and plans because it will help firms to reduce operational risk, market risk, and then serve clients better. This is the relationship between risk management and marketing strategy.

From competitor analysis, our marketing can make recommendations for competitive strategy. For instance, we can choose product differentiation strategy to allow us to have higher premium pricing.

Or we can focus on technology and supply chain relationship to have low pricing strategy and catch the medium market. In addition, our firm can choose focus strategy with unique products/services offering to clients.

6. External and Global Macroeconomic Factors Affecting Marketing

The more economic growth and the more industrial manufacturing development, the more marketing activities.

Next is interest rate and exchange rate. Exchange rate increases or declines will affect trade balance, export -import of goods so it will influence on marketing and sales activities of corporations.

Lending interest rates go up or go down also affect the size of loans and lending need of companies to expand their business operation and branches, so it also affect marketing and sale strategy.

Also the relationship between supply chain sources and marketing and sale strategy also vital for businesses because cheaper supply resources will cause more competitive selling products price. That's why many corporations try to find out and control more supply resources (also including material and human resources).

Next is legal framework and regulation within specific industry will affect on the expansion plans of corporations in that sector so put an impact on market and marketing plans of firms.

Last but not least, technology and innovation will create more business opportunities (looking at Wechat, Facebook, Google, Instagram, Zalo, etc. And robotics, AI, IoTs, ICT, etc. as examples). These technology innovations will influence not only on new methods of communicating with clients but also new methods of producing and distributing goods and services.

Finally, we see effects of other factors such as tax policy, income per capita, and government expenditures: these will affect market demand of goods and products and profits of individuals and firms, so will influence their marketing plans and market research budget. Moreover, business ethics and CSR - corporate social responsibility are also considered as new factors that affect on corporation image and marketing and branding strategy.

And Priporas et al (2020) found out that respondents hold a strong scepticism toward CRM campaigns and they are more negative toward the CRM campaigns initiated by foreign enterprises as compared to the domestic ones. This can be attributed to ethnocentrism, or even antipathy or animosity towards foreign companies due to crisis. Furthermore, results reveal that the political and legal elements of the macro-environment have an impact on consumer scepticism towards CRM campaigns, while the impact of the economic crisis itself did not seem to be equally significant.

7. The Compounding Impacts of Covid 19 and China-Trump Commerce War

During covid 19, many production activities have been interrupted and global supply chain has been cut. Therefore, there are big effects on marketing activities and people tend to use online and digital marketing much more.

Because the global economic growth is slow down and covid impacts, many more home delivery and shopping online have been used by households. So clients will need reliable websites to buy goods and products online.

Covid has affected not only on public and community health but also on the way they purchase and consume products, as well as affect supply chain so both supply and production and demand of the corporations and of public are influenced.

Last but not least, covid 19 affects on production (declines) and oil price (declines) hence, there is transportation cost reduction and will affect pricing strategy of firms.

In reality, covid 19 has changed the perceptions and ways of shopping of consumers, even clients now they tend to buy more products based on competitive price with good quality and less brand and less familiar goods. So companies also need to invest into more flexible actions and tailoring their marketing strategies to clients.

For instance, in tourism, airlines and hotels industries, revenues reduced caused by covid impact. And marketing strategies ad business depend much on the linkage with medical sector for more prevention vaccines.

On the other hand, China-Trump commerce war also affected many Chinese and US firms, so they have to expand to other markets for example in Asian markets, so more marketing and market research activities are performed in these new market segments.

Chapter Three

Action Leadership in Marketing in Banking and Other Industries

8. Roles of Marketing in Banking

Banking sector normally have much investment into technology applications and marketing activities. Digital technology has affected the way clients interact with banks, from ATMs, credit and debit cards to Mobile App and machine learning.

Like other industries, banking industry in Vietnam received much impacts from Covid 19. Many working hours at banks has been cut. Bank officers spend more time to stay at home and sale/marketing strategy has been delayed. Bank offices has implemented programs for clean and fresh offices with caring policy for old people.

According to international experts, marketing strategies is the necessary living condition of corporations, of their business results and of status and global brand.

Therefore, banks nowadays try to apply digital technology and esp. AI and machine learning into marketing activities to personalize clients experience, let them engage more and share experiences.

Vietnam Report Joint Stock Company (Vietnam Report) has pointed out the Top 6 top priority strategies of banks in the current period. That is continuing to accelerate the process of bank digital transformation, designing measures to encourage customers to use more digital products; innovate, diversify products, expand operating markets; increase charter capital; restructuring the bank's operations; strengthen risk management; strengthen training of human resources to adapt to digital transformation.

Next, also according to a survey by Vietnam Report, a number of Vietnam banks (big banks such as Vietcombank, BIDV, HDbank, Vietinbank, Sacombank, VPBank) have implemented innovation and market expansion strategies by continuing to exploit their strengths and multiplying their operating models in rural and agricultural markets. sponsor the chain and link with platform partners, well exploit ecosystem customers.

Putting more investment into new product development is also another way to respond to post covid 19 time, for instance, why banks only receive money as deposits, while assets such as house and land and trucks, automobiles are another form of money and can produce profits for banks so they can consider these assets as money and receive as deposits with interest paid to clients.

Last but not least, banks need to pay attention to team marketing, push and pull marketing strategies in post covid 19 stage. Nätti and Lähteenmäki (2016) stated Banks are shifting from risk management to focusing on customers. Empathetic leadership, employee training, excellent cooperation between and among different departments and teams, and technological readiness and capability are seen as necessities for creating value for customers.

Mahbub (2021) also said in case Bangladesh, Banks often sponsor different events, educational programmes, trade shows, charity proceedings etc. to reach specific business goals and increase their competitive advantage to reach the targeted niche market and the local audiences9 . Sponsorship style marketing is different from advertisements which persuades customers by sharing specific messages about a product/service the bank renders. 'Television and

Radio Ads' is the second concentrated area for bank's publicity; yet, it is very volatile in developing countries due to its dependency on political and many other external factors (Friedman, 2021). The 'Promotional Material and Gifts' in different occasions and festivals is considered the third highest spending sector for advertisements in the precrisis period for the listed PCBs in Bangladesh. Besides these, PCBs (Private commercial banks) also do 'Paper Advertisements' on newspapers, magazines and via leaflets. The tendency of advertising through direct postal mails are diminishing due to the amplified implementation of paper-free campaigns. In recent years, 'Cross Selling Marketing Programme that includes In-Branch Marketing and Point of Sales Marketing' are gaining much attention as banks' marketing tools.

9. Marketing responding to competitors in Vietnam Banking -Commerce -Investment -Finance -Tourism -Airlines -Hotels- Manufacturing-Hardware-Medicine-Agriculture -Electric-Gas & Oil and other fields

We would like to mention strength and role of marketing communication in responding to competitors:

In marketing communication, we consider to use sale marketing with languages showing importance of clients and the match between our products features and their demand....

Beside, During the pandemic customers, publics, and governments required and, in some cases, forced, collaboration for the benefit during this regard, past competitors became collaborators (see de Menzies,2020). Lynn, R.A. (1987) mentioned that Competition is a key factor that marketing strategists face. Competitors' market moves demand timely and creative reaction. To get usable advance estimates of such probable moves, it is essential to have a system for careful monitoring of competitors. All proactive strategic actions should anticipate the market reactions that competitors are likely to make to them. Then Gatignon et al (1989) explained how established competitors in an oligopoly react to a significant new entry in their market. It has been suggested that at least some established competitors will react to a market entry positively and at least some competitors will react negatively or not at all.

In Vietnam not only bank sectors , there are changes and innovative ideas in marketing of Medicine and pharmacy sector, for instance, a system of Pharmacity shops has been established, the values is normal but necessary for patients.

Beside, firms note that doing a good job in customer service also keep clients loyalty and increase retention.

Bala et al (2021) proposed a conceptual model for customer service below:

Figure 5- Customer service in covid 19 pandemic

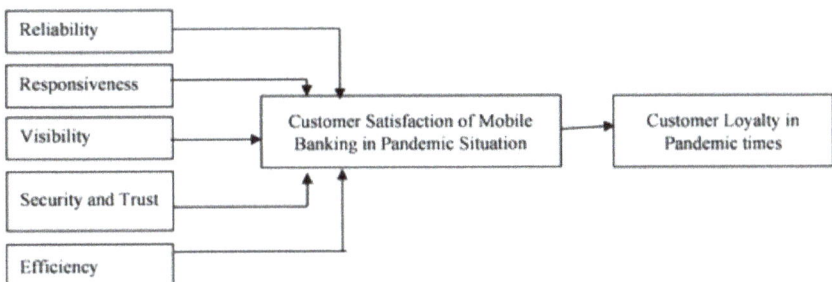

(source: Tapas Bala et al., 2021)

10. Marketing in global leading firms in Various industries

Walmart - a big retailer case: Walmart sell various products such as groceries, furniture, hardware,appliances, health goods, wellness, to entertainment and they did a good job in marketing with innovation, AI and Mobile App, so this is one success factor. With Mobile App, clients can have more engagement and share customer experience and involving in discussion as well. To increase loyalty and retention, customer can enter My local store and find their goods available in stocks. Its pricing strategy comprising of: bulksales and friendly price to maximize profits (buy many products) and diversification pricing (buy complementary products to promote others). Walmart also sale product with discounts in large number. For advertising, they used TV ads, billboards, social media, and even their eCommerce platform. Walmart has many trucks for delivery door to door (ver safe) and good IT platform to see products in inventory or in transportation. In general they did well in marketing mix.

Amazon- a big online retailer: Amazon win the market very fast and deliver products to clients quickly and rely on digital advertising. The company also pay attention much to its competitors.

Figure 6- Amazon shopping with products

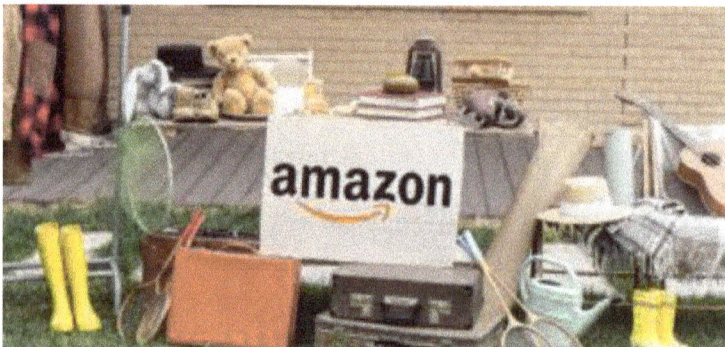

(source: internet)

P&G case: the company learn quickly and like fresh ideas from employee and then they build trust with partners so they can success. It came to a time when the firm used radio show to marketing products for female at home. So it likes creative marketing campaigns.

Figure 7- P&G design

(source: internet)

Pepsi Co case: success in partnership and sponsorship and in packaging products (reduce, reuse, recycle, renew, remove). It used a low price policy with Walmart by reducing overhead and reengineering production.

Figure 8- Pepsi Products

(source:internet)

Figure 9 - Display products

(source: internet)

Citibank case - a global brand presence in Latin America, Asia Pacific, North America, Europe, Middle East and Africa. They have diversified products and premium pricing strategies over competitors. They did good job in marketing 7P with nice physical building , ATMs and credit cards all showing brand, and marketing on newspaper, billboards, internet and TVs.

Gucci case: a successful example for luxury brand. The company also uses word of mouth , social media and engage clients successfully. With Gucci, clients will get status, image and prestige.

Figure 10 - Gucci shop

(source: internet)

Samsung case: its pricing strategy is flexible: competitive pricing with LG in various products (refrigerators, TVs, air conditioners), and skimming pricing to get high value when it first enter the market.

11. Extra Analysis of Strengths and Weaknesses in Marketing of Vietnam Banking-Commerce-Investment-Finance-Tourism-Airlines-Hotels-Manufacturing-Hardware-Medicine-Agriculture -Electric-Gas & Oil and Other Sectors

12. The ultimate goal of a marketing strategy is to achieve and communicate a sustainable competitive advantage over rival companies (investopedia.com, access date 14/1/2021).

We make analysis below in case Vietnam:

Strengths:

Let's look at some examples. Vinamilk has performed an effective 4P marketing strategy, in which their products (esp. VFresh) are rich in vitamin and minerals which are healthy for people and public, with competitive price because of stable supply chain and material (fresh milk).

The firm pay attention to CSR with donations for study encouraging, scholarships and programs (trial use) at schools.

Vinamilk also make advertisement through TVs, poster, internet and newspaper and at point of sale.

Figure 11- Vinamilk products

(source: internet)

For distribution development: The firm expanded markets to rural areas. It developed many trucks for distributors and delivery. And The system of freezers, refrigerators, and refrigerated trucks was also expanded to meet the growing demand for yogurt group. The company is always looking for and expanding export markets through other countries in the region and the world. to maintain and develop export revenue.

Let's see 2nd example: Biti's focused on young generation and used KOL for communication campaign with hot idols on internet. Then it can introduce various shoes to clients. Biti' salso used PR messages/ writings.

Third example: GrabTaxi, GrabCar, GrabBike, GrabExpress , Grab food has passed Uber brand in Vietnam market and did a good job in covid 19 time. They have reasonable and cheap prices and competitive to taxi. Also they use technology on Mobile App and allow clients with flexible payment to pay by cash or credit card.

Fourth example: Tan Hiep Phat products such as C2, Green tea an Dr Thanh tea, various products to provide more options for clients.

Figure 12- Dr Thanh tea

(source: internet)

All above companies ave identified new trend of market and converted it into business opportunities. This shows a business capacity of these corporations and marketing team. They focus on long , lasting relationship with clients.

Identification of new demand of clients will show roles of modern marketing.

Weaknesses

First, some people and young people still have negative think of marketing people and marketing job. Some people still consider internet is unreal environment and be afraid of internet marketing. In fact, young generation and officers nowadays use internet much more and see its influence.

Second, some SMEs still have limited budget for marketing campaigns, not like big corporations.

Third, Point of sales marketing still is preferred by firms than internet marketing.

Fourth, advertising companies still familiar with traditional marketing, not really specialized in internet marketing so it is hard to consult clients and firms.

Fifth, advertising on internet still limited with banners and pop-ups and not developed much. But more and more email marketing and SEO google have been used.

Sixth, there are not so many programs showing difference in 2 segments: old people and young generation.

Seventh, in society there are still negative views on network marketing/sale; company -distributor-customers. This is a kind of multilevel marketing so there is risk and also change to get high profits if we are based on qualified products.

13. Further Analysis on Relation between Marketing and Leadership

We refer to below McKinsey loop model that keep people interact and put people back into the funnel to engage:

Figure 13- McKinsey loop model vs. linear

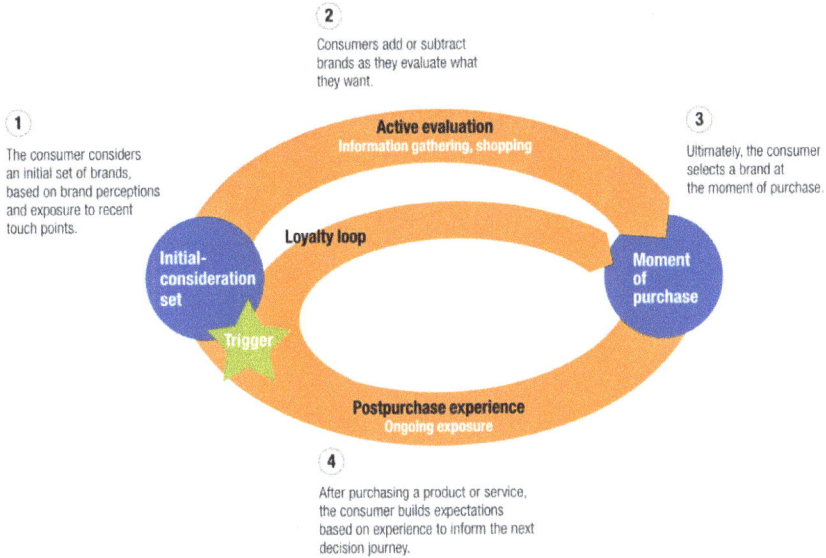

2
Consumers add or subtract
brands as they evaluate what
they want.

1
The consumer considers
an initial set of brands,
based on brand perceptions
and exposure to recent
touch points.

Active evaluation
Information gathering, shopping

3
Ultimately, the consumer
selects a brand at
the moment of purchase.

Loyalty loop

Initial-
consideration
set

Trigger

Moment
of
purchase

Postpurchase experience
Ongoing exposure

4
After purchasing a product or service,
the consumer builds expectations
based on experience to inform the next
decision journey.

(source: McKinsey & Company, 2009).

Chapter Four

Common Techniques and Tools for Marketing

14. Common Techniques and Tools for Marketing

First we see marketing techniques by goals including several techniques such as:

A) Individual -based marketing: this is marketing technique aims to personal/individual client and make them feel important, so it is not aiming to huge number of clients. Therefore it will go together with personal selling and consulting.

Leaders in the AMA's leaders' survey specified: 'Proactive emails with personalized ideas and strategy recommendations have been appreciated and have generated new opportunities with current clients' (Steimer 2020, p. 51). Authors of the survey concluded that one-to-one personalized communication is most effective.

B) Content marketing: this is a technique to deliver content of products/services to clients (mass) in various ways: podcast, blog, e-book, articles, case studies, video, etc. Sometimes content marketing can be conducted with telling stories, and so it helps to build community around and restated our leading position by answering as many questions as possible.

C) Email marketing: this is a cost-effective marketing tactic and help us to reach a large number of audiences and clients and build our community in order to promote our products or share information or tell stories. On special days and events you can send email to offer discounts for customers, as well as postcards to them.

Figure14 - Using email marketing effectively

(source: internet)

D) Event marketing: will focus on mass, a big number of clients and allow face to face communication with clients at conferences, trade shows, exhibition, etc. It is different from digital marketing which might take place online via social media channels.

E) Word of mouth marketing: this is traditional method to increase our brand awareness, can be done via messages on mobiles among clients.

F) Pull strategy in marketing (inbound marketing): many people prefer this marketing tactic instead of pushing clients to business. So this pull strategy can be start with newspaper, television and radio ads, or flyers/brochures, website posts, and other advertisements, mass social media, promotion and discount and customer relationship management programs. Customers review , google /website and word of mouth review will make long term customers values and help our business growth. Other examples of pull marketing including: using social media, influencer content with video guiding clients how to use products, and using blogs to educate clients and prove them with knowledge. Then we could consider to use SEO (Search Engine Optimization) to optimize our web pages when clients search with key words, phrases and terms.

G) Push strategy in marketing (outbound marketing): it might be in a form of direct selling which means pushing products/services to customers before or after clients tried it. Sometimes marketing officer can use money award-based (paid in advance) marketing to push clients try to use their services. For instance, we see billboards on high ways is a kind of pushing strategy, or direct marketing at showrooms, trade shows, etc.

Beside, Corniani (2008) also stated A push strategy refers to the development of processes that emanate from the company and go towards the market: the company invents, develops and proposes a product that is destined to find purchasers. Supply is therefore sustained by the company.

A pull strategy is the opposite, because it refers to processes that start from the market and go towards the company: demand requests supply and 'pulls' it out of the company. We could say that the market stimulates the needs that prompt the company to develop a particular product, which emerges as a response to the pull action of demand.

In this sense, the two strategies are alternatives, because they are founded on very different market assumptions (the characteristics of demand, of competition, of the financial system, of the supplier system, etc.) that require very different capabilities and resources from companies. Push strategies presuppose comprehensive knowledge of the market, of the needs of its major players (demand and competition) and of their dynamics. This then makes it possible to plan in advance the corporate activities necessary to perform all the processes oriented to the realisation of a product that allows a company to strive to achieve good commercial results.

Pull strategies are based on the opposite premise. The company is not able to develop comprehensive knowledge of the market and its players, which are characterised by the changeability and dynamism of their actions and needs. Planning corporate activities is therefore a very risky business and cannot be performed for very long periods of time. The premise for application of pull strategies is therefore an unstable context, in which the same corporate processes cannot be reiterated successfully. Corporate competitiveness is not founded on the development of rigid cost structures that are gradually reduced over time: the competitive force of pull strategies therefore lies in their ability to respond to the market and in rapid action. Experience in manufacturing and communications is not built up, but experience is developed in flexible responses, both with regard to manufacturing processes, and to information and communications. The competitiveness of pull solutions lies in the ability to respond before the competition to the changing needs of demand, and this applies both to material flows and to flows of information and communications.

We see below figure:

Figure 15 - Push and pull strategies

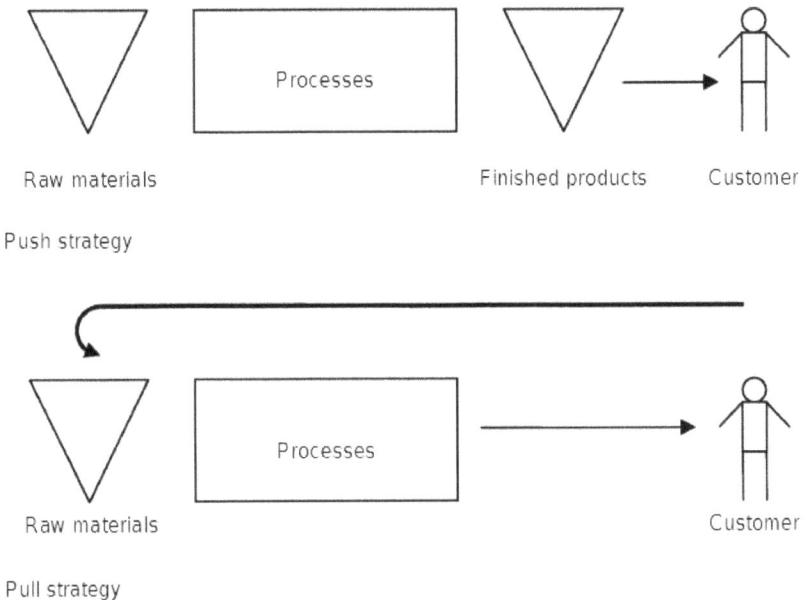

Raw materials   Processes   Finished products   Customer

Push strategy

Raw materials   Processes   Customer

Pull strategy

(source: Elaboration of A. by P.G. Brabazon, B. MacCarthy, Order Fulfillment Models from the

Catalog Mode of Mass Customization–A Review, in T. Blecker, G. Friedrich (eds.), Mass

Customization: Challenges and Solutions, Springer, New York, 2006, pp. 211-231, p. 214)

H) Team marketing: We might see some small team on the street who make advertisement on their products to many clients. In insurance or banking credit product selling, people also used small team to give advice on their products and close sale.

On the other hand, we will consider factors in an effective marketing campaign they include: social media, TV shows, radio, printed newspapers, journals, direct mail, etc. For instance, in case of Coca Cola, they use effective unchanged font, printing names on products, bottles types, etc.

Figure 16- Marketing campaign

(source: internet)

The buying process for all above marketing techniques will go from client awareness to their consideration and then closing deal.

15. Several key indices, measurements and KPIs in marketing management activities of firms

Initially, Establish marketing goals will follow SMART, which means : Specific-Measurable-Achieveable-Relevant-Time bound.

Then we identify financial budget for marketing campaign/plans within timeline and in selected markets.

Some measurements of marketing can be: number of times visiting website or store, number of orders/purchases, number of re-visiting, number of appointments, etc.

Also Return on investment (ROI) and ratio of sales over marketing costs + production cost + admin cost is another measurement. Also other KPIs such as revenues and number of sales/clients.

16. The Role of Digital Technology, and IT in Marketing

Everything nowadays connect to internet so there are new opportunities for marketing strategies with Internet of Things (IoTs). Digital technology has boosted e-commerce transactions and therefore, push marketing online more in economic downturn and covid 19 pandemic.

Google , Facebook and other electronic devices such as mobile, tablet, computers, etc. has been used more for digital marketing and motive creativity of firms. Businesses and organizations also use more Zoom, Google meet, Skype, and Microsoft team , video conferences for business meeting and communication platform.

More firms (online education, retails, supermarkets, bookstores, clothing stores, etc.) consider to use AI and technology application such as robots and chatbots in marketing and communicating with clients. Online advertising including video content, infographics, images, GIF, etc. are promoted.

Whereas travel and hospitality has been affected by corona, customers also have more time stay at home and use more internet. Online entertainment channels (HBO, Spotify, Netflix, etc.) also has bee developed more. Online conferences and online healthcare and doctors also used more.

And because clients now spend more time to read newspapers, magazines, and watching TVs, businesses can use these means for advertising, marketing, selling.

17. Benefits Vs. Cost of Effective Marketing Strategy

At the beginning, we see below figure a marketing strategy example proposed:

Figure 17- Marketing strategy

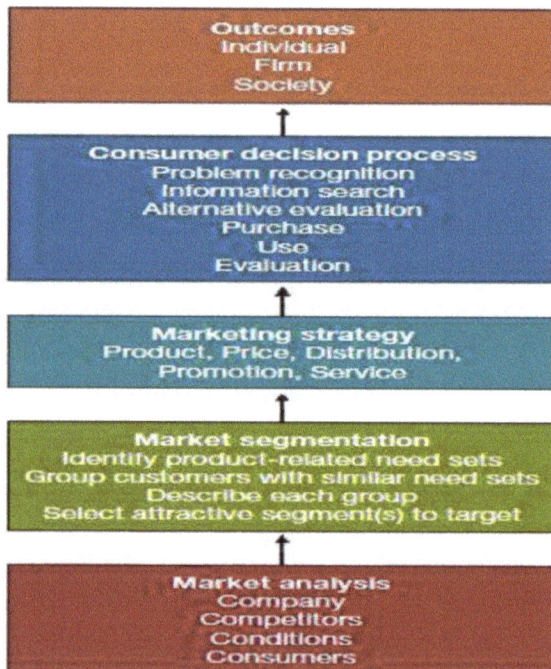

(source: Mihalj, Bakator, 2016)

Then we can see various benefits a marketing campaign or strategy can bring values to clients including: easy to use, convenience, healthcare, option choices, relaxation, friendliness, etc. And other benefits go with products features such as: safety, exiting, peace of mind, time and money saving, etc. Moreover, marketing research strategy on future clients will help our firm maintain growth. And there is opportunity to increase revenues when company launch new products/services.

However there are costs attached such as: repaired frequently, charges, unfriendly officers, long time waiting, delivery costs, low quality, etc.

Beside, there is Opportunity Costs which implies lost benefits, or opportunities, that we lost when we choose this strategy instead of another. It comes when a company pursues one product or strategy over another.

Chapter Five

SWOT Analysis and Conclusion Part I

18. Analysis of Opportunities and Threats in Marketing in Industry 4.0

Still many opportunities for digital marketing in industry 4.0 as we see in below figure more than 70% population in Vietnam using internet and social network in year 2020.

Figure 18- Statistics of Vietnam population using social network and mobile

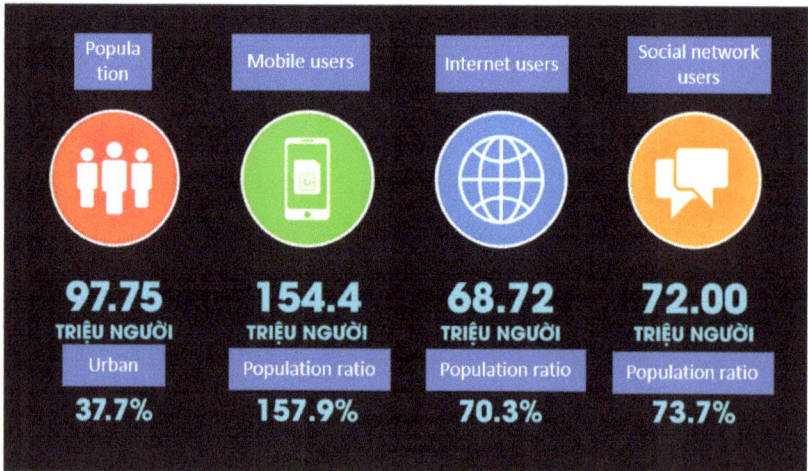

(source: Report of Hootsuite- Dgital in Vietnam 2021)

We see in below analytical table:

Table 2- O & T

Opportunities	Threats
- Development of mobile, smartphones and google and IoTs allow firms to offer more advertising programs via mobiles to attract more clients - Covid 19 cause people tend to use TVs more and Youtube more so there is rooms for developing marketing plans - Transaction costs may be lower because of digital banking - Digital technology revolution can benefit banks through cloud technology, saving big data and internet of things - Many companies can increase sales and revenues from e-commerce so much - Corporations can increase investment for machine learning and market research to understand internet users and buyers behaviors - Companies can increase investment for advertising and AI, IoTS to increase or boost their sales and profits - Cooperate with banks and credit institutions to increase clients credit to boost consuming sales	- Covid 19 pandemic still put negative impacts on marketing field - Facebook advertising may reduce - Investment in technology in industry 4.0 will cost budget and need to consider effectiveness

(source: author analysis)

39. Analysis of Strengths and Weaknesses of Marketing in Vietnam Banking-Commerce-Investment-Finance-Tourism-Airlines-Hotels-Manufacturing-Hardware-Medicine-Agriculture -Electric-Gas & Oil and Other Industries

Next, We see in below analytical table:

Table 3- S & W

Strengths	Weaknesses
- Vietnam banks invested in innovations in ATMs and chip cards. - Using Google Ads and put our products on top search - Digital and corebanking and technology has helped bans and firms to develop new products and marketing activities - Some Vietnam firms transfer advertising budget to covid prevention programs, so CSR will be good tool help them in marketing - Several Companies understand deeply behaviors and process of purchasing of consumers so they can win market - More businesses cooperate with e-commerce platform such as Tiki, Lazada, Shopee in Vietnam to increase communication channels and advertising to clients to boost sales - Offering Sale programs with gifts or discount to clients	- Slow trend in improving innovative ways of marketing - Slow down movies activities in cinemas - Needs high security software to protect data - High risks if hackers enter platform and steal online data

(source: author analysis)

40. **Conclusion Part I**

We present marketing theories, perspectives and SWOT analysis of marketing strategies taking place at this current time under covid 19 context, in which client behaviors has transferred from offline to online transactions.

There are both chances and challenges for companies to develop marketing activities with e-commerce while they also face a reduction in human resource due to technology revolution in industry 4.0.

We come to know that marketing strategy under governance concept, esp. Corporate governance context, will help firms more confidence to win market with new directions and stronger risk and corporate governance system.

The economic crisis from 1997-1998 to 2008-2009 and now 2020-2021happen again (cycle we see every 10-12 years then economic downturn taking place). We can expect that 2022-2027 is the time economic recover with stronger marketing strategies and activities from global economy as well as the trend that marketing and risk management and corporate governance show more connection.

Part Two

Eleven (11) Case Studies in marketing in Banking and Various Industries: Commerce-Investment-Finance-Tourism-Airlines-Hotels-Manufacturing-Hardware-Medicine-Agriculture-Electric-Gas & Oil and Other **Industries**

PART II - CONTENTS

DATE

JAN 09, 2022

The cases are presented in the following order:

19. Case no. 6: Marketing Strategy based on Competitor Analysis - A Case in Vietnam Medicine Sector

20. Case no. 7: Beta Evidence in Viet Nam Three Insurance and Financial Service Industries After Crisis 2007-2009 and Low Inflation Period 2015-2017

21. Case no. 8: A One Factor Model Affect The Risk Level of Viet Nam Hardware Industry During and After The Global Crisis 2007-2011

22. Case no. 9: Various Industrial Competitors Affect The Risk Level of Viet Nam Non-Banking Investment and Financial Service Industry During The Economic Crisis 2007-2009

23. Case no. 10: A Two Factors Model On The Risk Level of Viet Nam Electric Power Industry During and After The Global Crisis 2007-2011

24. Case no. 11: Selecting Various Industrial Competitors Affect The Risk Level of Viet Nam Water Industry During and After The Global Crisis 2007-2011

25. Refer Appendix for Implementation form and case user manual.

	CASE QUESTIONS	DATE
		JAN 09, 2022

These questions for teaching purpose only: Below are, but not limited to, among recommended case questions for appropriate Professors to use in case write-ups, class discussion, presentation, analytical paper, homework or group meeting

Case 1 "Management Issues of Tea Planting and Tea Crops in Vietnam in the Concept of Sustainable Agricultural Development – and Recommendations on Marketing 4P"

Question 1: Discuss marketing 4P solutions in case of Tea Planting and Tea Crops in Vietnam and in Developing Countries?

Question 2: Discuss about internal and external factors that might affect tea crops?

Question 3: What are Concept of Sustainable Agricultural Development?

Case 2 "Insects Alcohol Traps, Sustainable Agricultural Value Chain in Coffee and Tea Crops in the Northern Regions of Vietnam – and Solutions for Marketing Mix"

Question 1: Discuss business environment of Coffee and Tea Crops in the Northern Regions of Vietnam.

Question 2: What are Solutions for Marketing Mix?

Question 3: Analyze and describe more solutions for Sustainable Agricultural Value Chain in Coffee and Tea Crops in the Northern Regions of Vietnam .

Case 3 "DISCUSSION ON TEA AND COFFEE PLANTING IN LAM DONG AND THAI NGUYEN PROVINCES IN VIETNAM – FDI INVESTMENT, ECONOMIC VALUES, NATURAL CONDITIONS, FARMING TECHNIQUES FOR AGRICULTURAL SUSTAINABILITY"

Question 1: What are opportunities and threats for TEA AND COFFEE PLANTING IN LAM DONG AND THAI NGUYEN PROVINCES IN VIETNAM?

Question 2: What are strengths and weaknesses of TEA AND COFFEE PLANTING IN LAM DONG AND THAI NGUYEN PROVINCES IN VIETNAM?

Question 3: Give suggestions to enhance ECONOMIC VALUES, NATURAL CONDITIONS, FARMING TECHNIQUES FOR AGRICULTURAL SUSTAINABILITY in this industry.

Case 4 "ICT AND DIGITAL TECH EFFECTS ON MARKETING STRATEGIES AND CHOOSING COMPETITOR AFFECTING ON BUSINESS OPERATION - A CASE IN HOTEL AND ENTERTAINMENT SECTOR "

Question 1: Discuss what kinds of competitor risk for HOTEL AND ENTERTAINMENT SECTOR.

Question 2: What are strengths and weaknesses of ICT AND DIGITAL TECH EFFECTS ON MARKETING STRATEGIES?

Question 3: What are sound recommendations for MARKETING STRATEGIES in this case?

Case 5 "DIGITAL MARKETING APPLICATIONS IN TOURISM INDUSTRY VIA A CASE STUDY OF MTC - MY TRA COMPANY IN VIETNAM "

Question 1: What are sound recommendations or suggestions for DIGITAL MARKETING APPLICATIONS IN TOURISM INDUSTRY?

Question 2: What are competitor risks for MTC - MY TRA COMPANY IN VIETNAM?

Question 3: What are strengths and weaknesses of DIGITAL MARKETING APPLICATIONS IN TOURISM INDUSTRY?

Case 6 "Marketing Strategy based on Competitor Analysis - A Case in Vietnam Medicine Sector"

Question 1: What are key aspects in marketing in Vietnam Medicine Sector?

Question 2: What are potential competitor risk for Vietnam Medicine Sector?

Question 3: Give recommendations for enhancing Marketing Strategy based on Competitor Analysis in this case.

Case 7 "Impacts of Competitor Selection Strategy on Firm Risk - Case in Vietnam Investment and Finance Industry"

Question 1: In term of competitor risk, what are Impacts of Competitor Selection Strategy on Firm Risk in this above sector?

Question 2: What are factors affecting Vietnam Investment and Finance Industry?

Question 3: What suggestions you make to improve business strategy case?

Case 8 "A One Factor Model Affect The Risk Level of Viet Nam Hardware Industry During and After The Global Crisis 2007-2011"

Question 1: What are key elements affecting marketing strategies of Viet Nam Hardware Industry ?

Question 2: What are business and competitor risks? Give recommendations to deal with this risk.

Question 3: Give recommendations for policies in Viet Nam Hardware Industry.

Case 9 "Various Industrial Competitors Affect The Risk Level of Viet Nam Non-Banking Investment and Financial Service Industry During The Economic Crisis 2007-2009 "

Question 1: What are key elements driving marketing strategies of Viet Nam Non-Banking Investment and Financial Service Industry?

Question 2: What are strengths and weaknesses of current marketing activities at Viet Nam Non-Banking Investment and Financial Service Industry?

Question 3: What are competitor risks? Give recommendations to deal with this risk.

Case 10 "A Two Factors Model On The Risk Level of Viet Nam Electric Power Industry During and After The Global Crisis 2007-2011"

Question 1: Drawing a picture of competition and risk environment of Viet Nam Electric Power Industry.

Question 2: Analyzing potential risks from internal and external environments for this sector.

Question 3: What are your suggestions to enhance marketing activities of Viet Nam Electric Power Industry ?

Case 11 "Selecting Various Industrial Competitors Affect The Risk Level of Viet Nam Water Industry During and After The Global Crisis

2007-2011"

Question 1: What are key elements affecting marketing strategies of Viet Nam Water Industry?

Question 2: Analyzing potential risks from internal and external environments for this sector.

Question 3: What are competitor risks that Affect The Risk Level of Viet Nam Water Industry? Give recommendations to deal with this risk ?

	GLOSSARY AND ABBREVIATION	**DATE**
		JAN 01, 2022

Glossary and Notes

CP	Corporate Performance
CRM	Customer Relationship Management
ERM	Enterprise Risk Management
RG	Risk Governance
RC	Risk Control
RP	Risk Prevention
CG	Corporate Governance
CEO	Chief Executive Officer, or Chief Executive
CMO	Chief Marketing Officer
CFO	Chief Financial Officer, or Finance Director
CRO	Chief Risk Officer
HR	Human Resource
MIS	Management Information System
ESR	Environmental and Social Risks
CSR	Corporate Social Responsibility
4P	Price-Product-Place-Promotion
7P	4P + People + Process + Physical
KPIs	Key Performance Indicators
PCB	Private Commercial Bank

Abbreviations

FAQs	Frequently Asked Questions
b.t	between
w/o	without
esp.	especially

(published in SSCI/SCIE, Tobacco Regulatory Sciences, 7(6), 2021)

Management Issues of Tea Planting and Tea Crops in Vietnam in the Concept of Sustainable Agricultural Development - and Recommendations on Marketing 4P

Duong Thi Huyen , PhD Thai Nguyen University of Sciences, Vietnam. huyendt@tnus.edu.vn **Nguyen Dinh Trung** , PhD
National Economics University (NEU), Hanoi Vietnam
trungnd@neu.edu.vn **Pham Van Tuan** , PhD, Asso.Prof
National Economics University, Hanoi Vietnam phamvantuan@neu.edu.vn
Dinh Tran Ngoc Huy , MBA, (corresponding)
Banking University HCMC, Ho Chi Minh city Vietnam   – Internat
ional University of Japan, Niigata, Japan dtnhuy2010@gmail.com

Nguyen Thi Hang , PhD
Thai Nguyen University, University of Information and Communication Technology, Vietnam
nthang@ictu.edu.vn

Nguyen Bich Hon g , PhD
Thai Nguyen University of Economics and Business Administration (TUEBA), Vietnam
nguyen.bich.hong85@gmail.com

Bui Thi Suu , Master
Tay Bac University, Quyet Tam Ward, Son La City, Son La Province,
Vietnam. **Le Thu Ha** , PhD
Faculty of Basic Science, Thai Nguyen University of Economics and Business Administration,
Vietnam. Lethuha.cva@gmail.com

ABSTRACT

Thai Nguyen and Lam Dong provinces are two biggest ares of Vietnam to have tea crops planting. Farmers produce various tea products and among them, Green tea contains polyphenols and catechins as well as caffeine, but green tea has less caffeine than coffee, and many extracts are decaffeinated. Our research goal is to find out real situation of tea planting in Vietnam in the concept of sustainable agricultural development in Vietnam and recommendations and marketing 4P Research results show us that CPI and R (lending rate) and Risk free rate (Rf) have negative correlation with tea export price, while GDP growth has positive impacts. Next, the State plays an important role in supporting and promoting contractual

linkages. Government policies must hold farmers and businesses accountable for

the performance of the contract. In Vietnam, with a still agricultural fragmented, backward, the link between farmers and businesses is still loose, the determination of The right direction and support of the Government will create a great impetus to promote development economic links between businesses and farmers.

Our research limitation is that we can expand for other crops, industries and markets as well.

Key words: sustainable development,

agricultural value chain, tea and coffee planting, tea products, Vietnam

JEL: M21, G30, G32, G38

*Tob Regul Sci."2021;7(5):*1784 - 1803

DOI: doi.org/10. 18001/TRS.7.5.102

1.Introduction

First, we recognize the importance of tea crops and other crops in Vietnam in the concept of sustainability. Green tea is made from the dried leaves of the same plant (Camellia sinensis) as traditional tea, a green shrub in Asia. However, the traditional tea leaves are fermented, and the green tea leaves are steamed but not fermented. Green tea can be brewed and taken orally or taken as an extract tablet or capsule. It has many components that are believed to have antioxidant and anti-cancer effects. Green tea contains polyphenols and catechins as well as caffeine, but green tea has less caffeine than coffee, and many extracts are decaffeinated.

Le Thi Thanh Huong,Vu Quynh Nam,Dinh Tran Ngoc Huy, Pham Van Tuan,Pham Van Hong. (2021) explored explore not only strengths, weakness, opportunities and threats of Coffee and tea growing in the northwestern region of Vietnam, but authors also would suggest that Tay Bac provinces need to have both medium term and long term strategies in agriculture development esp. When Vietnam enter free trade agreements such as EVFTA and UK agreements.

Thai Nguyen province in Vietnam is specialized in tea crops.

Authors find out there are Limited product support services int he field. With the current development trend, products or manufacturing industries all need the system.

ecology to support. This is very important for products that have a need to promote participation enter the international market. However, from the practical study of tea products in the province shows that some necessary support services are still lacking.

With increasing requirements for food safety and hygiene, tests and analyzes for tea products with essential requirements. However, tea exporting companies in Thailand

Nguyen can only do simple tests in Thai Nguyen province or must down to Hanoi. Even quality management agencies lack the equipment for quality assessment, especially for tests with higher requirements.

Studies on policies for production inputs, agricultural development commodity-oriented industry and participate in the value chain: the agricultural sector, Rural areas are home to over 70% of the labor force and a large concentration of poor people. This is an area where the government has won many policies to encourage development such as investment in infrastructure construction, land policy, capital support, support for farmers

access to capital and credit policies, tax exemptions and reductions, technical assistance, seed, farming methods,... (Dang Van Thanh, 2010). Even so, not a few of the main

The policy to support farmers is not suitable with the characteristics of regions, localities and ethnic groups or with seasonal characteristics of crops and livestock. For example, coffee is one of the key export products, but the loan policy

Agricultural production, hunger eradication and poverty reduction are still not suitable with the characteristics of the Western region. Preferential loan programs with small loan sizes, but how to support through many lending channels has dispersed the loan and resulted in The level of lending in each channel is still low, making it difficult to meet the demand for agricultural products export (Nguyen Dinh Hoa and Dang Hoang Giang, 2013).

Studies show that the volume of agricultural products exported is large but low added value, mainly China market

After doi moi, Vietnamese agriculture has achieved great success in terms of production

export volume and value. From a country suffering from hunger, Vietnam has become one of the 5 the world's largest exporter of agricultural products such as coffee, rice, shrimp, etc.

However, compared to other countries in the region, Vietnam's agriculture is still inferior to other countries countries in the region in terms of land, labor and water efficiency. The industry is mainly sold in its raw form at a lower price than other countries due to its high quality. Even for the domestic market, food safety is still getting many concerns (World Bank, 2016). According to Pham Ngoc Tuan (2016), China is gradually become the leading country in importing agricultural and aquatic products of Vietnam.

However, this is considered to be a volatile market, with supply and demand information Vietnamese enterprises have very little access to it, with many potential risks. While, Exports to China are mostly raw materials, with very high value.

Research issues

Issue 1: What are real situation of tea planting in Vietnam in the concept of sustainable agricultural development in Vietnam?

Issue 2: What are recommendations and marketing 4P solutions for agriculture and tea products!

2. Literature review

Further discussion on Agricultural value chains and tea crops issues:

First, According to Tran Hoang Hieu and Nguyen Thanh Son (2014), the "large sample fields" shaped formed under the association between farmers, between farmers and enterprises, or State intervention has initially contributed to land accumulation and concentration and this model has shown to contribute to the formation of product chains to supply the market and participate in the international market. According to Phuoc Minh Hiep (2013), the implementation of this model still faces some difficulties such as: small area; production level is not uniform leading to limited ability to absorb and apply science and technology and consequently to uneven product quality; there is no real connection between producers and processing and consuming establishments;...

Next We summarize previous studies as follows:

Table 1 — Summary of previous studies

Authors	Year	Contents, results
Carr	1999	With the reference of more than 30 articles published in international journals, which present subjects such as weather and climate for tea planting (drought and irrigation) scientists have been equipped with modern techniques and also, they train staff within tea sector.
Khoi, NV et al	2015	Despite of small scale (operation), fragmentation and weak connection, Vietnam tea sector has long history and helped many farmers to escape poor life and poverty, esp. in the North and North East region of Vietnam.
Bien, N.C et al	2018	With the role as a major export (product), tea production has contributed to economy and foreign currency, as well as creating more employment for workforce increase. Hence it is important to develop tea value chain as well as adding values for tea production in the globalization and integration.
Tran Thi Quy Chinh et al	2020	The study propose solutions including increase credit access for farmers and technical training and reducing costs for farmers, based on recognition of 3 positive factors (credit access, productivity and technical training) and 2 factors with negative impacts (risk and tea area).

Katuwal	2020	Have emphasize important roles of organic farming in tea production in Jitpur and Mangalbare area of Ham district, with the recognition of factors for transferring to organic environment such as economic benefit awareness (environmental); bright market prospects, health consciousness and sustainability.
Chen ct al	2020	Realize that tea competitiveness was depending on specialization level, with strongest impacts. And next factors influencing competitiveness are Local governments' sectoral strategies and institutional policies .
Saha et al	2021	Recognized in Bngaladesh case, 2 factors vehicles such as yield and area expansion influenced tea production and and productivity increased significantly to 1.05, 1.89, and 0.98% respectively annually for the stage 1972-2018 than 1947-1970.
San Viet Le et al	2021	limited studies have been conducted to determine the viability of this conversion in Vietnam, particularly regarding technical aspects. Focusing on aspects of soil health, tea productivity and quality, here we highlight the benefits and challenges of conventional tea production system and provide a comprehensive evaluation of potential advantages agroecological tea management practices could have for Vietnam. The outcomes of this review are an informative resource for tea producers, tea production management authorities and other relevant organizations; enabling more informed decisions regarding the management methods, policies and programs to promote agroecological tea management in Vietnam and other tea producing nations

Last but not least, Le Thi Thanh Huong, Dinh Tran Ngoc Huy, Pham Van Tuan, Pham Van Hong (2021) stated that In Vietnam, esp. In the northwest region, tea and coffee crops have been increasing in both quality and quantity and scientists are trying to find ways to increase productivity, as well as eliminate damaging insects and coffee berry borer, etc in order to reduce damages for farmers. The fact in agriculture is that when farmers are in good crops, the coffee price is going down and vice versa.And Dinh Tran Ngoc Huy, Nguyen Thi Hang, Le Thi Thanh Huong, Pham Van Hong. (2021) mentioned important roles of agriculture project financing and emphasized roles of banks (Huy, D.T.N.; Loan, B.T.; Anh, P.T., 2020).
Methodology Method and *Data*

3. Methodology
3.1 Method and Data

Research object: identify barriers and causes inhibiting market participation to international market of tea products.

Research scope:

Space: Thai Nguyen province (tea) and Lam Dong province.
Time: At the industry level: from 2011 to 2018

At the level of tea and lychee product chains: 2018

About the content: Clarifying barriers and reasons for restricting tea products and

join the international market

Regarding to tea crops, This study mainly use combination of quantitative methods and qualitative methods including synthesis, inductive and explanatory methods.

For quantitative analysis, the study is supported

with OLS regression.

Data is collected from reliable internet sources and websites of Bureau Statistics, State Bank and Ministry of Finance and Vietnam banks.

4. **Main results**

4.1 Concepts of sustainability in agriculture and tea planting Studies on Vietnam's tea value chain

Ngo Thi Hong Hanh (2012) focuses on comparing and evaluating the economic efficiency of varieties of tea (midland tea and branch tea). Research results show that tea branches have higher criteria than midland tea trees, effective in production activities of Exporting tea branches brings higher economic efficiency than midland tea.

New planting, investment in renovating old tea, switching to intensive farming on Kinh tea area Business is being carried out by farmers at all levels. However, in practice This transformation is still facing many challenges that need to be solved, especially for with tea growers.

Nguyen Thi Phuong Thao, Do Thuy Linh (2015) research on the participation of the poor into the tea value chain. Research results show that the poor get difficult to join the chain and enjoy negligible benefits. The poor are productive, harvested yield per unit of cultivated area and total product income tea is lower than that of the average and well-off households.

Cause of the problem

This is because poor households lack production conditions or harvested tea is only preliminary processed for sale.

Meanwhile, well-off households have conditions to invest in tea production at all stages more fruitful.

There are some Recent studies focuses on researching the linkage in the tea supply chain of small and medium enterprises participating in the tea supply chain in Thai Nguyen province.

Originally Research shows the link between subjects in the above tea product chain In Thai Nguyen province, there is almost no tea, or if there is, it is very small and not really tight.

Research by MCG (2014) evaluates the tea value chain under the impact of climate change. Research shows that tea growing areas are mainly located in places with difficult topographical conditions (hills) and harsh weather conditions. Meanwhile, adaptive capacity of tea growers is still limited, the support policies are still inadequate and the system

As a result, tea growers face many risks and find it difficult to participate in the value chain, if participation is also only at the low value-added stage.

Do Thuy Ninh (2015) studies the value chain of tea industry in Thai Nguyen province. The author has analyzed the actual situation of the actors involved, the linkage between actors in the tea value chain in Thai Nguyen province. The research has in-depth economic analysis of the stages in the value chain, the added value of each stage and how the chain is managed. However, This study starts with the tea grower as a starting point and ignores the input supply chain of the chain (inputs for agricultural production, science and technology for tea growers) and thus the chain analysis lacks comprehensiveness. The author only focuses on value chain research with limited domestic market (economic analysis for consumers is the domestic market, not to mention the requirements and ability to penetrate the world market). In particular, the research has not specified the market requirements, the standards of the target markets

Research by To Linh Huong (2017) positioning Vietnam's tea industry in the value chain of global rule. Research results show that Vietnam is mainly involved in the production stage export and import of raw tea. From the actual survey results, the study shows that the actors in the cognitive chain are still very limited in terms of global value chains and requirements of international market demand. For that reason, from farmers to processing enterprises,variables, trade pays little attention to quality, branding and investment for science and technology for quality improvement and competitiveness enhancement.

Guo and Rato (2019) found out that tea culture tourism in Thai Nguyen is developing quickly as a multilevel tourism form combining scenery sightseeing, learning, and hands-on experiences. However, it is still in the emerging stage and faces challenges of infrastructure on its road to development.

The limitation of this study is that it has not been able to compare and evaluate the current situation of stages in the value chain with the requirements of the market, especially the market - international standards (for example, the level of satisfaction of food quality, safety and hygiene; number of households produce and obtain certificates of safe tea production and processing). Such comparisons and assessments aim to help better locate the status of stages in the global value chain, thereby making appropriate intervention policies

Table 2- Area of tea crops in Thai Nguyen Province

Area	Certified are a (ha)	Certificatio n valid in time	Ou of date certificate (ha)
Whole province	/35.6	394.3	341.3
Thai Nguyen city	82.7	26	56.7
Song Cong city	10	10	0
Pho Yen town	46.2	20	26.2
Dinh Hoa dist	89.3	31	58.3
Vo Nhai dist	24.7	0	24.7
Phu Luong dist	114.2	88.5	25.7
Dong Hy dist	114.7	44.06	70.6
Dai Tu dist	253.8	174.7	79.05

4.2 Tea planting in Vietnam

4.2.1 Tea planting in the northern region of Vietnam
Studies on tea industry development issues

For tea plants, up to now, there have been many studies dealing with each aspect production, processing, consumption and management of the tea industry. Researches by Nguyen Huu Tai (1993) discuss the management mechanism and the issue of land allocation and documentation production for tea growing households. These studies focus on solving problems about the mechanism for the tea industry in the early Doi moi period, that is, the transition from the next economy planning to a market economy and the issue of land allocation from farms for farm households.

On how to organize and manage production for tea growing households, research by Tran Quang Huy (2010) focuses on assessing the influence of production factors on demand for cooperation (participation in cooperatives cooperatives and the relationship between cooperatives and cooperative members) of the household farmers produce and consume tea in key tea areas in Thai Nguyen province.

Hai Ninh, N.T. et al (2018) explored evaluated the situation of tea production of tea growers in PhuTho Province, Vietnam. Average tea plantation area among the largest group of households is 0.61 ha. In production, the types of risks that tea growers encounter include: unfavorable weather (33.4%), diseases (13.2%), insects and worms(2.3%), capital (0.3%) and price which is the most major risk (50.8%). The survey of 1,000 tea growers identified that 46.7% of the households are in need toparticipate in tea production insurance. The average willingness to pay was estimated to be 2,407.07 (thousand VND/ha/year).If the agricultural program issuccessfully implemented in the province, it is estimated to have a total agricultural insurance fund of 34-35 billion VND/year. The survey results show that gender,education level, tea growing area and location are factors that affect the level of willingness to pay for agricultural insurance for tea trees.

Do Thi Thuy Phuong (2014) done a Research on production and business activities of cooperatives in Thai Nguyen province, including cooperatives producing and trading tea. These studies are pointing out the meaning and relationship between production relations (cooperatives) in accordance with the nature, presentation, level of productive forces (market power, competition and integration), thereby confirming determine the role of cooperatives in organizing tea growers to take advantage of production to scale, increase bargaining power, meet the requirements of the market economy, international economic integration.

Researching on enterprises in the tea industry, VBCS D (2015) focuses on analyzing,

evaluate the competitiveness of enterprises with weaknesses in production inputs (quality of human resources, scale of production capital and science - technology).

The study also pointed out barriers in the business environment for enterprises tea industry.

Positives and limiting factors binding tea products to participate in international markets

The positives/advantages of entering the market

Natural and climatic conditions for tea plants: Thai Nguyen has favorable natural conditions for tea plants, especially tea varieties imported from Phu Tho province, also known as Trung du tea. If the suitable temperature conditions for tea plants to grow are in the range of 22oC-28oC and the humidity reaches 80%-85%, the annual average temperature and degrees

The average annual humidity of Thai Nguyen is quite ideal, at 25°C and 81.2%, respectively.

The average annual rainfall in the province is about 2,000-2,500 mm, set from May to October. Therefore, tea plants of Thai Nguyen, especially Tan tea

Erect, usually grows and develops best in the summer (May to July).

thanks to enough sun, enough temperature and enough water. Tea buds at this stage also develop strongest and most nutritious. As a result, the Midland tea tree when grown in Thai Nguyen grows better and gives a more distinctive and delicious flavor than tea - The same species is grown in Phu Tho.

Tea growers have many years of production experience: With experience and technique of Growing and processing tea is accumulated over a century of history, tea plants from the Originally planted to green the bare lands and hills, it has now become the world strong and is one of the strategic crops of Thai Nguyen province. Hitherto, Tea trees have been planted in all 9 cities/districts/towns of the province with a total area of Cultivation area has been continuously expanded over the years. In 2018, the total cultivated area of The province's tea reaches 22,027 hectares, accounting for about 14.3% of the total cultivated area and 57.9% of the total cultivated area Of perennial industrial crops in the province. Tea industry of Thai Nguyen currently attracts the participation of 95,000 households, or 40% of the total number of households in the agricultural villages, including individual production households as well as production households participating in cooperatives (43) and craft villages (140) (Thai Nguyen Department of Industry and Trade, 2017).

And we analyze challenges and benefits in tea sector as below:

Table 3 - Benefits and challenges for tea production

Benefits	Challenges
- Increase employment	- Land area
- Improve farmers income	- Technical training for farmers
- Increase linkages among producers	- Credit access, credit channels

(source: author analysis)

2.0.1 Tea crops in Lam Dong province, Vietnam

Lam Dong is one of the provinces with the largest and oldest tea growing area in Vietnam. Favored by nature, fertile soil, suitable climate and especially with the advantage that the province is located at an altitude of 800-1,000m, Lam Dong's tea quality is confirmed to be delicious, fragrant, and sweet.

According to statistics, Currently, the total tea area in the province is 25,929 hectares, down more than 1,000 hectares compared to the previous year. Of which, the tea area is 23,791 hectares for trading, and annually supplied to the domestic and foreign markets is reached. 183,571 tons. In fact, Lam Dong province's tea trees account for 25% of the area and 27% of the country's tea production. Lam Dong tea has been famous for a long time with famous brands such as: Tann Chau, Le Ky, Quoc Thai... Among the famous tea brands, Lam Dong has also contributed high-value products, which are appreciated by many connoisseurs. Acceptable teas such as oolong tea, green tea, black tea, etc.

In Lam Dong, tea is grown mainly in Bao Loc, Bao Lam, and Di Linh. Because tea trees have been planted since the 20s of the last century, many tea areas here are now old, with low productivity. In the past years, especially from 2002 up to now, in the programs and projects to support the development of tea, the province has focused on expanding the area while promoting the "variety revolution", improving the tea garden to achieve high productivity. productivity, high quality and gradually building safe and clean tea material areas. Up to now, the area of new varieties of tea in the province accounts for 32%, with 6,340 hectares of high-yielding branched tea and 2,075 hectares of high-quality Taiwanese oolong tea. And according to the Project on developing tea material areas by 2020, the total tea area will be raised to 28,000 hectares, of which high-quality and productive tea varieties account for 55%, and at the same time implementing many projects to improve tea gardens

(source: agro.gov.vn,access date 20/11/2021)

4.3 Tea products and benefits

A. in the North of Vietnam

In Thai Nguyen, there are many tea regions with very high quality. Because Tan Cuong commune is the first tea growing area of the province. Therefore, Tan Cuong Thai Nguyen Tea brand is also known more.

Besides Tan Cuong, Thai Nguyen tea area also has other delicious tea regions. Like La Bang, Hoang Nong, Trai Cai or Khe Coc tea areas. Although it is the same green tea, each region has its own unique flavoy. The most famous tea of the Tan Cuong Thai Nguyen green tea region is Thai Nguyen Hook Tea. hook Tea is a type of tea that is crushed until the finished product, the tea leaves curl like a fishing hook.

Figure 3 - Tan Cuong tea in Thai Nguyen province

B. In Lam Dong province

Bao Loc Oolong Tea

Oolong tea is a famous tea of Lam Dong tea region, popular in many parts of the world. Oolong tea originated in Fujian province, China, then imported to Taiwan and prospered. The worldwide demand for tea has brought the oolong tea variety to Vietnam, and the land of Bao Loc, Lam Dong is the most suitable locality for the wonderful growth of this plant.

In Bao Loc, there are 3 famous varieties of oolong tea: Kim Tuyen oolong tea, Long Thuan oolong tea and Tu Quy oolong tea. Bao Loc oolong tea is famous because it grows at an altitude of 1,000m above sea level, the climate is foggy all year round, the soil is fertile, suitable for tea tree growth. Along with that is the processing process that goes through many stages: withering, turning incense, frying to kill yeast, jarring bells, shaping jars, drying, etc. To get a delicious oolong tea, Bao Loc people must comply with it. rigorous processing process from harvesting to finished tea products.

(so nice: fi*ttps://*yen rravier.ve/vung-cue-Jam-dong/, *access* date *2011 112021)*

4.4 Regression model for tea - export price versus macro factors: First of all, we see below correlation matrix and see that:

	TEA_EXPO...	CPI	G	R	RF
TEA_EXPO...	1.000000	-0.783433	0.262450	-0.819496	-0.299648
CPI	-0.783433	1.000000	0.099628	0.744833	0.509105
G	0.262450	0.099628	1.000000	0.095911	0.426732
R	-0.819496	0.744833	0.095911	1.000000	0.678900
RF	-0.299648	0.509105	0.426732	0.678900	1.000000

(source: author *analysls from* Vietnam *economy)*

4.5 Process of making green tea

Like Tan Cuong Thai Nguyen green tea, the flavor is considered the easiest to drink. Easy to drink here can be understood in the sense that the taste is easily liked by many people.

In Tan Cuong Thai Nguyen tea, there is always a prominent flavor, that is: the aroma of nuggets is passionate, greasy, and sweet. In it, there is less bitterness.

Overall, green tea is low in caffeine compared to other caffeinated beverages. As long as you're consuming caffeine within the recommended limits above, the amount of caffeine in green tea shouldn't be a concern.

In summary, Green tea contains less caffeine than other beverages. As long as you stay within

the recommended caffeine limit, the amount of caffeine in green tea should not be a concern.

A 230ml cup of green tea mixed with 2g of tea contains 30-50mg of caffeine. The maximum recommended amount of caffeine per day is 400mg, which is equivalent to about 8 230ml cups of green tea.

However, it's best not to drink 8 cups at a time, especially if you're sensitive to caffeine. Overall, green tea is a nutritious drink that contains safe amounts of caffeine.

Best of all, drinking green tea may even have some amazing benefits for your health. (Source:

https://www.healthline.com/nutrition/caffeine-in-green-tea). How *to choose to* huy *Fresh green* tea leaves

Fresh green tea leaves are not shiny, small leaves, dark green in color.

Should choose the top part that is old, has a lot of flat leaves (which are neither too old nor

too young).

Avoid choosing leaves that are too old, crushed, when cooking the tea will be acrid.

Then, Follow below steps:

Preliminary processing of tea leaves

Tea leaves pick up the leaves, remove old branches and damaged leaves and then wash a few times with water. Then, soak the tea leaves in water for 10 minutes before steeping and then draining.

Kettle tea

Gently rub the tea leaves and put them in the jar.

Next, to rinse the tea, pour 0.5 liters of boiling water into the pot, shake it gently, and pour the water into the glass.

Then, pour into the pot 2.5 liters of boiling water, leave for 10-20 minutes for the tea to infuse. Finally, pour the boiling water over the tea before to fill the tea pot.

Green tea juice has a beautiful light yellow color, has a slightly sweet taste and a slight aroma of tea leaves. Sitting and sipping a cup of green tea, eating a piece of cake with family and friends is great.

Figure 5 - Green tea made

(Source; internet)

5 . Discussion and Conclusion

The environment and policies for agricultural development are still limited.

Vietnam's agriculture is still facing major obstacles in the process of restructuring

structure and improve global competitiveness. According to Diaz-

Bonilla and Kwieciñski (2014), growth-encouraging environment and agricultural competitiveness of Vietnam is much less favorable than its main competitors in the market such as China, Thailand, Brazil,

Mexico, Chile,... Obstacles bring fundamental factors such as human resources, capital, agricultural institutions, the operation of markets (goods, labor, financial services) is still limited.

Studies on planning and planning management of crops and livestock for Stabilizing supply in the market:

Planning is a tool of the state used for development orientation, in line with the socio- economic development strategy, and at the same time ensure essential balances in the economy and the ecological environment. Identify important roles the importance of planning work, in recent years, central and local agencies

The province has implemented many plans for almost all sectors, fields and agriculture industry is no exception. However, many studies have shown the status of

The planning for the development of crops and livestock in the agricultural sector is not yet guaranteed

Due to poor quality, reliability and management, plans are often destroyed.

On the quality of human resources in the agricultural sector. Results of the survey of rural, agriculture and fishery shows the number of people of working age in the agricultural sector

Villages with the ability to work with professional and technical qualifications have a very slow increase and only a small percentage. Number of people of working age who are able to work with qualifications - technical expertise from elementary level upwards in 2011 accounted for 2.95% (in 2006 it was

2.48%. The region has the highest percentage of workers who are trained in skills from elementary to high is the Southeast with 5.25%. The lowest is the Mekong Delta with only 1.71%. rate of workers with intermediate education is 1.23% (in 2006 it was 0.89%); university degree reached 0.21%

(in 2006 it was 0.11%) (TCKT, 2012). Thus, there are more than 97% of agricultural workers Currently, there is no professional training, no professional certificate. Lack of labor

Having professional qualifications will be a major obstacle in applying the production method modernity, especially modern production thinking in the context of integration.

Factors affecting participation in the global agricultural value chain

To promote and improve the agricultural value chain, key factors play a supporting role and influence the entry of agricultural products into international markets,

especially the market of developed countries including:

Support services

Input support services

Availability of input services (seeds, fertilizers, pesticides, raw materials/fuels production, ..) is an important basis to help producers and processors of products

Agriculture increases production efficiency by reducing transaction costs. However, The quantity of input products is an important factor for agricultural products

produced to meet export standards to international markets, especially the domestic market and developed countries. Availability of responsive production input supply services meet the standards of export markets, especially markets of other countries

development is an important condition for producers to access. If the services provided inadequate levels or they provide unqualified inputs also affect quality of agricultural outputs. Post-harvest and processing support services Unlike other value chains, agricultural products are often seasonal, easy to damaged, so normally, agricultural product chains are not continuous.

Moreover, the time of harvesting is concentrated, so the harvested output is often very large in very short period of time. Due to asymmetries in terms of supply and demand in the market, prices of agricultural products have been greatly reduced. This trend occurs quite often in many locations

In the locality, the phrase "good harvest" is still a haunting obsession of many businesses agricultural authorities as well as farmers. To relieve pressure and master

become more active in the production, processing and consumption of agricultural products, supporting services -Post-harvest support (cold storage, transport vehicles, preliminary

processing/processing techniques, chemical testing, etc.) play an important role in helping agricultural products last longer in storage, processing and consumption of products. On the one hand it reduces the failure rate for post-harvest products for farmers, partly to help prolong the processing time transform and consume products to improve efficiency and add value in the value chain.

Marketing 4P recommendations

Using this marketing strategy will help firms to understand the market, needs and wants of consumers. Since then, manufacturers have constantly created products to satisfy that desire of consumers. Products must be standardized, the quality of products put on the market must be guaranteed. Products bring benefits that even exceed consumer expectations. Moreover, Enhance brand value, company reputation in the market.

Beside, Dao Thi Huong, Dinh Tran Ngoc Huy (2021) said that The goal of internal marketing is to satisfy internal customers and retain employees. When internal customers are satisfied, they will become more loyal and committed to the company. Internal customers will be ready to serve to satisfy and create loyalty of customers outside the business. Thus, internal marketing needs to be done before doing external marketing. The function of internal marketing is that the internal communication between the business and its employees must function effectively before the business can succeed in realizing its goals in relation to the external market.

Table 4- Marketing 4P suggestions for tea and agricultural products

Products (coffee, tea,...)	Price
-Naming products can be done via combination between product names and company names - Can expand width and depth of products (categories)	- Follow various pricing strategies - When determining the selling price, the business owner carefully determines the costs to perfect the product: the cost of materials, labor, transportation, design, etc. to make a profit. For example, The profit rate is about 15-30% of the total product value.
Place	Promotion
- Online marketing for agricultural products - Choose either Direct distribution: manufacturers sell products directly to customers without any intermediaries, businesses have stores, organize a sales team, and sell websites. Indirect distribution: manufacturers distribute their products through intermediaries such as supermarkets, shops, restaurants,	- change social media, communication - Advertising online - Individual sale need to be enhanced - PR through events connecting to clients

*(source: authors **analysis**)*

Research limitation

Authors can expand model for tobacco products as well.

ACKNOWLEDGEMENTS

I would like to take this opportunity to express my warm thanks to Board of Editors and Colleagues in assisting convenient conditions for my research paper.

References

[1]. Buu Thi Suu, Vu Quang Giang, Vu Phương Lien, Dinh Tran Ngoc Huy, Ha Thi Lan. (2021). The Auto-infection Trap with the Native Entomopathogenic Fungus, Beauveria Bassiana for Management of Coffee Berry Borer (Stephanoderes Hampei Ferrari) in the Northwest Region of Vietnam, Alinteri Journal of Agriculture science, 36(1): 11-198.

[2]. Bui Thi Suu, Dinh Tran Ngoc Huy, Nguyen Thi Hoa. (2021). SUSTAINABLE VALUE CHAIN ISSUES, INSECT TRAPS AND SOLUTIONS FOR COFFEE BERRY BORER IN THE NORTH

OF VIETNAM, Plant Cell Biotechnology and Molecular Biology 22(55&56), 7s-83

[3]. Bien, N.C., Phuong, N.T.M., & Cuc, N.T.T. (2018). Developing Tea Market through Analyzing the Value Chain of Vietnam Tea Industry, PSAKU International Journal of Interdisciplinary Research, 7(2)

[4]. Carr, M.K.V. (1999). Evaluating the impact of research for development: tea in Tanzania, Experimental

Agriculture , 35(3): 207 - 264. DOI: https://doi. org/10.1017/50014479799003051

[5]. Chinh, T.T.Q., Cuong, T. and Chen, J.C. (2020). Factors Affecting to Tea-Growing Household's Financial Efficiency: A Case Study from Thai Nguyen Province. *Open Access Library JoutRH, I,* 1-12. dot: 10.4236/oalib.1106969.

[6]. Chen Y., Li M., Abu Hatab A. (2020). A spatiotemporal analysis of comparative advantage in tea production in China. Agric. Econ. — Czech, 66: 550-561.

[7]. Dao Thi Huong, Dinh Tran Ngoc Huy. (2021). MEASUREMENT OF INTERNAL MARKETING INGREDIENTS AT GARMENT ENTERPRISES IN THAI NGUYEN PROVINCE, Journal of

Organizational Behavior Research, 6(2)

[8]. Dinh Tran Ngoc Huy, Nguyen Thi Hang, Le Thi Thanh Huong, Pham Van Hong. (2021). FOOD AND DRINK PROCESSING FROM LYCHEE PRODUCTS IN THE NORTHERN PROVINCES OF

VIETNAM - AND ROLES OF AGRICULTURE PROJECT FINANCING, Revista de Investigaciones Universidad del Quindio, 33(1), 187-195. https://doi.org/10.33975/riuq. vo133n1.555

[9]. Do Thu Huong, Nguyen Thi Hang, Duong Thi Ngu, Dinh Tran Ngoc Huy, Pham Thi Huyen Trang. (2021). Discussion on Case Teaching Method in a Risk Management Case Study with Econometric Model at Vietnam Listed Banks—Issues

Of Economic Education for Students , Review of International Geographical Education Online, 11(5), 2957-2966

[10]. Guo, Y., & Rato, M. (2019). The Development of Tea Planting and Tea Culture Tourism in Thai Nguyen, Vietnam, Journal of Mekong Societies, 15(3). doi:10.14456/jms.2019.19

[11]. Hac, L.D.; Huy, D.T.N.; Thach, N.N.; Nhung, P.T.H.; Thang, T.D. & Anh, T.T. (2021). Enhancing risk management culture for sustainable growth of Asia commercial bank -ACB in Vietnam under mixed effects of macro factors. Entrepreneurship and Sustainability Issues, 8(3). https://econpapers.repec.org/article/ssijouesi/v_3a8_3ay_3a2021 3ai_3a3_3ap_3a291-307.htm

[12]. Hang, T.T.B.; Nhung, D.T.H.; Nhung, D.H.; Huy, D.T.N.; Hung, N.M. & Dat, P.M. (2020). Where

beta is going - case of Vietnam hotel, airlines and tourism company groups after the low inflation period. Entrepreneurship and Sustainability Issues, 7(3). 2282-2298.

https://ideas.repec.org/a/ssi/jouesi/v7y2020i3p2282-2298.html

[13] Hai Ninh, N.T., Song, N.V., & Lebailly, P. (2018). NEEDS OF TEA GROWERS FOR PARTICIPATING IN TEA PRODUCTION INSURANCE: A CASE STUDY IN PHU THO PROVINCE, VIETNAM, AGROFOR 2(2). DOI:10.7251/AGRENG1702082V

[14] Ha, T.T.H, Khoa, N.B., Huy, D.T.N., Nhan, V.K., Nhung, D.H., Anh, P.T., Duy, P.K (2020) Modern

Corporate Governance Standards and Role of Auditing-Cases

in Some Western European Countries After Financial Crisis, Corporate Scandals and Manipulation, International Journal of Entrepreneurship 23(1S).

[15]. Huy, D.T.N.; Loan, B.T.; Anh, P.T. (2020). Impact of selected factors on stock price: a case study of Vietcombank in Vietnam. Entrepreneurship and Sustainability Issues, 7(4): 2715-2730.

https://ideas.repec.org/a/ssi/jouesi/v7y2020i4p2715-2730.html

[16] Huy, D. T. N., & Hang, N. T. (2021). Factors that affect Stock Price and Beta CAPM of Vietnam Banks and Enhancing Management Information System—Case of Asia Commercial Bank. REVISTA Geintec- Gestao Inovacao E Tecnologias, 11(2), 302-308

[17] Huy, D.T.N. (2015). The critical analysis of limited south asian corporate governance standards after financial crisis. International Journal for Quality Research, 15(1), 741-746.

http://www.ijqr.net/paper.php?id=378. Access: Jan. 11, 2021.

[18]. Hong, P.V., Nguyen, N.T., Huy, D.T.N., Thuy, N.T. and Huong, L.T.T. (2021). Evaluating Several Models of Quality Management and Impacts on Lychee Price Applying for Vietnam Agriculture Products Value Chain Sustainable Development. Alinteri Journal of Agriculture Sciences, 36(1): 122- 130. doi: 10.47059/alinteri/V36I1/AJAS21018

[19]. Huy, D.T.N.; Dat, P.M.; & Anh, P.T. (2020). Building and econometric model of selected factors' impact on stock price: a case study. Journal of Security and Sustainability Issues, 9 (M), 77-93.

https://cibg.org.au/index.php/cibg/article/viewFile/9/journal/article_8416.html

[20]. Huy, D.T.N.; Hien, D.T.N. (2010). The backbone of European corporate governance standards after financial crisis, corporate scandals and manipulation. Economic and Business Review, 12(4), 2015-2040. http://ojs.ebrjournal.net/ojs/index.php/ebr/article/download/101/30

[21]. Hien, D. T., Huy, D. T. N., & Hoa, N. T. (2021). Ho Chi Minh Viewpoints about Marxism Moral Human Resource for State Management Level in Vietnam. Psychology and Education Journal, 58(5), 2908-2914. Hoang, N. T., & Huy, D. T. N. (2021). Determining factors for educating students for choosing to work for foreign units: Absence of self-efficacy. JETT, 12(2), 11-19.

[22] Huy, D. T. N., Hanh, N. T. T., Hang, N. T., Nhung, P. T. H., Thao, N. T. P., Han, L. T., & hang, D.

T. (2021). General Solutions for Enhancing Quality of Teachers During Globalization in Emerging Markets Including Vietnam-and Some Pedagogy Psychological Issues. Psychology and Education Journal, 58(4), 2343-2349.

[23] Humphrey, J., and H. Schmitz. 2002. "How Does Insertion in Global Value Chains Affect Upgrading in Industrial Clusters." Regional *Studies* 36 (9): 1017-27

[24]. Humphrey va Memedovic (2006), Global value chains in *the* agri%od *sector.* Working papers 2006, UNIDO.

[25]. Huy, Dinh T.N., (2012), Estimating Beta of Viet Nam listed construction companies groups during the crisis,

Journfi of/n *tegtatior* and *DeveJopnien t, 15(1).*

[26] Huy D.T.N., Nhan V.K., Brett N.T.N., Hong N.T.P., Chung N.T., Huy P.Q. (2021). 'Impacts of Inter nal and External Macroeconomic Factors on Firm Stock Price in an Expansion Econometric model—A Case in Vietnam Real Estate Industry', *Data Screw ce Not financial Econ oinettics-Studies* in *Compute* rionaJ /n *telligen ce,* vol.898, Springer. http://doi-org-043.webvpn.fjmu.edu.cn/10.1007/978- 3-030-48853-6 14

[28]. J.K.SahaaK.M. MehediAdnanaSwati AninditaSaikerbShefaliBunerjee. (2021). Analysis of growth trends in area, production and yield of tea in Bangladesh, Journal of Agriculture and Food Research, 4

[29] Khoi, N.V., Lan, C.H., & Huong, T.L. (2015). International Journal of Managing Value and Supply Chains, 6(3)

[30] Le Thi Thanh Huong,Vu Quynh Nam, Dinh Tran Ngoc Huy, Pham Van Tuan, Pham Van Hong. (2021). Increasing Agricultural Productivity, Quality and Quantity of Coffee and Tea Crops Planting and Marketing Mix Solutions - Methods of Eliminating Coffee Berry Borer and Insects in Vietnam, Alinteri JOurnal of Agriculture Science, 36(1)

[31] Le Thi Thanh Huong, Dinh TRan Ngoc Huy, Nguyen Thi Hang, Nguyen Tien Dung. (2021). Marketing Strategy based on Competitor Analysis - A Case in Vietnam Medicine Sector, Revista geintec- gestao Inovacao E Tecnologias, 11(3)

[32] Ngu, D.T., Huong, D.T., Ngoc Huy, D.T., Thanh, P.T., Dongiil, E.S. (2021). Language Teaching Application to

English Students at Master's Grade Levels on History and Macroeconomic-Banking Management Courses in Universities and Colleges , Journal of Language and Linguistic Studies, 17(3)

[33]. Phuong, N.T.T., Huy, D.T.N, Tuan, P.V. (2020). The evaluation of impacts of a seven factor model on nvb stock price in commercial banking industry in vietnam-and roles of discolosure of accounting policy in risk management, Intl. Journal of Entrepreneurship, Q3 scopus, Special issue, Vol.24(1)

[34] Porter, Michael E., "Competitive Advantage". 1985, Ch. 1, pp 11-15. The Free Press. New York.

[35] San Viet Le, Lesueur, D., Herrmann, L., & Hudek, L. (2021). Sustainable tea production through agroecological management practices in Vietnam: a review, Environmental Sustainability, 3. DOI:10.1007/s42398-021-00182-w

[36]. Tinh, D. T., Thuy, N. T., & Ngoc Huy, D. T. (2021). Doing Business Research and Teaching Methodology for Undergraduate, Postgraduate and Doctoral Students- Case in Various Markets Including Vietnam. Elementary Education Online, 20(1), 1414-1418. doi: 10.17051/ ilkon1ine.2021.01.148

[37] Thach, N.N., Hanh, H.T., Huy, D.T.N., ...Huong, L.T.T., Nam, V.Q. (2021). TECHNOLOGY QUALITY MANAGEMENT OF THE INDUSTRY 4.0 AND CYBERSECURITY RISK MANAGEMENT ON CURRENT BANKING ACTIVITIES IN EMERGING MARKETS – THE CASE IN VIETNAM, /n *rernarionfi* Journñ for Qu£ity *Research,* 5(3), pp. 845-856

[38]. Tran, D.N.L.; Nguyen, T.D.; Pham, T.T., Rañola, R.F., Jr.; Nguyen, T.A. (2021). Improving Irrigation Water Use Efficiency of Robusta Coffee (Coffea canephora) Production in Lam Dong Province,

Vietnam. Sustainability, 13, 6603. https://doi.org/10.3390/su13126603

[39]. Trung, N.D., Huy, D.T.N., Hang, N.T. and Ha, L.T. (2021). Effective Management via a Business Model of Food and Drink Processing from Lychee Products in the Northern Areas of Vietnam. Alinteri Journal of Agriculture Sciences, 36(1): 406-411. dot: 10.47059/alinteri/V36I1/AJAS21061

[40] Tuan, P.V., Huy, D.T.N., Trung, N.D., & Hoa, N.T. (2021). MARKETING STRATEGIES FOR TOURISM AND DIGITAL TECH APPLICATIONS IN TOURISM INDUSTRY - A CASE OF OCH TOURISM CORPORATION IN VIETNAM, Design engineering, Issue 7

[41] Thi Hang, N., Thi Tinh, D., Ngoc Huy, D. T., & Hong Nhung, P. T. (2021). Educating and training labor force Under Covid 19; Impacts to Meet Market Demand in Vietnam during Globalization and Integration Era. Journal for Educators, Teachers and Trainers, 12(1), 179-18a. doi: 10.47750/jett.2021.12.01.023

[42] Thi Hoa, N., Hang, N. T., Giang, N. T., & Huy, D.T.N. (2021). Human resource for schools of politics and for international relation during globalization and EVFTA. Ilkogretim Online, 20(4)

[43] Van Tuan, P., Huy, D.T.N., & Duy, P. K. (2021). Impacts of Competitor Selection Strategy on Firm Risk Case in Vietnam Investment and Finance Industry. Revista Geintec-Gestao Inovacao E Tecnologias, 11(3), 127-135.

[44] Yong-Yan. F., Manafian, J., Zia, S.M., Huy, D.T.N., Le, T.-H. (2021). Analytical Treatment of the Generalized Hirota-Satsuma-Ito Equation Arising in Shallow water Wave, Advances in Mathematical Physics, 2021 issue

Exhibit

Exhibit 1 - Inflation, CPI over past 10 years (2007-2017) in Vietnam

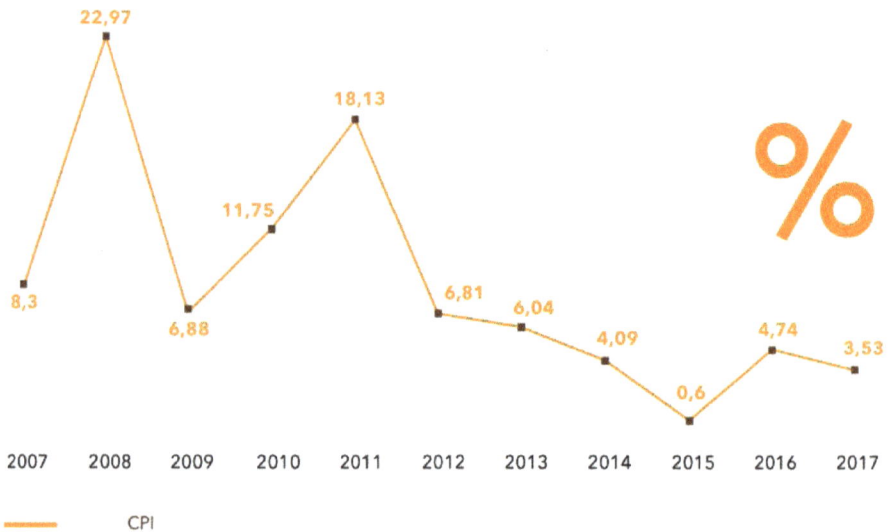

Exhibit 2 – GDP growth rate past 10 years (2007 - 2018) in Vietnam

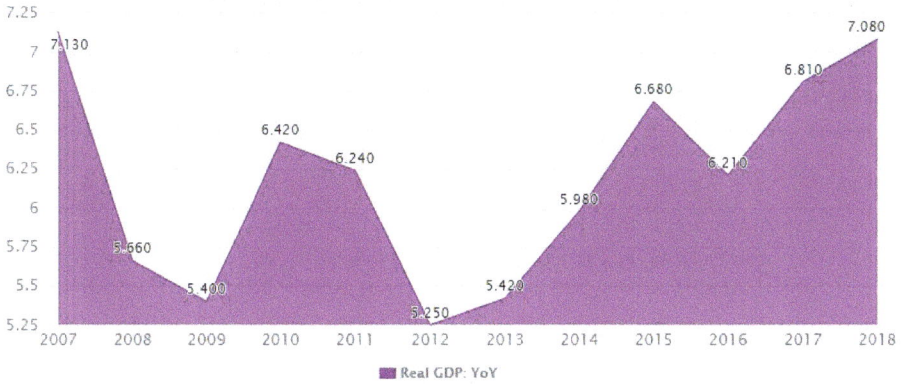

SOURCE: WWW.CEICDATA.COM | General Statistics Office

CASE NO. 2

DATE

7 Jan, 2022

INSECTS ALCOHOL TRAPS, SUSTAINABLE AGRICULTURAL VALUE CHAIN IN COFFEE AND TEA CROPS IN THE NORTHERN REGIONS OF VIETNAM - AND SOLUTIONS FOR MARKETING MIX

Dinh Tran Ngoc Huy, MBA,

Banking University HCMC, Ho Chi Minh city Vietnam – International University of Japan, Japan

dtnhuy2010@gmail.com

Pham Van Tuan, PhD, Asso.Prof

National Economics University, Hanoi Vietnam

phamvantuan@neu.edu.vn

Bui Thi Suu, Master

Tay Bac University, Quyet Tam Ward, Son La City, Son La Province,

Vietnam.

buithisuu@utb.edu.vn

Nguyen Ngoc Thach, PhD, Asso.Prof

Banking University HCMC, Ho Chi Minh city Vietnam

thachnn@buh.edu.vn

Bui Thi Thom, PhD

Thai Nguyen University of Forestry and Agriculture Science, Vietnam

buithithom@tuaf.edu.vn

Nguyen Dinh Trung, PhD

National Economics University (NEU), Hanoi Vietnam

trungnd@neu.edu.vn

Nguyen Thuy Duong, PhD

Thuongmai University, Hanoi Vietnam

Duong.nt@tmu.edu.vn

ABSTRACT

To ensure sustainability in tea and coffee crops as two main crops in the northern region of Vietnam, for instance in Son La and Thai Nguyen Provinces, we need to explore changing traditional production methods (manufacturing according to own experience) by a new way of production according to the production process cleaner, safer (VietGAP, GlobalGap, ..). This production process helps households, Farmers use the right inputs at the right time, reducing costs as well as product quality improvement.

The next solution is to replace gradually chemical pesticides (at least reduce proportion) in agricultural using, with insect traps such as insect alcohol traps or bottle traps in order to eliminate female insects (Coffee berry borer- CBB) that are harmful and their next generation as well.

Research results show us that CPI and R (lending rate) have negative correlation with tea export price, whereas G (GDP growth) and Rf (Risk free rate) have positive correlation with tea price. Besides, this study also give out recommendations for reduction in CPI and R and increase in G to push tea export price.

Our research limitation is that we can expand for other crops, industries and markets as well.

Key words: agricultural value chain, sustainability, tea crops, coffee crops, insect alcohol traps, Vietnam

JEL: M21, G30, G32, G38

1.Introduction

First, we recognize the importance of developing sustainable agricultural value chain for coffee, tea and lychee crops in the North of Vietnam in recent years, under effects from covid 19.

Pham Van Hong, Nguyen Thao Nguyen, Dinh Tran Ngoc Huy, Nguyen Thu Thuy, Le Thi Thanh Huong (2021) stated that In Vietnam, we will evaluate the effectiveness of VIETGAP and GLOBAL GAP models, principles and standards applying in Vietnam agriculture value chain in a specific case study. The research results show a strict condition for applying VIETGAP and GLOBAL GAP for better quality in agriculture, including: Conditions for soil, irrigation water, fertilizers, pest control, etc.

Next, Nguyen Dinh Trung, Dinh Tran Ngoc Huy, Nguyen Thi Hang, Le Thu Ha (2021) mentioned Vietnam agriculture has been growing in 2012-2020, however according to World bank, overall agricultural productivity (TFP) has been in a declining trend since the year 2000. Vietnam's tea exports are mainly and for a long time focused on markets Easy-going market, does not set strict standards on food safety and hygiene.

Then, Duyen Nhat Lam Tran et al (2021) presented study findings further suggest that mitigating water shortages in coffee farms require subregional and national policy support such as better access to credit and extension services, training, land management, and household-level efforts to improve farming practices through the application of appropriate technologies and traditional knowledge

And Perez and Viana (2012) showed a cross-country study comparing Colombia and Vietnam, two of the major coffee exporting countries in the world, in terms of their infrastructures, the roles of external shocks, technology adoption at different stages of production, added value, positioning in both domestic and global markets, internationalization patterns, marketing and branding innovations, regulatory frameworks, and policy environments.

Research questions

Question 1: What are principles of sustainable value chain applying in coffee, tea and lychee crops in the North of Vietnam?

Question 2: What are benefits of insect alcohol traps used for Coffee berry borer?

2. Literature review

Activities to improve global agricultural value chains

For developing countries (production enterprises/organizations or households)

family) when participating in the global value chain is a successful step. Participating in this network, the actors participate in the stages in the chain will have the opportunity to access knowledge, management skills and production technology higher. Since then, the capacity and working skills of enterprises, farming households as well as workers in general gradually approach the common standards of developed countries.

According to Humphrey and Schmitz (2002), there are three main groups of methods to improve value growth in global value chains.

Specifically:

Upgrade/Improve production process:

Improve added value through changing production methods more efficiently.

For example, in farming, changing traditional production methods

(manufacturing according to own experience) by a new way of production according to the production process cleaner, safer (VietGAP, GlobalGap, ..). This production process helps households, Farmers use the right inputs at the right time, reducing costs as well as product quality improvement.

In the stages of post-harvest preservation and product processing, changes in technology

or modern and appropriate processing and preservation process will help improve product quality agricultural products, long-term product sales, thereby avoiding the quantity supplied to the market massively in a short time. The extension of time will help to increase the selling price of the product higher.

In fact, changing and improving the production process depends quite a lot on the requirements of the customer market. Even in the domestic market or the export market, if consumers and retailers have a need to consume clean products, clearly stating the origin and clear production process, the production stage will be forced. must meet if you want to participate in the value chain. In developed countries, the regulations and supervision on food safety, counterfeit goods as well as strict management and enforcement policies force the products supplied to consumers to ensure quality and quantity. The state's legal corridor helps protect consumers and promote Brand investors.

We summarize previous studies as follows:

Table 1 – Summary of previous studies

Authors	Year	Contents, results
Perez & Viana	2012	Using value chain analysis, it was found that Colombia and Vietnam produce different types of coffee, and that both have implemented diverse strategies in order to be more competitive in domestic and foreign markets via product differentiation. These differences make explicit room for cooperation between these two countries in an international environment where fierce competition persists. Originality/value – Cooperation between producing countries is an under-researched subject. These findings will be useful both for policy makers in coffee-producing countries and agribusiness researchers.
Doan Ba Toai et al	2019	investigate the Vietnam tea export from 2010 to the world. The Vietnam tea overview research Vietnam tea production, domestic consumption and Vietnam tea export volume to more important recommendations for the future of the Vietnam's tea. The Result, we found that volume of Vietnam's tea and average volume per person in Vietnam is going up.

Nguyen Hung Anh et al	2019	highlight the fact that farmers' decisions to participate in sustainable coffee farming are mainly driven by economic benefits. Sustainable farming is more cost-effective and profitable than conventional farming, despite the insignificant difference in production efficiency. Improvement of education, farming knowledge, and collective actions could mitigate negative effects of small-scale production for sustainable coffee farmers. Pesticide management, shade coffee encouragement, and reduction of excessive fertilization, over-irrigation, and unproductive coffee varieties are recommended for sustainable development of the sector.
Azrag et al	2019	Although the coffee berry borer, *Hypothenemus hampei* (Ferrari) (Coleoptera: Curculionidae: Scolytinae) is the most destructive insect pest of coffee worldwide, there is much to learn about its thermal biology.

Johnson et al	2019	estimated that 49.5% of the total coffee berry borer load was present in dripline raisins, 47.3% in tree raisins, and 3.2% in center aisle raisins. Our findings confirm the importance of whole-farm sanitation in coffee berry borer management by demonstrating the negative impact that poor postharvest control can have on the following season's crop.
Tran, D.N.L et al	2021	The production function analysis using Cobb–Douglas shows that the volume of irrigation water, amount of working capital, labor, and farm size significantly influence coffee productivity. Indigenous farmers are more efficient in utilizing irrigation water than migrant farmers. The Tobit result indicates that farmers' experience, education level, the distance of farm to water sources, security of access to water sources, extension contact, and credit access significantly affect IWUE.
Pham Van Hong, Nguyen Thao Nguyen, Dinh Tran Ngoc Huy, Nguyen Thu Thuy, Le Thi Thanh Huong	2021	Sustainability of Vietnam agriculture value chain will be dependent on various factors such as skills and experience of farmers, advanced technology, agricultural engineering, standards and models such as VIETGAP or GLOBAL GAP, etc

Nguyen Dinh Trung, Dinh Tran Ngoc Huy, Nguyen Thi Hang, Le Thu Ha	2021	emphasizes positive and healthy aspects of lychee products and lychee fruit juice in our country, Vietnam. And also roles of banks in project financing is also a good way to support microfinancing for star-ups and our business model.

Last but not least, Johnson, M.A et al (2020) stated that Coffee berry borer (*Hypothenemus hampei* (Ferrari), CBB) has invaded nearly every coffee-producing country in the world, and it is commonly recognized as the most damaging insect pest of coffee.

3. Methodology

Method and Data

This study mainly use combination of quantitative methods and qualitative methods including synthesis, inductive and explanatory methods. And it emphasizes again important roles of internet data in sustainable modern bank management

For quantitative analysis, the study is supported with OLS regression.

Data is collected from reliable internet sources and websites of Bureau Statistics, State Bank and Ministry of Finance and Vietnam banks. See below figure 1, we recognize that standard deviation of variable - tea export price has highest value while that of GDP growth is lowest:

Figure 1 - Descriptive data statistics

	TEA_EXPO...	CPI	G	R	RF
Mean	1627.650	0.053530	0.061090	0.115260	0.046905
Median	1645.100	0.038150	0.064800	0.100000	0.053350
Maximum	1724.500	0.181300	0.070800	0.190000	0.065350
Minimum	1466.000	0.006300	0.029100	0.080000	0.012200
Std. Dev.	89.43470	0.048052	0.012441	0.039225	0.018595
Skewness	-0.572756	2.051303	-1.843628	1.138882	-0.570545
Kurtosis	2.050915	6.308044	5.524584	2.705184	2.017240
Jarque-Bera	0.922067	11.57272	8.320575	2.197970	0.944960
Probability	0.630632	0.003069	0.015603	0.333209	0.623454
Sum	16276.50	0.535300	0.610900	1.152600	0.469050
Sum Sq. Dev.	71987.08	0.020781	0.001393	0.013847	0.003112

(source: Ministry of Industry and Trade, Ministry of Agriculture and Rural Development)

4.Main results

4.1 Coffee crops planting in Vietnam

Monitoring coffee berry borer with alcohol trap

Son La province, located approximately 300 km westward from Hanoi and borders Laos to the south, is the largest province in northwestern region with a total area of 14,055 km2, and the provincial population of 1,024 million.

Thai ethnic minority people account for approximately 55% which is more than half of provincial population. The main crops are cassava, sugarcane, and coffee beans.

There are a lot of nations who used Traps in order to monitor CBB, and in some cases, to manage these populations by "Mass-trapping" to reduce females lead to reduce next generations.

Scientists and researchers have formed Traps , using 2.0 litter bottles which are transparent and plastic (initially a container - soft drink) and used a small window (13 x 18 cm) of 9.0 cm above the bottom. Then they form a killing agent by Water (200 ml) with liquid detergent (2 ml) added to bottom of the bottle trap , this is for preserving dead adult CBB. A 15 ml amber glass vial with a rubber cover (originally used as a medicine antibiotic powder container) was used as a alcohol dispenser. Absolute Ethanol and Methanol (1:1) were used in average about 868mg day. Inside bottle - The vial was hung, 20cm above the trap bottom. 12 m was distance b.t traps within a block, and 30 m b.t blocks. Plots were laid out in a completely randomized design with three replicates. Scientists set / arranged 20 traps for every coffee farm. Scientists have to replace Water with liquid detergent and alcohol weekly. In order to

perform research assessments, researchers has removed water with dead insects for counting and the weighted vial to determinate mean volatile release rates. Nuber CBB adults captured per trap and proportion berry infestation were record once a week.

(source: Suu Thi Bui, Dinh Tran Ngoc Huy, Lan Duc Doan, 2021)

Insects Alcohol traps in agricultural crops

In planting coffee, tea, etc. there are many harmful insects which previously can be killed by chemical pesticides.

But nowadays scientists develop more tools and traps to eliminate harmful insects, for example, alcohol traps to hold female insects and kill next generation.

Bottle trap using alcohol attractants will help farmers track CBB populations and monitor CBB adult flight to determine the best timing for insecticide (chemical, entomopathogenic fungi) spray.

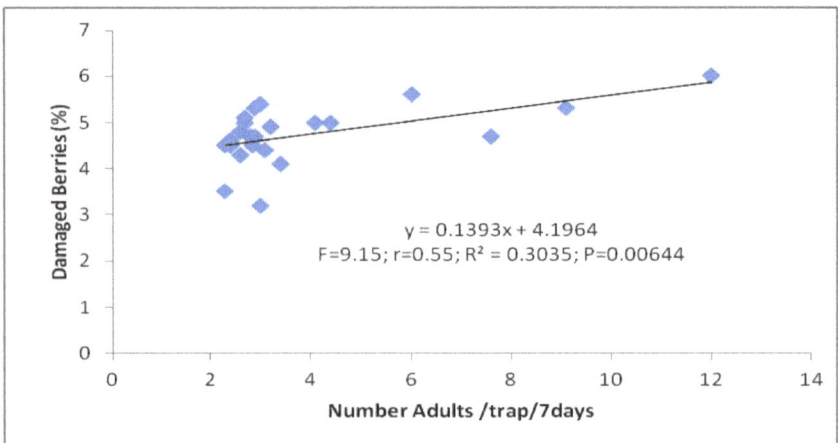

Within the figure:
$y = 0.1393x + 4.1964$
$F = 9.15; r = 0.55; R^2 = 0.3035; P = 0.00644$

Y-axis: Damaged Berries (%)
X-axis: Number Adults /trap/7days

Figure 2- The regression of the mean of infested coffee berries proportion and the no. of CBBs captured

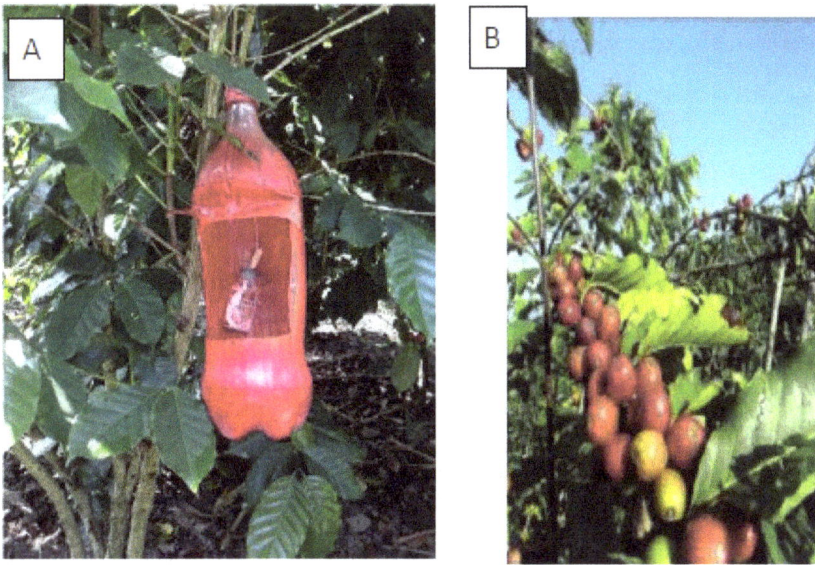

Figure 3-Monitoring CBB in Son La province, Vietnams using red bottle traps. (A) The bottle trap using monitoring CBB; (B) Coffee tree with matured berries.

(Source: Bui Thi Suu, Lan Duc Doan, Dinh Tran Ngoc Huy, 2021)

Beside, Bui Thi Suu, Dinh Tran Ngoc Huy, Nguyen Thi Hoa (2021) stated that scientists has thought of using traps, alcohol traps to reduce generations of insects, reduce female insects that are harmful. There are some factors that influence traps for example: wind direction, climate, etc. The reason for scientists to limit chemical pesticides and move to other methods to eliminate coffee berry borer is that chemicals will be harmful for coffee products, for farmers and for consumers.

Then, Johnson et al (2019) said that Coffee berry borer, Hypothenemus hampei Ferrari (Coleoptera: Curculionidae: Scolytinae), is the most damaging insect pest of coffee worldwide. Old coffee berries (raisins) are widely acknowledged as coffee berry borer reservoirs, yet few studies have attempted to quantify coffee berry borer populations in raisins remaining on farms postharvest.

4.2 Tea crops planning in Vietnam

The change in the structure of Vietnam's tea export market to developing countries

development has a negative trend even though the import tax rate is increasingly reduced.

From 2007 onwards, the output exported to countries with high requirements for

standards such as EU, Japan, Australia, Canada,... tend to decrease significantly (see also table 2). The cause of this decrease can be attributed to an increase in the number of

regulations on food safety and hygiene as well as lowering the MRL for some types of Plant protection products. In particular, in 2009, exports from Vietnam to the EU countries (as well as the UK, France) and Japan have significantly decreased due to the inability to passed the food safety and hygiene tests.

Table 2- The largest tea export markets of Vietnam (% by volume)

	2013	2014	2015	2016	2017
Total Markets	100	100	100	100	100
Pakistan	16.2	26.5	29.2	29.7	23
Taiwan	15.9	17.4	14.1	9.6	12.6
Russia	8.3	8.6	12	12.5	12.5
China	9.9	9.7	6.2	6.3	7.7
Indonesia	8.3	4.3	7.8	11.9	6.9
USA	7	7.5	6.3	4.8	5.0
UAE	2.7	2.7	4.9	2.3	4.8
Malaysia	2.6	2.6	2.3	3.4	2.6
India	0.8	0.8	0.1	1.9	1.2
Arab xeut	1.6	1.7	1.6	1.1	1.2

(source: Vietnam General custom)

Key actors in the tea value chain

Input provider

Because tea producing households all have long-term experience in growing tea (many households have 30-40 years of experience) so many households are able to self-seed their growing areas new or renovate tea garden. However, most households buy new varieties to replace Traditional tea varieties (Middleland tea) are often easily purchased from households other businesses, or seed agents in the locality or neighboring communes and districts.

Fertilizers, pesticides and simple production and processing tools can be easily purchased

at local shops (in the commune or in the district). Agricultural materials (fertilizers, pesticides) provided by private companies and other small merchants. Tea growers can buy and pay later (buy on credit) for the owners of agents of agricultural materials

Tea growers

Tea growers in Thai Nguyen province are still mainly households and businesses

The industry is also involved in tea growing, but the area is very small compared to the total area conscious. On average, the total tea growing area per household is only about 0.2-0.3 ha and is dispersed into about 2-3 small pieces. It is the fragmentation and small size of the area that Households also face difficulties in the cultivation process as well as in the application of public science technology into production.

Education level is an important factor for all economic activities and for production

Tea products are no exception. According to the survey results of the research team for

The average number of years of schooling of the head of a tea growing household is 7.6 years, which is only good junior high school career. The qualifications are quite low but most of them have 30 to 40 years of experience in tea growing.

The cultivation and care of tea has a fairly clear division of labor. Most activities

This movement is mainly performed by women. Female participants (in terms of time, number of days workers) compared with men is because tea picking is mainly done by hand, these jobs more suitable for women. In contrast, pesticide spraying for tea is mainly done by men (69% of pesticide spraying is done by men in the household).

Table 3- Division of labor in tea planting and processing

	By stage (%)	By gender		
DIY	*100*	*Male*	*Female*	*Total*
Tea planting and caring	*92.38*	*34.17*	*65.83*	*100*
Tea processing-Homemade	*7.62*	*34.42*	*65.58*	*100*
Hire labors	*100*			
Tea planting and caring	*88.25*	*6.76*	*93.24*	*100*
Tea processing	*11.75*	*0.71*	*99.29*	*100*

(source: Le Van Hung, Pham Van Hong, Project, 2019)

Trader (Trader)

Tea collectors can either buy fresh tea or dry tea from households. Because the majority of Tea growing households have processed to dry tea, so the main collectors are:

for dry tea. They can directly come to buy at tea growing households, buy at the market

wholesalers (weekly markets like Dai Tu district), or tea growing households bring them to sell for them. Traders can resell to processing and packaging establishments/enterprises tea or resell it to tea shops and retailers in Thai Nguyen province as well as in other provinces.

For tea enterprises and processing establishments in Thai Nguyen province, they mainly buy directly from tea growing households (both fresh and processed tea).

Processors

For Thai Nguyen province, tea production at the household level is the main type of tea production.

The total output of processed tea in the province is over 42,000 tons. Of these, 80%

tea production is processed by 45 cooperatives, 95 groups of cooperatives and 216 craft villages (with more than 60,000 participating households). Enterprises engaged in industrial processing Industry accounts for only about 20% of total production (8,400 tons). Processing is on a large scale small, scattered leading to difficulties in quality control, reputation and security brand protection. In the domestic market, there are many jars labeled Thai Nguyen but do not specify the unit, production and packing facility. Even many tea products There is no information about the person who processes and produces the tea product packing and tea packing. Tea products processed at households by traditional methods, The system is mostly loose tea products packed in large bags, without packaging and labels.

Processing establishments/cooperatives usually have business registration and product labels pack. They mainly process traditional tea (dried green tea) and create brand in the local or domestic market. Processing scale of each establishment/cooperative is not too large, so the raw materials used are usually purchased from relatives, people acquaintances in the commune or members of the cooperative.

Wholesaler/retailer

The people who play the role of distributing tea products of Thai Nguyen province are including: wholesalers, retailers in the domestic market and companies that play the role of intermediary to export to the international market. Distribution is difficult

about equipment for maintaining and preserving tea quality. The people

Wholesalers/retailers can pack and label themselves to improve added value. Also

Like households/processors and businesses, distributors can also pack

dry tea by foil bags and vacuum.Currently packing tea in various types

bags of organic origin are still modest, only used by a few businesses.

Consumers

There is a relative difference in the type of tea consumed in the domestic market with tea exported

For domestic consumption, due to the taste of Vietnamese people, most tea is consumed

The domestic tea is dried green tea. Meanwhile, the export tea of Thai Nguyen province has two main product categories are raw tea for export (bag tea), dip tea and tea group

packaged dried greens. Thai Nguyen tea has become a famous brand for

tea drinkers in the country. Demand for Thai Nguyen tea in the country

This is one of the reasons for reducing tea export motivation of the province.

Because the quality of tea depends quite a lot on the land, weather and care techniques of the farmers. Even within the province, the distance between the two districts is only 25km, but the quality and yield of tea in the two districts are different. While, the average selling price of fresh tea in Thai Nguyen city is 42.5 thousand VND/kg of fresh tea, while the selling price of fresh tea in Dai Tu district is only 29.2 thousand VND/kg. Thanks to the high selling price but low maintenance cost, the profit of tea growers in Thai Nguyen city is much higher than in Dai Tu district. Another important reason leading to the difference in selling prices between the two areas is that Thai Nguyen city has a famous Tan Cuong tea brand in the country.

Table 4- Comparison of profits of tea growing households by different groups

1,000 VND/kg (fresh tea)

	Cost	Revenue	Profit
General	18.556	37.190	18.634
By location			
Thai Nguyen city	15.863	42.454	26.591
Dai Tu district	22.515	29.455	6.940
By ethnicity			
Kinh	17.707	37.610	19.903
Minority	25.851	33.588	7.738
Education level of household			
Secondary school or lower	18.804	36.409	17.604
High school or upper	17.249	41.308	24.059
Join the link			
Linked	16.083	41.816	25.733
Not linked	19.308	35.784	16.476

(source: Le Van Hung, Pham Van Hong, Project, 2019)

According to population groups, Kinh people have a higher profit from tea cultivation than ethnic minority groups. Ethnic minority groups often live in disadvantaged areas

(Ethnic people often live in mountainous areas of Dai Tu district, far from the center, markets,...) compared to Kinh people in Xinjiang, Thai Nguyen city, so the land is less fertile fat and tea quality are also worse.

Under the same natural conditions, the profits from tea cultivation for ethnic minorities are still low than the Kinh people living there. The reason is that the ethnic minority group has more limited techniques for planting and taking care of tea trees than the Kinh people. Low level of education and capacity is also the reason leading to lower profits from tea cultivation of households headed by a householder with a secondary education or less than that of a household head with a high school education level or higher.

Constraints restricting participation in international markets

Small scale production but weak production links

With a large number of farmers engaged in tea production, it is understandable why

The scale of tea production of households is still very limited, although the area of tea cultivation in the province is very limited

Thai Nguyen has continuously increased over the years. According to the survey results of the Year 2018, on average, a production household has only 0.36 hectares, scattered into two or three different plots (maybe near or far from where they live). Even, the average area of each tea growing household in Thai Nguyen province is only 0.11 ha (Thai Nguyen Provincial People's Committee, 2017).

Moreover, the small size of the area and the lack of centralized production lead to higher production costs and reduced efficiency. Due to the limited and unsynchronized common irrigation system, households often hire people to drill wells and buy pumps to get water for irrigation without sharing water sources. It is also difficult because the scale is not large enough. Currently, more than 77% of surveyed households report a lack of water for irrigation, especially during the dry season months (November to April).

Moreover,in areas lacking electricity connection infrastructure, farmers have to invest in generators to generate electricity to run water pumps. Recently, the manifestations of climate change such as prolonged heat and cold, harmful cold, extreme weather phenomena and the frequency of natural disasters (floods, droughts) are increasing in Vietnam. some places in Thai Nguyen province in recent years. According to the Hydrometeorological Station of Thai Nguyen province; the average annual temperature in 9 districts, cities and towns in the province increased gradually, from 1959 to 2016 it increased by about 20 C; In the last 9 months of 2018 and the first 3 months of 2019, the rainfall is only 66% compared to the average rainfall of previous years.

Meanwhile, the abuse of pesticides is still happening and at a very low level

worthy of attention. On average, each tea growing household was sprayed 19.2 times/year (for 7 tea batches), 1.38 times higher than the recommended level of 14 times/year. The pre-harvest quarantine period is shorter, with an average of only 12.4 days compared to the recommended level of 15 days. If based on the results of this survey, it can be concluded that the production stage in the tea value chain of Thai Nguyen province has not yet ensured the recommended safe thresholds in the use of pesticides for tea plants and harvested tea products.

4.3 Econometric model for tea - export price:

First of all, we see below scatter charts and see that:

Chart 1 - CPI vs tea export price

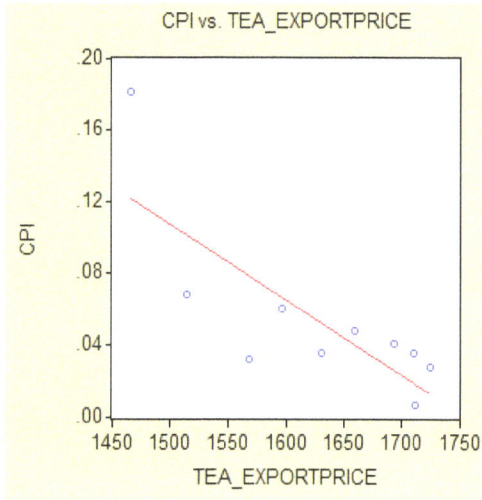

(source: Ministry of Industry and Trade, Ministry of Agriculture and Rural Development)

Chart 2 - Lending rate vs tea export price

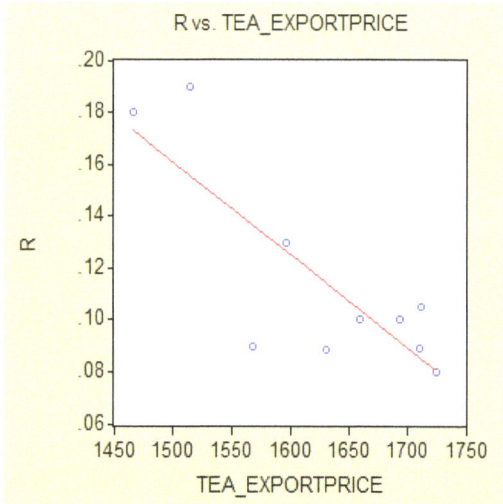

(source: Ministry of Industry and Trade, Ministry of Agriculture)

Chart 3 - GDP growth vs tea export price

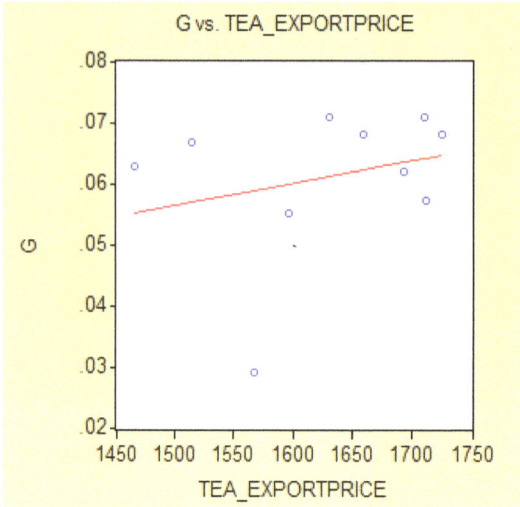

(source: Ministry of Industry and Trade, Ministry of Agriculture and Rural Development)

Second we analyze from below correlation matrix:

- Correlation between tea export price and R is lower than that between tea export price and CPI and Rf (figure 2).

Figure 2 - correlation matrix

Correlation Matrix					
	TEA_EXPO...	CPI	G	R	RF
TEA_EXPO...	1.000000	-0.783433	0.262450	-0.819496	-0.299648
CPI	-0.783433	1.000000	0.099628	0.744833	0.509105
G	0.262450	0.099628	1.000000	0.095911	0.426732
R	-0.819496	0.744833	0.095911	1.000000	0.678900
RF	-0.299648	0.509105	0.426732	0.678900	1.000000

(source: Ministry of Industry and Trade, Ministry of Agriculture and Rural Development)

We analyze from below regression results that:

- CPI and R have negative correlation with tea export price, whereas G and Rf have positive correlation with tea price.

Figure 3 - Regression results for tea price

Dependent Variable: TEA_EXPORTPRICE
Method: Least Squares
Date: 10/05/21   Time: 11:15
Sample: 1 10
Included observations: 10

Variable	Coefficient	Std. Error	t-Statistic	Prob.
CPI	-756.2119	384.3429	-1.967545	0.1063
G	1723.285	1145.063	1.504970	0.1927
R	-1723.106	570.4374	-3.020675	0.0294
RF	1529.279	1037.685	1.473742	0.2006
C	1689.729	75.74046	22.30946	0.0000

R-squared	0.905267	Mean dependent var		1627.650
Adjusted R-squared	0.829480	S.D. dependent var		89.43470
S.E. of regression	36.93123	Akaike info criterion		10.36284
Sum squared resid	6819.578	Schwarz criterion		10.51414
Log likelihood	-46.81422	F-statistic		11.94493
Durbin-Watson stat	2.145434	Prob(F-statistic)		0.009014

(source: Ministry of Industry and Trade, Ministry of Agriculture and Rural Development)

4.4 Drinking Products from green tea

From green tea and lychee, we can make delicious lychee tea product, a favorite drink for many people.

Steps to Make rose tea:

Put 1 packet of rose tea in a glass jar, pour hot water to cook dried rose buds, steep the tea for about 3 minutes, then remove the filter bag.

Put 150ml of rose syrup, 50ml of sugar syrup, 50ml of fresh lychee juice, 50ml of yellow lemon juice into the tea pot. Stir until the mixture comes together. The tea has a beautiful bright pink color and a faint rose scent.

The last step, put the lychee into the glass depending on your preference more or less. Add ice cubes and then pour in rose tea, add mint leaves or basil to increase the taste and beauty.

Figure - Make Rose tea drink with ice

(source: internet)

5. Discussion and Conclusion

Dinh Tran Ngoc Huy, Nguyen Thi Hang,Le Thi Thanh Huong, Pham Van Hong (2021) stated that lychee and tea planting policies and capital financing policies in the country, esp. In the north of Vietnam. For instance, the nation needs to continue to negotiate with countries that have not yet allowed Vietnam's fresh lychee to be imported into developed countries (such as Korea, ...); The state/ province cooperates with donors and businesses in trade promotion activities in potential export markets for Vietnamese lychee and fruit products (Japan, Korea, US, EU, ASEAN)

In the context of product distribution and consumption activities of production networks and The value chain is led and dominated by most large corporations in developed countries, If Vietnam wants to really take advantage of the opportunities from integration, it needs to be able to participate in global value chains. Therefore, agriculture needs comprehensive changes from production to processing to meet strict standards and technical requirements of markets, especially developed countries.

The common group of solutions to the agricultural industry:

Linking and forming concentrated commodity production areas

The problem of land consolidation and change of plots: to ensure that rural people still have land

"self-defense" agriculture has just transformed agricultural production according to the collective model. Vietnam should encourage and create favorable conditions for investors, businesses, and capable farmers to stand out to rent land from farmers, mobilize farmers to participate in concentrated production according to regulations. business processes to create product homogeneity.

Production linkage between farmer households, between farmers and enterprises

Invest in the synchronous construction of infrastructure for agricultural production (irrigation, transport and connection in production and with the market).

Alcohol traps

Johnson, M.A et al (2019) mentioned Coffee berry borer (CBB) is the most serious insect pest of coffee worldwide, causing more than US$500M in damages annually. Reduction in the yield and quality of coffee results from the adult female CBB boring into the coffee fruit and building galleries for reproduction, followed by larval feeding on the bean itself.

Authors conclude, based on findings, that alcohol traps (bottle)

and Beauveria bassiana could be used to eliminate new generation of insects (killing female Coffee berry borer-CBB) and replace for chemical pesiticides solutions, then serving for agricultural sustainability.

Bui Thi Suu, Vu Quang Giang, Vu Phuong Lien, Dinh Tran Ngoc Huy, Ha Thi Lan (2021) stated that Among main cultivated crop in northwest area of Vietnam is coffee crop, then we have to deal with the negative factor, or insect, coffee berry borer (CBB), which cause losses and damages for farmers with negatively significant impact.

Marketing mix solutions

The process of having an agricultural product goes through many steps such as planting, planning, harvesting, packing, transporting, storing and distributing. So what are the marketing mix strategy of the agricultural industry?

Products (coffee, tea, lychee,...)	Price
- Develop product chain or categories	- Apply penetration policy
- Improve quality control	- Payment time flexible
- Product positioning	- Customer type based
- Branding	- Price for loyal clients
	- Discount policy and price based on psychology

Place	Promotion
- Online marketing for agricultural products	- change approach way
- Change distribution channel	- change social media, communication
- Indirect and direct channels	

Research limitation

We need to expand further analysis for other crops as well.

ACKNOWLEDGEMENTS

I would like to take this opportunity to express my warm thanks to Board of Editors and Colleagues in assisting convenient conditions for my research paper.

References

Buu Thi Suu, Vu Quang Giang, Vu Phương Lien, Dinh Tran Ngoc Huy, Ha Thi Lan. (2021). The Auto-infection Trap with the Native Entomopathogenic Fungus, Beauveria Bassiana for Management of Coffee Berry Borer (Stephanoderes Hampei Ferrari) in the Northwest Region of Vietnam, Alinteri Journal of Agriculture science, 36(1): 191-198.

Bui Thi Suu, Dinh Tran Ngoc Huy, Nguyen Thi Hoa. (2021). SUSTAINABLE VALUE CHAIN ISSUES, INSECT TRAPS AND SOLUTIONS FOR COFFEE BERRY BORER IN THE NORTH OF VIETNAM, Plant Cell Biotechnology and Molecular Biology 22(55&56), 74-83

Dinh Tran Ngoc Huy, Nguyen Thi Hang, Le Thi Thanh Huong, Pham Van Hong. (2021). FOOD AND DRINK PROCESSING FROM LYCHEE PRODUCTS IN THE NORTHERN PROVINCES OF VIETNAM - AND ROLES OF AGRICULTURE PROJECT FINANCING, Revista de Investigaciones Universidad del Quindío, 33(1), 187-195. https://doi.org/10.33975/riuq.vol33n1.555

Hac, L.D.; Huy, D.T.N.; Thach, N.N.; Nhung, P.T.H.; Thang, T.D. & Anh, T.T. (2021). Enhancing risk management culture for sustainable growth of Asia commercial bank -ACB in Vietnam under mixed effects of macro factors. Entrepreneurship and Sustainability Issues, 8(3). https://econpapers.repec.org/article/ssijouesi/v_3a8_3ay_3a2021_3ai_3a3_3ap_3a291-307.htm

Hansen, H. and Tarp, H. (2001), Aid and growth regressions, *Journal of Development Economics*, 2001, 64, 547-570.

Hang, T.T.B.; Nhung, D.T.H.; Nhung, D.H.; Huy, D.T.N.; Hung, N.M. & Dat, P.M. (2020). Where beta is going - case of Vietnam hotel, airlines and tourism company groups after the low inflation period. Entrepreneurship and Sustainability Issues, 7(3). 2282-2298. https://ideas.repec.org/a/ssi/jouesi/v7y2020i3p2282-2298.html

Huy, D.T.N.; Loan, B.T.; Anh, P.T. (2020). Impact of selected factors on stock price: a case study of Vietcombank in Vietnam. Entrepreneurship and Sustainability Issues, 7(4): 2715-2730. https://ideas.repec.org/a/ssi/jouesi/v7y2020i4p2715-2730.html

Huy, D.T.N. (2015). The critical analysis of limited south asian corporate governance standards after financial crisis. International Journal for Quality Research, 15(1), 741-746. http://www.ijqr.net/paper.php?id=378. Access: Jan. 11, 2021.

Hong, P.V., Nguyen, N.T., Huy, D.T.N., Thuy, N.T. and Huong, L.T.T. (2021). Evaluating Several Models of Quality Management and Impacts on Lychee Price Applying for Vietnam Agriculture Products Value Chain Sustainable Development. Alinteri Journal of Agriculture Sciences, 36(1): 122-130. doi: 10.47059/alinteri/V36I1/AJAS21018

Huy, D.T.N.; Dat, P.M.; & Anh, P.T. (2020). Building and econometric model of selected factors' impact on stock price: a case study. Journal of Security and Sustainability Issues, 9 (M), 77-93. https://cibg.org.au/index.php/cibg/article/viewFile/9/journal/article_8416.html

Huy, D.T.N.; Hien, D.T.N. (2010). The backbone of European corporate governance standards after financial crisis, corporate scandals and manipulation. Economic and Business Review, 12(4), 2015-2040. http://ojs.ebrjournal.net/ojs/index.php/ebr/article/download/101/30

Humphrey, J., and H. Schmitz. 2002. "How Does Insertion in Global Value Chains Affect Upgrading in Industrial Clusters." *Regional Studies* 36 (9): 1017–27

Humphrey và Memedovic (2006),*Global value chains in the agrifood sector*. Working papers 2006, UNIDO.

Huy, Dinh T.N., (2012), Estimating Beta of Viet Nam listed construction companies groups during the crisis, *Journal of Integration and Development, 15(1).*

Huy D.T.N., Nhan V.K., Bich N.T.N., Hong N.T.P., Chung N.T., Huy P.Q. (2021). 'Impacts of Internal and External Macroeconomic Factors on Firm Stock Price in an Expansion Econometric model—A Case in Vietnam Real Estate Industry', *Data Science for Financial Econometrics-Studies in Computational Intelligence*, vol.898, Springer. http://doi-org-443.webvpn.fjmu.edu.cn/10.1007/978-3-030-48853-6_14

Mendesil, E.; Jembere, B.; Seyoum, E. Population dynamics and distribution of the coffee berry borer, Hypothenemus hampei (Ferrari) (Coleoptera: Scolytidae) on Coffea arabica L. in southwestern Ethiopia. Sinet 2004, 27, 127–134.

Posada-Flórez FJ. 2008. Production of *Beauveria bassiana* fungal spores on rice to control the coffee berry borer, *Hypothenemus hampei*, in Colombia. 13pp. *Journal of Insect Science* 8:41, available online: insectscience.org/8.41

Yobana A. Mariñoa , Maria-Eglée Pérezb, Fernando Gallardoc, Marella Trifilioa, Michelle Cruza, Paul Bayman (2015). Sun vs. shade affects infestation, total population and sex ratio of the coffee berry borer *(Hypothenemus hampei*) in Puerto Rico. Agriculture, Ecosystems and Environment 222 (2016) 258–266

Perez, M.A.G., & Viana, S.G. (2012). Cooperation in coffee markets: The case of Vietnam and Colombia, Journal of Agribusiness in Developing and Emerging Economies 2(1):57-73. DOI:10.1108/20440831211219237

Robert G. Hollingsworth, Luis F. Aristizábal, Suzanne Shriner, Gabriel M. Mascarin, Rafael de Andrade Moral and Steven P. Arthurs (2020). Incoporating *Beauveria basssiana* into an intergreated pest managerment plant for coffee berry borer in Hawaii. Frontiers in sustainable foof systerms, volume 4, Article 22

Johnson, M.A., Ruiz-Diaz, C.P., Manoukis, N.C., and Verle Rodrigues, J.C. (2020). Coffee Berry Borer (*Hypothenemus hampei*), a Global Pest of Coffee: Perspectives from Historical and Recent Invasions, and Future Priorities. *Insects*, 11(12), 882. https://doi.org/10.3390/insects11120882

Kulandaivelu Velmourougane, Rajeev Bhat and Thirukonda Nannier Gopinandhan (2010). Coffee Berry Borer (Hypothenemus hampei)—A Vector for Toxigenic Molds and Ochratoxin A Contamination in Coffee Beans. FOODBORNE PATHOGENS AND DISEASE Volume 7, Number 10, 2010

Nguyen Hung Anh, Bolkemann, W., Nga, D.T., & Minh, N.V. (2021). Toward Sustainability or Efficiency: The Case of Smallholder Coffee Farmers in Vietnam, *Economies* 2019, 7(3), 66; https://doi.org/10.3390/economies7030066

Tran, D.N.L.; Nguyen, T.D.; Pham, T.T., Rañola, R.F., Jr.; Nguyen, T.A. (2021). Improving Irrigation Water Use Efficiency of Robusta Coffee (Coffea canephora) Production in Lam Dong Province, Vietnam. Sustainability, 13, 6603. https://doi.org/10.3390/su13126603

Trung, N.D., Huy, D.T.N., Hang, N.T. and Ha, L.T. (2021). Effective Management via a Business Model of Food and Drink Processing from Lychee Products in the Northern Areas of Vietnam. Alinteri Journal of Agriculture Sciences, 36(1): 406-411. doi: 10.47059/alinteri/V36I1/AJAS21061

Vu, H.T. (2013). The Research on Arabica coffee cultivation technical toward sustainable development for Northwest ecological region. In national conference on Crop Science I, 897-906.

Vega, F.E.; Benavides, P.; Stuart, J.A.; O'Neill, S.L. Wolbachia infection in the coffee berry borer (Coleoptera:Scolytidae). Ann. Entomol. Soc. Am. 2002, 95, 374–378.

Vega, F.E.; Infante, F.; Johnson, A.J. The genus Hypothenemus, with emphasis on H. hampei, the coffee berry borer. In Bark Beetles: Biology and Ecology of Native and Invasive Species; Vega, F.E., Hofstetter, R.W., Eds.; Academic Press: San Diego, CA, USA, 2015; pp. 427–494.

Exhibit

Exhibit 1 – Inflation, CPI over past 10 years (2007-2017) in Vietnam

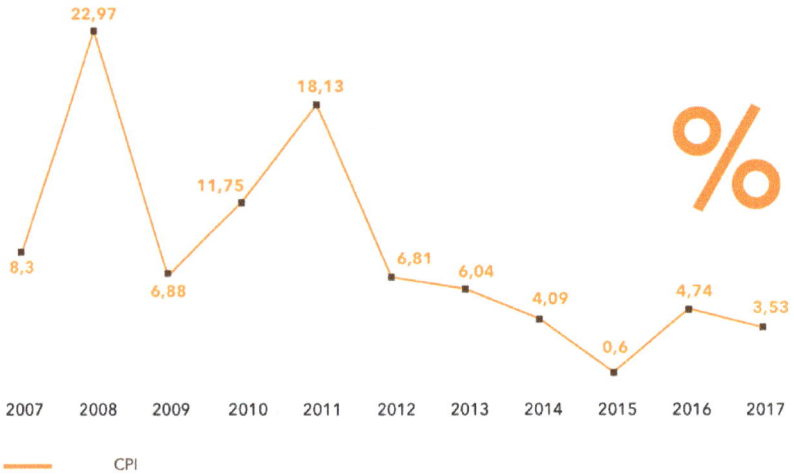

Exhibit 2 – GDP growth rate past 10 years (2007-2018) in Vietnam

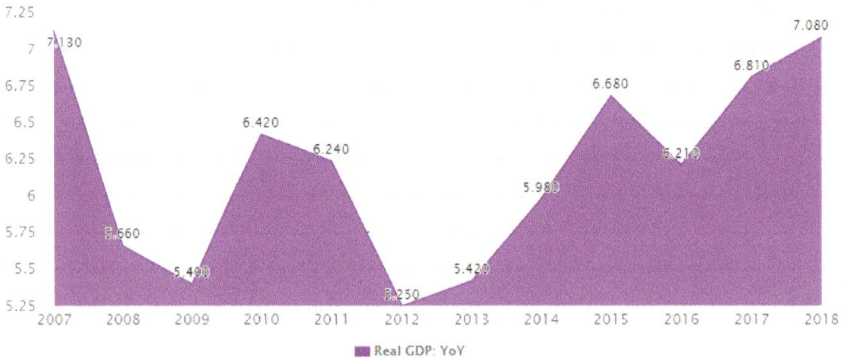

CASE NO. 3

DATE

7 Jan, 2022

(PUBLISHED IN SSCI/SCIE TOBACCO REGULATORY SCIENCE 2021)

DISCUSSION ON TEA AND COFFEE PLANTING IN LAM DONG AND THAI NGUYEN PROVINCES IN VIETNAM - FDI INVESTMENT, ECONOMIC VALUES, NATURAL CONDITIONS, FARMING TECHNIQUES FOR AGRICULTURAL SUSTAINABILITY

Nguyen Dinh Trung[1], Dinh Tran Ngoc Huy[2], Nguyen Kim Phuoc[3], Pham Van Hong[4], Le Thi Thanh Huong[5], Tran Duc Thang[6], Nguyen Thanh Hoang[7]

[1]*National Economics University (NEU), Hanoi Vietnam . Email: trungnd@ neu.edu.vn*

[2]*Banking University HCMC Ho Chi Minh city, Vietnam - International University of Japan, Niigata, Japan. Email: dtnhuy2010@gmail.com. ORCID: 0000-0002-2358-0699 (corresponding)*

[3]*Ho Chi Minh city Open University, Vietnam . Email: phuoc.nk@ou.edu.vn*

[4]*Thai Nguyen University of Agriculture and Forestry, Vietnam . Email: buithithom@tuaf.edu.vn*

[5]*Dai Nam University, Vietnam . Email: lethanhhuong@dainam.edu.vn*

[6]*National Economics University (NEU), Hanoi Vietnam . Email: tranducthang@neu.edu.vn*

[7]*The University of Social Sciences and Humanities National University of Ho Chi Minh City, Vietnam. Email: hoangnguyenfir@hcmussh.edu.vn*

ABSTACT

In order to propose suitable policies for sustainability of coffee and tea in Vietnam, we could perform both qualitative and quantitative analysis. We analyze tea and coffee planting in Thai Nguyen, Lam Dong and Daklak provincies in Vietnam where are biggest locations.

In this study, we used an econometric model to suggest suitable policies to be in favor of tea export price.

The study results show that although long years with experiences in planting coffee and tea crops, The area, productivity and output of coffee all decreased compared to 2019 and did not meet the plan. The reason is that some areas of re-cultivated coffee have not yet been harvested and converted to effective crops such as vegetables, flowers, etc., and at the same time, due to low coffee prices, people's investment in caring for gardens is limited. Next in a five factor model regression, we find out a reduction in exchange rate and CPI while increase in VNIndex will be in favor of tea export price. And correlation between exchange rate and tea price is higher than that between VNIndex and tea price.

Last but not least, Limitation of our research is we can expand research model for other agricultural products as well.

Keywords: tea and coffee crops, planting, value chain, marketing solutions, econometric, tea price, SWOT

JEL: M21, G30, G32, G38

1.INTRODUCTION

Lam Dong and Thai Nguyen provinces are two biggest tea planting locations where there are suitable natural conditions and climate change. Whereas Daklak, Tay Nguyen are big locations for coffee crops and planting.

There are some benefits of green tea:

Tea also helps you lose weight effectively. One of the benefits of tea is that it boosts metabolism and burns fat. According to a study, drinking tea every day will help you reduce 75-100 calories per day. Green tea contains less caffeine than coffee but enough to keep you awake and improve brain function.

Next drinking coffee have benefits:

Studies have shown that coffee brings more benefits every day than people imagine. Coffee is full of substances that help protect against common health problems, especially in women, including Alzheimer's disease and metabolic cardiovascular diseases including hypertension, coronary heart disease, dyslipidemia...

Many people will immediately think of caffeine when talking about coffee, but that's not the only thing that exists in this top popular beverage. Coffee contains many antioxidants and compounds with anti-inflammatory as well as disease-fighting properties. This assertion has been confirmed by leading experts and professors of the Johns Hopkins University School of Medicine. In addition, studies also show that people who have the habit of enjoying a cup of coffee every morning have a much lower risk of some serious diseases than those who do not have this habit.

(source: vinmec.com, access date 22/12/2021)

Related to FDI investment into coffee crops:

In Daklak, The construction of coffee processing factories, besides improving product quality and value, also forms direct purchasing points, limiting intermediaries, contributing to reducing economic losses for coffee growers. However, the number of coffee investment projects is still not much; Only a few enterprises are capable of processing high-quality coffee, the rest are mostly small-scale establishments, unsynchronized equipment lines, and deep processing accounts for about 2.3% of total output. export coffee. In addition, FDI projects have large scale in terms of capacity and investment capital, but the number is small, while domestic investment projects are larger in number but limited in operational capacity. The reason for this situation is that coffee processing requires large capital (average investment of roasted coffee is about 15-17 billion VND for a capacity of 1,000 tons/year; for instant coffee, it is 150 billion VND for a capacity of 1,000 tons/year. capacity of 2,000 tons/year), so it is difficult for domestic enterprises with financial disadvantage to compete in long-term investment with foreign investors.

The land is still fertile

According to experts in the coffee industry, FDI investment is still limited in number because countries previously only imported Vietnamese green coffee as raw materials and protected the processing stage in their countries. Therefore, Vietnamese roasted and ground coffee products are often subject to 20% tax when exported to those countries. However, recently with the participation in free trade agreements, the tax rate has been reduced to 0%, which has created great opportunities for foreign enterprises to invest in deep processing of Vietnamese coffee to fully exploit local resources of raw materials and labor.

(source: baodaklak.vn/channel, access date 23/12/2021)

Research question:

What are factors influencing tea export price and policy implications for agri sustainability?

What are real situation of tea and coffee planting in Vietnam?

2. LITERATURE REVIEW

First, Dinh Tran Ngoc Huy et al (2021) stated we need to develop Sustainable Agricultural Value Chain in Coffee and Tea Crops in the Northern Regions of Vietnam. While Huy, D.T.N (2015) stated many solutions for better business management in the field.

Currently we need to improve coffee planting field. To acquire coffee raw materials, FDI enterprises in Dak Lak only export raw coffee with low technological content and low added value.

Next we can summarize related studies in below table:

Table 1- Previous studies

Authors	Year	Content, result
Jolliffe et al	2010	International Tourists have experience with Vietnam coffee
an et al		

Nguyen Thi Thao		
Guo & Rato	2019	Experience-based tea culture tours in Thai Nguyen
		are becoming popular, mainly among foreign tourists seeking knowledge and
		beautiful scenery. The tea culture destinations and the tour packages provide
		sightseeing as well as opportunities to try tea-related activities, such as
		harvesting, production, and tasting. This article suggests that tea culture tourism
		in Thai Nguyen is developing quickly as a multilevel tourism form combining
		scenery sightseeing, learning, and hands-on experiences
Dinh Tran Ngoc Huy et al	2021	We need marketing solutions in agri products (coffee and tea)

| Bui Thi Suu et al | 2021 | We can use insect alcohol traps instead of chemical pesticides in coffee planting |
| Hoang Quoc Tuan et al | 2021 | Compositions of fatty acids and amino acids compound were investigated in coffee beans included Arabica and Robusta cultivars grown in three region of Vietnam |

(source: author synthesis)

3. MATERIALS AND METHODS

This paper uses 2 approaches: first is value chain approach in agriculture, and second is sustainability approach in agriculture

Hence, authors also use econometric model to estimate effects of macro factors on price of tea for a sustainable suggestions.

Beside, the study also analyze and compare previous related studies.

Last but not least, for qualitative approach authors use inductive and synthesis methods.

Finally, authors construct an econometric model for tea price as follows:

$Y = f(x1, x2, x3)$ where y : price of tea (export), x1: x2: x3:

4. RESULTS AND DISCUSSION

4.1 Area, production and distribution of tea crops in Thai Nguyen region

Vietnam has three famous tea growing regions: Northwest, Thai Nguyen and Lam Dong. With suitable soil conditions, Thai Nguyen has long been famous for its vast green tea areas.

There are quite a few different types of processed tea that establishments/cooperatives process from different types of products from the general to the special ones. Selling prices of different products

quite big difference. To make this difference, the input material (fresh tea) must

are carefully selected, classified and the technique/know-how of tea copying/drying are the most important to create a private brand.

For special tea, the selling price and profit are much higher than pine dry tea

usually. However, this type of tea has a very small yield (accounting for only 3-5% of total tea production).

output). These teas are usually ordered by customers to be used as gifts or sold to high-income people.Cost and benefits of export processing enterprises

Only tea processing enterprises have the capacity to participate in exporting. There are two main groups of products that enterprises export: raw tea (exported to Pakistan, Sri Lanka, etc. let them process black tea, dip tea, ..) and dry green tea. In fact, the volume of tea exporting enterprises in the province is still very limited.

There are many different reasons leading to this situation: first, exporting finished tea to developed markets, despite high profits, is very risky. Because the importing countries have very strict regulations on the content of residues of chemicals and pesticides, if they take samples for testing but fail to meet the requirements, the loss to enterprises is huge. Meanwhile, enterprises do not have enough material areas to meet the requirements due to lack of land or limited linkages with farmer households. Second, for the group of tea raw materials for export, the profit is very low due to the low selling price, so businesses do not pay much attention. Third, a number of other deeply processed products such as matcha tea, tea bags, etc., enterprises in the province have not yet created a brand name in the international market, so their competitiveness is still low. Fourth, trade promotion in developed countries' markets is still limited due to costly costs.

As a result, there are not many enterprises focusing on export processing, but mainly focus on exploiting the domestic market, where tea consumption is still relatively easy and not costs and risks compared to exporting (chemical testing, customs, research market research,...)

Cost and benefits from exporting finished products of processing enterprises (premium tea)

Obviously, export tea brings the highest selling price and profit for the whole business

processing and tea growing households. Specifically, the selling price and profit from exporting dried green tea

of the same type sold in the domestic market from 1.5-2 times. However, the export output is still very small compared to the total tea output of the province due to difficulties in linking to ensure the material area meets the standards. To ensure quality, businesses rent land for their own material areas or cooperate with tea growing households and control the care process. However, due to weak linkages and limited area, the raw material area to meet export requirements is still difficult.

Furthermore, processed tea products such as tea bags, matcha tea and tea products

are still limited, have not yet created reputable brands in other developed markets. Even in the domestic market, these products still cannot compete with imported products (such as British lipton tea, Sri Lankan Dilmad tea or Japanese matcha tea).

Cost and benefits from exporting raw tea of enterprises

(Firm=>exporting to Pakistani countries)

Raw tea is usually prepared from old tea leaves after tea buds (fresh tea) are processed households that harvest or have poor quality tea materials are collected, preliminarily processed, and exported to other developing countries such as Pakistan so that they can process other finished products for export. The export price for this type of tea is quite low, only from 1.5 to 2 USD/kg. Due to the low selling price, the profit from this tea is also quite low, the profit is only 10-15 thousand VND/kg.

Positives and limiting factors for tea products to enter the international market

The positives/advantages of entering the market

Natural and climatic conditions for tea plants: Thai Nguyen has favorable natural conditions for tea plants, especially tea varieties imported from Phu Tho province, also known as Trung du tea. If the suitable temperature conditions for tea plants to grow are in the range of 22oC-28oC and the humidity reaches 80%-85%, the average annual temperature and average humidity of Thai Nguyen are quite ideal. are 25°C and 81.2% respectively. The average annual rainfall in the province is about 2,000-2,500 mm, concentrating from May to October. Therefore, Thai Nguyen's tea plants, especially Tan Cuong tea, often grow and develop the best. in summer (May to July) thanks to enough sunshine, enough temperature and enough water. Tea buds at this stage also develop the strongest and have the most nutrients. As a result, the Midland tea tree grown in Thai Nguyen grows better and gives a more distinctive and delicious flavor than tea of the same type grown in Phu Tho.

Tea growers have many years of production experience: With the experience and techniques of growing and processing tea accumulated over a century of history, tea trees were planted from the original purpose of planting to cover bare lands and hills. bald, has now become a strength and is one of the strategic crops of Thai Nguyen province. Up to now, tea trees have been planted in all 9 cities/districts/towns of the province with the total cultivated area continuously expanding over the years. In 2018, the province's total tea cultivation area reached 22,027 hectares, accounting for about 14.3% of the total cultivated area and 57.9% of the total area of perennial industrial crops in the province. Thai Nguyen's tea industry currently attracts the participation of 95,000 households, or 40% of the total number of households in rural areas, including individual producers as well as production households participating in cooperative models. Communes and craft villages (Thai Nguyen Provincial Department of Industry and Trade, 2017).

Gradually change the way of caring for tea plants in the direction of safe products: A survey in Thai Nguyen province shows that the trend of converting conventional tea production to safe tea production is increasingly clear, especially in the past 10 years. this. Safe tea area currently accounts for 80% of the total tea area of the province and about 34% of the total area has been certified to Vietnam Good Agricultural Practices (VietGAP) and other standards, of which has the UTZ Certified Certification Protocol – a sustainable farming program and label that is recognized worldwide. The survey results also show positive changes in the farming habits of tea growers in Thai Nguyen when the use of chemical fertilizers has tended to decrease in the last three years (2016-2018). Specifically, the percentage of households reducing the use of chemical fertilizers accounts for approximately one third of the total surveyed households. The number of households increasing the use of green manure and micro-organism fertilizers accounts for 77.25% and 72.46%, respectively, while the number of households increasing the use of manure accounts for nearly 50%.

Constraints restricting participation in international markets

Small scale production but weak production links

With a large number of farm households engaged in tea production, it is understandable why

The scale of tea production of households is still very limited, although the tea cultivation area in Thai Nguyen province has continuously increased over the years. According to the survey results of the 2018 Project, on average, a production household has only 0.36 hectares, scattered into two or three different plots (maybe near or far from where they live). Even, the average area of each tea growing household in Thai Nguyen province is only 0.11 ha (People's Committee of Thai Nguyen province, 2017).

Moreover, the small size of the area and the lack of concentration of production lead to higher production costs and reduced efficiency. Due to the limited and unsynchronized common irrigation system, households often hire people to drill wells and buy pumps to get water for irrigation without sharing the water source, applying current technology and techniques. It is also difficult because the scale is not large enough. Currently, more than 77% of surveyed households report a lack of water for irrigation, especially during the dry season months (November to April).

Not to mention that in areas lacking electricity connection infrastructure, farmers have to invest in generators to generate electricity to run water pumps. Recently, the manifestations of climate change such as prolonged heat and cold, harmful cold, extreme weather phenomena and the frequency of natural disasters (floods, droughts) are increasing in Vietnam. some places in Thai Nguyen province in recent years. According to the Hydrometeorological Station of Thai Nguyen province; the average annual temperature in 9 districts, cities and towns in the province gradually increased, from 1959 to 2016 it increased by about 20 C; In the last 9 months of 2018 and the first 3 months of 2019, the rainfall is only 66% compared to the average rainfall of previous years.

Climate change affects production and people's lives in many fields and economic sectors. For tea plants, climate change is most evident in the water for tea plants and in land degradation. Drought causes a shortage of water for tea plants. In Tan Cuong commune (especially in Doi Can and Soi Vang hamlets) due to lack of water supply from the irrigation system, people here had to drill deep wells to get water for tea plants. This groundwater is rarely treated, but directly irrigated tea plants, so there is a risk of iron and minerals contamination, affecting the quality of tea.

The effects of climate change must include drought causing land degradation.... Due to this impact, in order to maintain and improve the yield of tea, people have increased the use of chemical fertilizers. study and use of growth stimulants.

Although the area is small, but the linkage in production between households and the link between households and enterprises in production is very weak. The survey results of tea growing households show that the percentage of households participating in the association is still low. quite low, only 1.8% of households in the sample have links with enterprises; 12.57% join cooperatives and 8.98% join cooperative groups. Up to 76.65% of surveyed households do not participate in any type of association. The linkage is weak, the certified and non-certified tea growing households are intertwined and do not form a concentrated production area. Therefore, it is difficult for households to grow according to VietGap, UTZ or organic tea certificates to ensure standards due to the influence of spraying, chemical fertilizers, etc. from surrounding households. Processing enterprises do not have a long-term raw material area, leading to passivity in processing quality management and branding.

Tea qualified for export to developed countries is still limited (most of them have not met the demand from export markets).

Although households are more aware of safe tea production.

However, these

This change has not really been well controlled according to international standards. Ratio of tea production area is high, but the number of certified areas is still valid

very small. As of 2017, the area of tea certified according to real standards

Good agricultural practice (VietGAP and other standards) accounts for just over 735 hectares, equivalent to 3.34% of the total tea area of the province. It is worth noting that almost half of this total tea area now has expired certification. The results of in-depth interviews with enterprises show that, if they continue to organize tea production as at present, Thai Nguyen's tea has very little opportunity to expand to developed countries' markets.

(source: Le Van Hung, Pham Van Hong et al., Project, 2019)

4.2 Area, production and distribution of tea crops in Lam Dong region

Lam Dong is a mountainous province in the South Central Highlands, with an altitude of 200-2,200m above sea level. With the tea growing area surpassing Thai Nguyen, the tea area in Lam Dong, tea is considered the main crop in Lam Dong province.

Currently, tea varieties of Lam Dong province for processing account for about 90% of the total annual output, mainly high yielding and high quality tea varieties. The main processed tea products are black tea (11.05%), green tea (1.41%), Olong tea and other tea (87.54%).

(source: yeutraviet.vn, access date 22/12/2021)

Hence, Currently, the total tea area of Lam Dong province is more than 12,400 hectares with an output of about 180,000 tons of fresh bud tea, of which more than 49% of tea is high-tech application, with more than 150 tea processing companies with a production scale of 29,800 tons/ year of finished products and 90 tea processing facilities with a scale of 17,400 tons of finished products/year, mainly in Da Lat, Bao Loc and Bao cities. Forestry, etc. Processed products are also diverse such as oolong tea, flavored green tea, preliminarily processed green tea... accounting for 60% of tea output is processed semi-finished products for export, the rest is mainly consumed in Central provinces, including many tea processing factories with modern production lines, have contributed to creating many famous brands for tea products of Lam Dong province.

(source: http://lamdongtv.vn/tin-tuc-n8590/lam-dong-hon-40-dien-tich-che-ung-dung-cong-nghe-cao.html, access date 22/12/2021)

Figure 1- Tea crops in Lam Dong province

(source: internet)

4.3 Area, production and distribution of coffee crops

In 2018, the country's coffee area was very large, about 720,000 hectares. In which, about 670ha Robusta (accounting for 93% of the area), reaching about 1.71 million tons (about more than 96% of output). Arabica coffee, area is 50,000 hectares (just nearly 7%), output is nearly 67,000 tons (only nearly 4%). (the figure is about 70,000 ha higher than the official data).

Table 2- Area and estimated production of Vietnam's robusta coffee

	Robusta coffee	Area 9 x1000 ha)	Quantity (x1000 tons)	Productivity (ton/ha)
1	Daklak	204	490	2.4
2	Lam Dong	164	443	2.7
3	Dak nong	158	417	2.6
4	Gia Lai	91	253	2.8
5	Kontum	17	51	3.1
6	Binh Phuoc	15	23	1.5
7	Binh Thuan	3	7	2.3
8	Dong Nai	11	21	1.9
9	Other provinces	5	8	1.7
		668	1.714	2.6

(source: https://tasacoffee.com/dien-tich-ca-phe-viet-nam-2018.html, access date 22/12/2021)

4.4 Sustainability concepts and value chain in agriculture

A global value chain differs from a value chain in that a value chain can include only a geographical location or even a single company (such as a a plant that is grown, packaged, and consumed only in one country. Meanwhile, a Global value chain can be divided by many different companies and geospatial can be spread across many different countries (Duke GVCC, 2019).

Previously, according to C. Miller and L. Jones (2010), "global value chains are activities that create added value from production to consumption, through processing and commercialization. Each stage of the chain has one or more forward and backward links.

That is, value chains increasingly have a close relationship between each other

stages, between the subjects in the chain.According to Backer and Miroudot (2014), a global value chain defines the full range of activities performed by businesses/participants to bring a product or service from production to the final consumer. together. All advantages such as technology, cost, access to resources have assigned production stages in the chain to see who has the advantage in each geographical area. This assignment helps to increase the efficiency and sustainability of the product chain. For policymakers, global value chains are a good opportunity to capture economic linkages. In particular, it is emphasized that the competitiveness of exported goods depends on an efficient input supply source, and good links between processors and exporters with distributors and final consumers abroad. Therefore, it is really important to specialize in the production and distribution of products in the chain of countries.

Currently, global agribusiness is increasingly dominated by relationship along this value chain. In which, the leading leading companies carry out longitudinal coordination of the chain. In many parts of agribusiness, companies engage in modern manufacturing practices such as promoting innovation and product differentiation, changing the way product quality is controlled based on on inspection and testing by managing risks, controlling production processes and on-time delivery (Humphrey and Memedovic, 2006).

Studies discuss types of linkages such as vertical coordination such as Van Roekel (2002) or Young and Hobbs (2002) to distinguish between extended market relationships or vertically integrated firms. However, there is currently a change in linkages in the agricultural value chain in the form of farming contracts, brand management by supermarkets (Doland and Humphrey, 2004), or linkages in consumption. such as marketing contracts, product sales. Henson (2006) argues that the coordinating role of corporations and large companies in global agricultural value chains is increasing, especially in the field of food, which is mainly distributed. by major retailers.

In a nutshell, global agricultural value chains are activities that create added value from production to processing and distribution of products to consumers. The stage in the value chain can be vertically or horizontally linked with together. The subjects in the chain can participate in one or more other stages -each other in the value chain; This depends on the objectives, strategies and participation capacity of those actors.

Basically, the global agricultural value chain is not much different from other countries in global value chains. However, the value chain of agricultural products has some distinctive characteristics that require businesses, farmers and chain stakeholders to have appropriate policies and strategies that will help them participate in the value chain. better global.

Because agricultural products are often seasonal, short harvest time and perishable, requiring competent post-harvest storage and handling and modern technology. Besides, agricultural productivity and output are also easily affected by weather, diseases, and food safety and hygiene. To create brands of agricultural products and participate in the international market, agricultural producing countries need to have synchronization from production, preservation technology, processing, packaging and good branding. . Global distributors and retailers often set their own product standards for their imported products to meet market standards and consumer tastes. These standards must at least pass applicable regulations in the country in which they do business.

Figure 2- Tea harvest in Lam Dong

(source: internet)

4.5 Steps to make good and delicious chicken egg-coffee

A) Egg coffee is made from extremely simple ingredients: fresh eggs, sugar, milk and coffee. With the egg yolks being beaten by hand, together with the talent of the bartender, it becomes a coffee with beautiful foam and a delicious taste that is irresistible.

Ingredients for Egg Coffee For 2 cups

Filtered coffee powder 15 gr

Condensed milk 25 ml

Chicken eggs 2

Honey 5 ml

Hot water

How to choose to buy delicious, standard coffee powder

Good coffee powder will usually be pure coffee powder, roasted and ground from coffee beans and not mixed with other ingredients, standard coffee powders will be less hydrated, so they will not clump, touch. It feels dry and spongy by hand.

To achieve the deliciousness, the coffee must be roasted through 1 burst, so the right coffee will have a brown color instead of a bright yellow like coffees that have not been roasted at enough temperature.

Should choose coffee with reputable brand in the market because it will ensure the quality of the product.

Step 2: Whip egg cream

Separate 2 egg yolks into a cup. Add 25ml condensed milk, 5ml honey. Using an electric mixer, turn on the lowest speed and beat in a certain direction for about 4-5 minutes until the egg cream mixture turns bright yellow. When picking up the whisk, the mixture flows downhill.

Step 3: Egg coffee

After the coffee is extracted, take the filter out of the mouth of the cup. Add the whipped cream and use a spatula to slow the melting of the custard.

Figure 3- Finished product

(Source: author collect)

Sprinkle a little coffee powder on top of the ice cream for a beautiful look. Enjoy while hot!

4.6 Build econometric model for tea crops

We see:

Figure 4- Descriptive data

	TEA_PRICE	CPI	EX_RATE	R	TRADE_B...	VNINDEX
Mean	1645.611	0.039333	2.289778	0.082900	-200.2222	734.7956
Median	1659.200	0.035400	2.292000	0.068100	-200.0000	664.8700
Maximum	1724.500	0.068100	2.323000	0.190000	498.0000	1067.500
Minimum	1515.000	0.006300	2.244000	0.029100	-1162.000	413.7300
Std. Dev.	73.27427	0.018173	0.028060	0.047969	561.8999	242.3730
Skewness	-0.552959	-0.095695	-0.171411	1.370917	-0.177630	0.108642
Kurtosis	2.018611	2.703527	1.764880	3.867829	1.989230	1.413489
Jarque-Bera	0.819817	0.046697	0.616143	3.101543	0.430450	0.961586
Probability	0.663711	0.976922	0.734863	0.212084	0.806360	0.618293
Sum	14810.50	0.354000	20.60800	0.746100	-1802.000	6613.160
Sum Sq. Dev.	42952.95	0.002642	0.006299	0.018408	2525852.	469957.4

(source: author analysis)

Figure 5 - Correlation matrix

Correlation Matrix						
	TEA_PRICE	CPI	EX_RATE	R	TRADE_B...	VNINDEX
TEA_PRICE	1.000000	-0.690199	0.321818	-0.597975	-0.460417	0.223101
CPI	-0.690199	1.000000	-0.181429	0.776208	0.128296	-0.464077
EX_RATE	0.321818	-0.181429	1.000000	-0.331760	0.120374	0.568159
R	-0.597975	0.776208	-0.331760	1.000000	0.232002	-0.671848
TRADE_B...	-0.460417	0.128296	0.120374	0.232002	1.000000	0.445029
VNINDEX	0.223101	-0.464077	0.568159	-0.671848	0.445029	1.000000

(source: author analysis)

Figure 6 - OLS regression

Dependent Variable: TEA_PRICE
Method: Least Squares
Date: 12/23/21   Time: 12:02
Sample: 1 9
Included observations: 9

Variable	Coefficient	Std. Error	t-Statistic	Prob.
CPI	-2913.212	2194.181	-1.327699	0.2763
EX_RATE	623.9376	1117.588	0.558289	0.6156
R	503.8060	1591.159	0.316628	0.7723
TRADE_BALANCE	-0.075007	0.090471	-0.829072	0.4679
VNINDEX	0.069416	0.308078	0.225319	0.8362
C	223.7289	2400.334	0.093207	0.9316

R-squared	0.694397	Mean dependent var	1645.611
Adjusted R-squared	0.185057	S.D. dependent var	73.27427
S.E. of regression	66.14774	Akaike info criterion	11.45638
Sum squared resid	13126.57	Schwarz criterion	11.58786
Log likelihood	-45.55371	F-statistic	1.363328
Durbin-Watson stat	2.639790	Prob(F-statistic)	0.424830

(source: author analysis)

Discussion:

- We find out: CPI and trade balance have negative correlation with tea export price while Lending rate R and exchange rate and VN Index have positive correlation (see figure 6)

- We also recognize: standard dev. Of trade balance and VNIndex are highest values (see figure 4)

- And we see: correlation between exchange rate and tea price is higher than that between VNIndex and tea price (see figure 5)

4. CONCLUSION

SWOT analysis in tea crops in Vietnam

Table 3- SWOT analysis

Opportunities	Threats
- Strengthen technical management, conduct trials to identify new generation drugs, biological drugs capable of preventing tea pests and diseases in order to improve the quality of raw materials in tea growing areas. Building tea production areas applying high-tech agriculture in Bao Loc city and Bao Lam district to reduce costs and increase product value	- The area, productivity and output of coffee all decreased compared to 2019 and did not meet the plan. The reason is that some areas of re-cultivated coffee have not yet been harvested and converted to effective crops such as vegetables, flowers, etc., and at the same time, due to low coffee prices, people's investment in caring for gardens is limited. .
- Lam Dong has been cooperating with international institutes and schools in research and application of science and technology on tea development. In the trend of international integration, Vietnam has signed trade agreements with China since 1991, especially with agreements such as the Comprehensive and Progressive Agreement for Trans-Pacific Partnership (CPTPP), the Comprehensive and Progressive Agreement for Trans-Pacific Partnership (CPTPP). The EU-Vietnam Free Trade Agreement (EVFTA)... is an opportunity to promote the development of the tea industry in Lam Dong province in the coming time.	According to aggregated results from localities in the province, in 2020, most people will not grow new coffee, but focus on replanting, grafting and improving on coffee areas with low yield and affected by pests and diseases. (source: http://dalatkettinhkydieutudatlanh.vn/vn/ca-phe-arabica/dien-tich-nang-suat-san-luong-ca-phe-deu-giam-so-voi-2019-40295.phtml, access date 22/12/2021)

Strengths	Weaknesses
- long years with experiences in planting coffee and tea crops - Vietnam's coffee yield is often among the highest in the world, averaging 2.6 tonnes per hectare for Robusta and 1.4 tonnes for Arabica. Robusta coffee has the highest yield in Kotum province, followed by Gia Lai, Lam Dong, Dak Nong and Daklak.	- With the current processing capacity, raw materials cannot meet the processing capacity due to a sharp decrease in area and output, so some processing facilities are short of raw materials, unable to operate, many facilities have stopped working due to insufficient raw materials and unable to sell products due to lack of price competition.

(source: made by authors)

Next, as we find out from econometric model (see figure 6): there is policy implications, for instance, a reduction in exchange rate and CPI while increase in VNIndex will be in favor of tea export price.

In addition, many technologies on varieties, genes and care techniques help plants to adapt better response to climate change, seasonal changes as well as crop yield grow. Post-harvest preservation and processing techniques have also helped many countries reduce failure rate, improve product quality and consumption time, avoid supply is too high for a short time.

The US experience shows that there is no contract manufacturing model

Which is suitable for all. Under the same conditions, but the economic linkage results will not be the same between crops and livestock. Therefore, the economic linkage

between enterprises and farmers, especially in-depth linkages will not be successful in all types of agricultural products.

Contract manufacturing can only be successful when businesses can afford it

ability to consume all agricultural products for farmers at reasonable prices. With a large scale, contract production helps entities avoid risks. It is necessary to actively establish cooperatives and negotiating associations to help increase the ability to strengthen the position and bargaining power of farmers in the linking process, ensure output for agricultural products as well as ensure the interests of farmers. farmers in the process of implementing economic linkages with enterprises.

The state plays an important role in supporting and promoting contractual linkages

copper. Government policies must require farmers and businesses to be responsible for the performance of contracts. In Vietnam, with a fragmented and backward agriculture, the link between farmers and businesses is still loose. However, the correct orientation and support of the Government will create a great impetus to promote the development of economic linkages between enterprises and farmers.

Limitation of research

Author can expand research model for other agricultural products as well.

Acknowledgement

Thank you editors, brothers and friends to assist this publishing.

Conflicts of interest

Authors declare there is no conflict of interest

REFERENCES

Arbona V., Iglesias DJ., Jacas J., Primo-Millo E., Talon M. và Gomez-Cadenas A., 2005. Hydrogel substrate amendment alleviates drought effects on young citrus plants. *Plant and soil* 270: 73-82.

Buu Thi Suu, Vu Quang Giang, Vu Phương Lien, Dinh Tran Ngoc Huy, Ha Thi Lan. (2021). The Autoinfection Trap with the Native Entomopathogenic Fungus, Beauveria Bassiana for Management of Coffee Berry Borer (Stephanoderes Hampei Ferrari) in the Northwest Region of Vietnam, Alinteri Journal of Agriculture science, 36(1): 191-198.

BUI THI SUU, DINH TRAN NGOC HUY AND NGUYEN THI HOA. (2021). SUSTAINABLE VALUE CHAIN ISSUES, INSECT TRAPS AND SOLUTIONS FOR COFFEE BERRY BORER IN THE NORTH OF VIETNAM, Plant Cell Biotechnology and Molecular Biology 22(55&56): 74-83

BUI THI THOM, DINH TRAN NGOC HUY, NGUYEN DINH TRUNG AND BUI THI SUU. (2021). THE ENHANCEMENT OF WILD PIG AND WILD PORK VALUE CHAIN IN THE CONCEPT OF SUSTAINABLE AGRICULTURAL DEVELOPMENT, Plant Cell Biotechnology and Molecular

Biology 22(55&56): 64-73

Bui Thi Thom, Dinh Tran Ngoc Huy, Nguyen Thi Hoa, Bui Thi Suu. (2021). THE PARTICIPATION OF PEOPLE IN DEVELOPING AGRICULTURE VALUE CHAIN OF WILD PORK AND WILD PIGS IN THE NORTH OF VIETNAM, International Journal of Ecosystems and Ecology Science, 11(4)

Dinh Tran Ngoc Huy et al. (2021). Insects Alcohol Traps, Sustainable Agricultural Value Chain in Coffee and Tea Crops in the Northern Regions of Vietnam - and Solutions for Marketing Mix, Tobacco regulatory science, 7(6-1)

DTN Huy, VK Nhan, NTN Bich, NTP Hong, NT Chung, PQ Huy. (2021). Impacts of Internal and External Macroeconomic Factors on Firm Stock Price in an Expansion Econometric model—A Case in Vietnam Real Estate Industry, Data Science for Financial Econometrics, 189-205

Dinh Tran Ngoc Huy ,Pham Van Tuan, Nguyen Dinh Trung, Duong Thi Huyen, Nguyen Thi Hang, Nguyen Bich Hong, Le Thu Ha, Bui Thi Suu. (2021). Management Issues of Tea Planting and Tea Crops in Vietnam in the Concept of Sustainable Agricultural Development – and Recommendations on Marketing 4P, Tobacco Regulatory Science, Vol.7(6-1)

D THI AI NHI, DTN HUY, N VAN DAT. (2021). Factors Affecting Banking Policies and Solutions for Banks in Agricultural Development in Vietnam, Journal of Contemporary Issues in Business and Government 27 (2), 1985-1988

DS Hoang, Z Tučková, DTN Huy, PT Pham. (2021). Factors to enhance tourist's ecotourism loyalty, an empirical study in Viet

Nam, Webology, 18 (special issue)

Dinh Tran Ngoc Huy, Nguyen Thi Hang, Le Thi Thanh Huong, Pham Van Hong. (2021). FOOD AND DRINK PROCESSING FROM LYCHEE PRODUCTS IN THE NORTHERN PROVINCES OF VIETNAM - AND ROLES OF AGRICULTURE PROJECT FINANCING, Revista de Investigaciones Universidad del Quindío, 33(1), 187-195

DT Tinh, NT Thuy, DT Ngoc Huy. (2021). Doing Business Research and Teaching Methodology for Undergraduate, Postgraduate and Doctoral Students-Case in Various Markets Including Vietnam, Elementary Education Online 20 (1)

Dinh Tran Ngoc Huy, Nguyen Thi Hang. (2021). Factors that affect stock price and Beta CAPM of Vietnam Banks and Enhancing Management information system - Case of Asia Commercial Bank, Revista geintec Inovacao E Tecnologias, 11(2).

Dinh Tran Ngoc Huy, Pham Ngoc Van, Nguyen Thi Thu Ha. (2021).Education and computer skill enhancing for Vietnam laborers under industry 4.0 and evfta agreement, Elementary education online, 20(4).

DTN Huy, TTN Linh, NT Dung, PT Thuy, T Van Thanh, NT Hoang. (2021). Investment attraction for digital economy, digital technology sector in digital transformation era from ODA investment-and comparison to FDI investment in Vietnam, Laplage em Revista 7 (3A), 427-439

DT Huong, DTN Huy, NT Hang, PTH Trang, DT Ngu. (2021). Discussion on Case Teaching Method in a Risk Management

Case Study with Econometric Model at Vietnam Listed Banks–Issues Of Economic Education for Students, Review of International Geographical Education Online 11 (5), 2957-2966

DTN Huy et al. (2021). Insects Alcohol Traps, Sustainable Agricultural Value Chain in Coffee and Tea Crops in the Northern Regions of Vietnam-and Solutions for Marketing Mix, Tobacco Regulatory Science (TRS), 6797-6813

DTNN Huy, D Tran, P Van Tuan, N Dinh Trung, D Thi Huyen, N Thi Hang. (2021). Management Issues of Tea Planting and Tea Crops in Vietnam in the Concept of Sustainable Agricultural Development-and Recommendations on Marketing 4P, Tobacco Regulatory Science 7 (5), 1784-1803

VTT Dung, DTN Huy, VTK Anh, NN Thach, HT Hanh. (2021). Quality of education of ethnic minority communities in vietnam-problems and recommendations, Elementary education Online 20 (4)

Dinh Thi Hien, Dinh Tran Ngoc Huy, Nguyen Thi Hoa. (2021). Ho Chi Minh Viewpoints about Marxism Moral Human Resource for State Management Level in Vietnam, Psychology, and education, 58(5).

DT Ngu, DT Huong, DTN Huy, PT Thanh, ES Döngül. (2021). Language teaching application to English students at master's grade levels on history and macroeconomic-banking management courses in universities and colleges, Journal of Language and Linguistic Studies 17 (3)

DT Ngoc-Huy, NT Hang, P Van Hong. (2021). FOOD AND DRINK PROCESSING FROM LYCHEE PRODUCTS IN

THE NORTHERN PROVINCES OF VIETNAM-AND ROLES OF AGRICULTURE PROJECT FINANCING, Revista de Investigaciones Universidad del Quindío 33 (1), 187-195

DTN Huy, NT Thuy. (2021). Education for students to enhance research skills and meet demand from workplace-case in vietnam, Elementary education Online, 20 (4)

DT Ngoc Huy, N Thi Thuy, LTM Phuong, PM Dat, VT Dung, PT Manh. (2020). A set of international OECD and ICGN Corporate Governance Standards after financial crisis, Corporate scandals and manipulation-applications for Nigeria and implications for developing countries,Management 24 (1)

Guo, Y., & Rato, M. (2019). The Development of Tea Planting and Tea Culture Tourism in Thai Nguyen, Vietnam, Journal of Mekong Societies, 15(3)

Hac, L.D., Huy, D.T.N., Thach, N.N., Chuyen, B.M., Nhung, P.T.H., Thang, T.D., Anh, T.T. (2021). Enhancing risk management culture for sustainable growth of Asia commercial bank -ACB in Vietnam under mixed effects of macro factors, Entrepreneurship and Sustainability Issues, 8(3).

Hang, T.T.B., Nhung, D.T.H., Hung, N.M., Huy, D.T.N., Dat, P.M. (2020). Where Beta is going–case of Viet Nam hotel, airlines, and tourism company groups after the low inflation period, Entrepreneurship and Sustainability Issues, 7(3).

HT Hanh, DTN Huy, MD Pham. (2020). Utilization of Energy Sources, Financial Stability and Prosperity in the Economy of Indonesia, International Journal of Energy Economics and Policy 10 (5), 631

HT Hanh, DTN Huy, NTT Phuong, LTV Nga, PT Anh. (2020). Impact of macro economic factors and financial development on energy projects-case in ASEAN countries, Management 24 (2)

Huy, D.T.N. (2015). The Critical Analysis of Limited South Asian Corporate Governance Standards After Financial Crisis, International Journal for Quality Research, 9(4): 741-764.

HT Hanh, BM Chuyen, DTN Huy, NTT Phuong, HTL Phuong, LN Nuong. (2020). CHALLENGES AND OPPORTUNITIES FROM IMPACTS OF FDI AND INCOME ON ENVIRONMENT POLLUTION: ROLE OF FINANCIAL ACCOUNTING TRANSPARENCY IN FDI FIRMS, Journal of Security & Sustainability Issues 10 (2)

Huy, D.T.N. (2012). Estimating Beta of Viet Nam listed construction companies groups during the crisis, Journal of Integration and Development, 15 (1), 57-71

Huy, D.T.N.; Loan, B.T.; Anh, P.T. (2020). Impact of selected factors on stock price: a case study of Vietcombank in Vietnam. Entrepreneurship and Sustainability Issues, 7(4): 2715-2730. https://ideas.repec.org/a/ssi/jouesi/v7y2020i4p2715-2730.html 16.

Huy, D.T.N.; Dat, P.M.; & Anh, P.T. (2020). Building and econometric model of selected factors' impact on stock price: a case study. Journal of Security and Sustainability Issues, 9(M), 77-93. https://cibg.org.au/index.php/cibg/article/viewFile/9/journal/article_8416.html 19.

Huy, D.T.N.; Hien, D.T.N. (2010). The backbone of European corporate governance standards after financial crisis, corporate scandals and manipulation. Economic and Business Review

Hoang Quoc Tuan et al. (2021). DIFFERENTIATION OF VIETNAMESE COFFEE ORIGIN AND CULTIVARS BY AMINO AND FATTY ACID PROFILE ANALYSIS PRELIMINARY STUDY, Vietnam Journal of Science and Technology, 58(6A)

Jolliffe, L. et al. (2010). Coffee in Vietnam: International tourist experiences, book: Coffee Culture, Destinations and Tourism, pp.86-98. DOI:10.21832/9781845411442-008

LTN Hanh, DTN Huy, DT Hien. (2021). Ho Chi Minh ideologies on public propaganda and organization, Review of International Geographical Education Online 11 (5), 2711-2718

Le Quoc Dien, Dinh Tran Ngoc Huy, Tran Nhan Dung. (2021). Differences And Similarities Of Bactrocera Carambolae And Bactrocera Tau In The Mekong Delta Of Vietnam Based On Polymorphism Of Mtdna, Natural Volatiles & Essent. Oils, 2021; 8(5): 3610 - 3621

Le Thi Thanh Huong, Vu Quynh Nam, Dinh Tran Ngoc Huy, Pham Van Tuan, Pham Van Hong. (2021). Increasing Agricultural Productivity, Quality and Quantity of Coffee and Tea Crops Planting and Marketing Mix Solutions - Methods of Eliminating Coffee Berry Borer and Insects in Vietnam, Alinteri Journal of Agriculture Science, 36(1)

Le, K., & Nguyen, M. (2021). Aerial bombardment and educational attainment, International Review of Applied Economics, 34(3), 361-383

LTV Nga, NTN Lan, LL Yen, DTN Huy, DM Thuy. (2020).

The measurement of successful management via a net profit maximization model with ten factors and financial accounting disclosure policy-case of Vinamilk in F&B Industry in Vietnam, Management 24 (2)

LT Lan, NT Hang, DTN Huy. (2021). Developing Local Cultural Features through Community Tourism Services in Ha Giang Province, Vietnam, Revista Geintec-Gestao Inovacao E Tecnologias 11 (3), 2261-2275

Le, K., & Nguyen, M. (2021). Educational and political engagement, International Journal of Educational Development, 85, 102441

Nguyen Thi Thao. (2017). DETERMINATION OF METAL CONTENT IN TEA LEAVES GROWN IN YEN BAI AND TUYEN QUANG PROVINCE, VIET NAM, Vietnam Journal of Science and Technology, 55(5A)

Nguyen Kim Phuoc, Phan Ngoc Thuy Nhu. (2021). STOCK INVESTMENT ACTIVITIES OF INDIVIDUAL INVESTORS -A CASE STUDY IN HO CHI MINH CITY VIETNAM, Review of International Geographical Education Online, 11(10).

N Van Dat, DTA Nhi, DTN Huy. (2021). Improving Tourism Entrepreneur's Competition during the COVID 19 Pandemic–A Case Study in Tourism Industry in Vietnam, Revista Geintec-gestao Inovacao E Tecnologias 11 (3), 112-126

MD Pham, N Van Tuong, NTP Hong, DTN Huy, TA Pham. (2020). Using an expansion econometric model with five factors to improve quality of measuring impacts of public debt on macro economic factors-case in Vietnam, International Journal for Quality Research 14 (3), 679

Nguyen Dinh Trung, Dinh Tran Ngoc Huy, Nguyen Thi Hang, Le Thu Ha. (2021). Effective Management Via a Business Model of Food and Drink Processing from Lychee Products in the Northern Areas of Vietnam, Alinteri Journal of Agriculture science, 36(1)

NN Thach, DTN Huy. (2020). Trade Openness and Economics Growth in Vietnam, PalArch's Journal of Archaeology of Egypt/ Egyptology 17 (1), 12-22

NT Hoang, DTN Huy. (2021). Determining factors for educating students for choosing to work for foreign units: Absence of self-efficacy, JETT 12 (2), 11-19

NTT Phuong, DTN Huy, P Van Tuan. (2020). THE EVALUATION OF IMPACTS OF A SEVEN FACTOR MODEL ON NVB STOCK PRICE IN COMMERCIAL BANKING INDUSTRY IN VIETNAM-AND ROLES OF DISCOLOSURE OF ACCOUNTING POLICY IN RISK MANAGEMENT, International Journal of Entrepreneurship 24, 1-13

NN Thach, N Van Bao, DTN Huy, BD Thanh, LTV Nga, TT Ha, NT Binh. (2020). Measuring the Volatility of Market Risk of Vietnam Banking Industry After the Low Inflation Period 2015– 2017, Review of Pacific Basin Financial Markets and Policies 23 (04)

NT Hoa, DTN Huy. (2021). Vietnam Tourism Services Development During and after Covid 19 Pandemic: Situation and Solutions, Revista geintec-gestao Inovacao E Tecnologias 11 (3), 23-34

NT Hang, DTN Huy, DT Tinh, DT Huyen. (2021). Educating Students in History and Geography Subjects through Visiting Historical Sites to Develop Local Economy and Community Tourism Services in Thai Nguyen and Ha Giang, Revista geintec-gestao Inovacao E Tecnologias 11 (3), 1-12

ND Dat, HC Cuong, DTN Huy, NT Thuy. (2020). Financial Development and Economic Growth in Asian Countries: A Panel Empirical Investigation, PalArch's Journal of Archaeology of Egypt/Egyptology 17 (1), 52-63

Phan, T.T.D et al. (2012). DETERMINATION OF CAFFEINE CONTENTS OF COFFEE BRANDS IN THE VIETNAMESE MARKET, Journal of Microbiology, Biotechnology, 1 (February Special issue)

PM Dat, ND Mau, BTT Loan, DTN Huy. (2020). COMPARATIVE CHINA CORPORATE GOVERNANCE STANDARDS AFTER FINANCIAL CRISIS, CORPORATE SCANDALS AND MANIPULATION, Journal of Security & Sustainability Issues 9 (3)

P Van Tuan, DTN Huy, PK Duy. (2021). Impacts of Competitor Selection Strategy on Firm Risk-Case in Vietnam Investment and Finance Industry, Revista Geintec-Gestao Inovacao E Tecnologias 11 (3), 127-135

Suu Thi Bui, Dinh Tran Ngoc Huy, Lan Duc Doan. (2021). Further Analysis on Alcohol Trap and application local Beauveria bassiana for Control Coffee Berry Borer (CBB) In the Concept of Agricultural Sustainable Value Chain, Nat. Volatiles & Essent. Oils, 2021; 8(5): 3630 - 3640

TTB Hang, DTH Nhung, DTN Huy, NM Hung, MD Pham. (2020). Where Beta is going–case of Viet Nam hotel, airlines and tourism company groups after the low inflation period, Entrepreneurship and Sustainability Issues 7 (3)

TTH Ha, NB Khoa, DTN Huy, VK Nhan, DH Nhung, PT Anh, PK Duy. (2019). Modern corporate governance standards and role of auditing-cases in some Western european countries after financial crisis, corporate scandals and manipulation, International Journal of Entrepreneurship 23 (1S)

VQ Nam, DT NGOC HUY. (2021). Solutions to Promote Startup for the Youth in Minoritty and Moutainous Region of Thai Nguyen Province-Vietnam, Journal of Contemporary Issues in Business and Government 27 (3), 2113-2118

CASE NO. 4

DATE

7 Jan, 2022

(Published in SCOPUS JOURNAL Design engineering, 2021)

ICT AND DIGITAL TECH EFFECTS ON MARKETING STRATEGIES AND CHOOSING COMPETITOR AFFECTING ON BUSINESS OPERATION - A CASE IN HOTEL AND ENTERTAINMENT SECTOR

Nguyen Dinh Trung, PhD

National Economics University (NEU), Hanoi Vietnam

trungnd@neu.edu.vn

Dinh Tran Ngoc Huy, MBA

Banking University HCMC, Ho Chi Minh city Vietnam - International University of Japan , Japan

dtnhuy2010@gmail.com

Pham Van Tuan, PhD

National Economics University (NEU), Hanoi Vietnam

phamvantuan@neu.edu.vn

Dao Thi Huong, PhD

Thai Nguyen University of Economics and Business Administration (TUEBA), Vietnam

dthuong2020@gmail.com

Abstract:

During the Covid 19 Pandemic, Vietnam tourism entrepreneurs need to develop suitable tourism package and tourism policies, going together with better management of tourism activities and with proper marketing and risk management strategies.

With a strategic vision, OCH is taking strong steps to confidently become a leading company in Vietnam in the hotel and food service business, and at the same time affirming its position in the golden opportunity. of the integrated economy.

This study will show digital technology and ICT will have certain effects on marketing activities of OCH tourism corporation as well as the whole tourism industry in general.

This research finding and recommended policy also can be used as reference in competition policy for tourism system in Vietnam based on the principle that better business management and better risk management will drive better competitiveness of these firms.

Keywords: tourism firm; marketing activities; digital technology; ICT effects;

JEL: M21, N1

1. Introduction

Together with tourism sector, Hotel and entertainment industry in Vietnam has attracted many more tourists, both local ad international over recent years.

However under effects of covid 19, this sector need to figure out new solutions to recover.

Looking back at the impact of the Covid-19 epidemic on Vietnam's tourism, it can be seen that when the epidemic occurred, travel bans and restrictions were applied to all tourist destinations. Activities in the hotel, motel, restaurant and transportation sectors have mostly been postponed due to the nationwide shutdown order. In addition, the aviation industry was also severely affected when a series of domestic and international flights to and from Vietnam were cancelled. The number of international visitors is only available in January and February, and from March there are almost no visitors. Domestic tourists also dropped sharply due to the complicated development of the epidemic and Vietnam implemented social distancing. Tourism businesses face difficulties, causing many employees of the tourism industry to lose their jobs and even have no income.

But Vietnam still has potential in post covid 19:

Figure 2 - Beautiful hotels in Ha Long (Bai Chay) in Vietnam

(source: internet)

The paper is organized with introduction , research questions, literature review and methodology. Next, main research findings/ results and some discussion and conclusion and policy suggestion will be presented.

2. Body of manuscript

2.1 Research questions

The scope of this study will cover:

Issue 1: What are market risk in hotel and entertainment sector?

Issue 2: What are impacts of digital technology on hotel and entertainment industry?

2.2 Literature review

Fama, Eugene F., and French, Kenneth R., (2004) also indicated in the three factor model that "value" and "size" are significant components which can affect stock returns. They also mentioned that a stock's return not only depends on a market beta, but also on market capitalization beta. The market beta is used in the three factor model, developed by Fama and French, which is the successor to the CAPM model by Sharpe, Treynor and Lintner.

Dimitrov (2006) documented a significantly negative association between changes in financial leverage and contemporaneous risk-adjusted stock returns. Aydemir et all (2006) identified in an economy with more realistic variation in interest rates and the price of risk, there is significant variation in stock return volatility at the market and firm level. In such an economy, financial leverage has little effect on the dynamics of stock return volatility at the market level. Financial leverage contributes more to the dynamics of stock return volatility for a small firm. Then, Maia (2010) stated the main determinants of firms' capital structures are related to firms' sensitivities to these systematic sources of risk and they affect asymmetrically low and high leverage firms. And temporary shocks are relatively more important for low leverage firms, and that financial distress risk seems to be captured by the sensitivity of firms' cash flow innovations to market discount rate news.

Umar (2011) found that firms which maintain good governance structures have leverage ratios that are higher (forty-seven percent) than those of firms with poor governance mechanisms per unit of profit. Chen et all (2013) supported regulators' suspicions that over-reliance on short-term funding and insufficient collateral compounded the effects of dangerously high leverage and resulted in undercapitalization and excessive risk exposure for Lehman Brothers. The model reinforces the importance of the relationship between capital structure and risk management. Then, Alcock et all (2013) found evidence that leverage cannot be viewed as a long-term strategy to enhance performance, but in the short term, managers do seem to add significantly to fund excess returns by effectively timing leverage choices to the expected future market environment. And Gunaratha (2013) revealed that in different industries in Sri Lanka, the degree of financial leverage has a significant positive correlation with financial risk.

Finally, financial leverage can be considered as one among many factors that affect business risk of consumer good firms.

3. Methodology and data

In this research, analytical research method is used, philosophical method is used and specially, leverage scenario analysis method is used. Analytical data is from the situation of listed hotel and entertainment industry firms in VN stock exchange and current tax rate is 25%.

Generally speaking, quantitative method is mainly used in this study whith a note that risk measure asset beta is mainly derive from equity beta and financial leverage.

Finally, we use the results to suggest policy for both these enterprises, relevant organizations and government.

4. Main results

4.1- Data analysis

Empirical Research Findings and Discussion

In the below section, data used are from total 12 listed hotel and entertainment industry companies on VN stock exchange (HOSE and HNX mainly). In the scenario 1, current financial leverage degree is kept as in the 2011 financial statements which is used to calculate market risk (beta). Then, two (2) FL scenarios are changed up to 30% and down to 20%, compared to the current FL degree.

Market risk (beta) under the impact of tax rate, includes: 1) equity beta; and 2) asset beta.

 A. Scenario 1: current financial leverage (FL) as in financial reports 2011

In this case, all beta values of 12 listed firms on VN hotel and entertainment industry market as following:

Table 1 – Market risk of listed companies on VN hotel and entertainment industry market

Order No.	Company stock code	Equity beta	Asset beta (assume debt beta = 0)	Note	Financial leverage (F.S reports)
1	DLD	0,181	0,109	VNG as comparable	35,0%
2	DXL	0,323	0,219	SGH as comparable	28,0%
3	MTC	0,386	0,374	SGH as comparable	2,8%
4	OCH	1,085	0,375	RIC as comparable	57,5%
5	SGH	0,392	0,362		7,9%
6	VIR	0,325	0,230	MTC as comparable	25,2%
7	VNG	0,234	0,181		28,4%
8	DNT	-1,072	-0,819		23,56%
9	DSN	0,447	0,401	FDT as comparable	10,26%
10	GTT	0,691	0,223	RIC as comparable	67,75%
11	RIC	1,779	1,434		19,42%
12	VPL	0,950	0,257		72,95%
				Average	31,55%

(source: Viet Nam stock exchange 2012)

(source: Viet Nam stock exchange 2012)

B. Scenario 2: financial leverage increases up to 30%

If leverage increases up to 30%, all beta values of total 12 listed firms on VN tourism industry market as below:

Table 2 – Market risks of listed hotel and entertainment industry firms (case 2)

Order No.	Company stock code	Equity beta	Asset beta (assume debt beta = 0)	Note	Financial leverage (30% up)
1	DLD	0,144	0,079	VNG as comparable	45,5%
2	DXL	0,275	0,175	SGH as comparable	36,4%
3	MTC	0,382	0,368	SGH as comparable	3,6%
4	OCH	0,552	0,139	RIC as comparable	74,8%
5	SGH	0,392	0,352		10,2%
6	VIR	0,280	0,188	MTC as comparable	32,7%
7	VNG	0,234	0,148		36,9%
8	DNT	-1,072	-0,744		30,62%
9	DSN	0,435	0,377	FDT as comparable	13,34%
10	GTT	0,272	0,032	RIC as comparable	88,08%
11	RIC	1,779	1,330		25,24%
12	VPL	0,950	0,049		94,83%
				Average	41,02%

(source: Viet Nam stock exchange 2012)

C.. Scenario 3: leverage decreases down to 20%

If leverage decreases down to 20%, all beta values of total 12 listed firms on the hotel and entertainment industry market in VN as following:

Table 3 – Market risk of listed hotel and entertainment industry firms (case 3)

Order No.	Company stock code	Equity beta	Asset beta (assume debt beta = 0)	Note	Financial leverage (20% down)
1	DLD	0,181	0,131	VNG as comparable	28,0%
2	DXL	0,323	0,250	SGH as comparable	22,4%
3	MTC	0,386	0,377	SGH as comparable	2,2%
4	OCH	1,085	0,586	RIC as comparable	46,0%
5	SGH	0,392	0,368		6,3%
6	VIR	0,325	0,259	MTC as comparable	20,1%
7	VNG	0,234	0,181		22,7%
8	DNT	-1,072	-0,870		18,85%
9	DSN	0,455	0,418	FDT as comparable	8,21%
10	GTT	0,943	0,432	RIC as comparable	54,20%
11	RIC	1,779	1,503		15,53%
12	VPL	0,950	0,395		58,36%
				Average	25,24%

(source: Viet Nam stock exchange 2012)

All three above tables and data show that values of equity and asset beta in the case of increasing leverage up to 30% or decreasing leverage degree down to 20% have certain fluctuation.

D. **Comparing statistical results in 3 scenarios of changing leverage:**

Table 4 - Statistical results (FL in case 1)

Statistic results	Equity beta	Asset beta (assume debt beta = 0)	Difference
MAX	1,779	1,434	0,3455
MIN	-1,072	-0,819	-0,2525
MEAN	0,477	0,279	0,1982
VAR	0,4495	0,2390	0,2105
Note: Sample size : 12			

(source: Viet Nam stock exchange 2012)

Table 5 – Statistical results (FL in case 2)

Statistic results	Equity beta	Asset beta (assume debt beta = 0)	Difference
MAX	1,779	1,330	0,4492
MIN	-1,072	-0,744	-0,3283
MEAN	0,385	0,208	0,1774
VAR	0,4121	0,2112	0,2009
Note: Sample size : 12			

(source: Viet Nam stock exchange 2012)

Table 6- Statistical results (FL in case 3)

Statistic results	Equity beta	Asset beta (assume debt beta = 0)	Difference
MAX	1,779	1,503	0,2764
MIN	-1,072	-0,870	-0,2020
MEAN	0,498	0,336	0,1626
VAR	0,4645	0,2709	0,1936
Note: Sample size : 12			

(source: Viet Nam stock exchange 2012)

Based on the above results, we find out:

Equity beta mean values in all 3 scenarios are low (< 0,8) and asset beta mean values are also small (< 0,6). In the case of reported leverage in 2011, equity beta value fluctuates in an acceptable range from -1,060 (min) up to 2,035 (max) and asset beta fluctuates from -0,888 (min) up to 1,532 (max). If leverage increases to 30%, equity beta moves in an unchanged range and asset beta moves from -0,836 (min) up to 1,497 (max). Hence, we note that there is an increase in asset beta min value if leverage increases. When leverage decreases down to 20%, equity beta value moves in a range between 0,056 and 0,545 and asset beta changes from 0,051 (min) up to 0,153 (max). So, there is an increase in equity beta min value and increase in asset beta min when leverage decreases in scenario 3.

Beside, Exhibit 4 informs us that in the case 30% leverage up, average equity beta value of 10 listed firms decreases down to -0,131 while average asset beta value of these 10 firms decreases little less to -0,137. Then, when leverage reduces to 20%, average equity beta value of 10 listed firms goes down little more to -0,46 and average asset beta value of 10 firms up to -0,416.

The below chart 1 shows us : when leverage degree decreases down to 20%, average equity and asset beta values decrease to 0,305 and 0,098 compared to those at the initial reported leverage (0,765 and 0,514). Then, when leverage degree increases up to 30%, average equity beta decreases little less and average asset beta value also decreases less (to 0,634 and 0,377). However, the fluctuation of equity beta value (0,767) in the case of 30% leverage up is higher than (>) the results in the rest 2 leverage cases. And we could note that the using of leverage in the case of 30% leverage up causes a decrease in asset beta var down to 0,473 (compared to 0,530).

Figure 1 – Comparing statistical results of three (3) scenarios of changing FL (period 2009-2011)

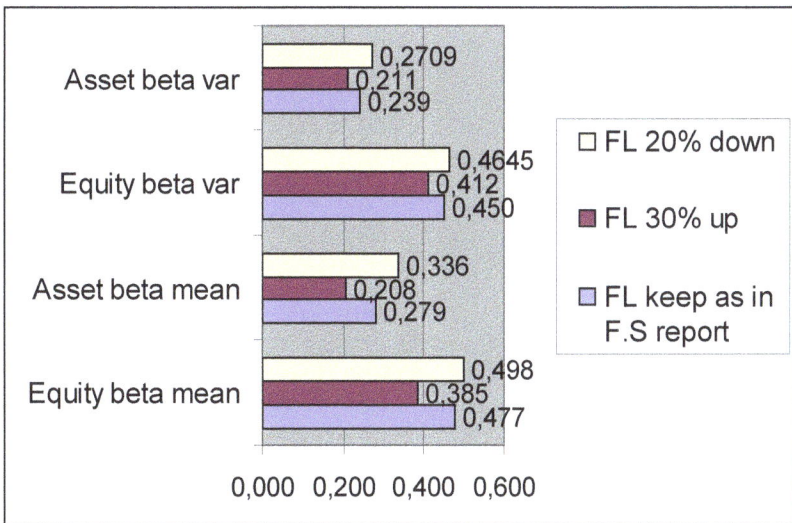

Figure 2 – Comparing statistical results of three (3) scenarios of changing FL (period 2007-2011)

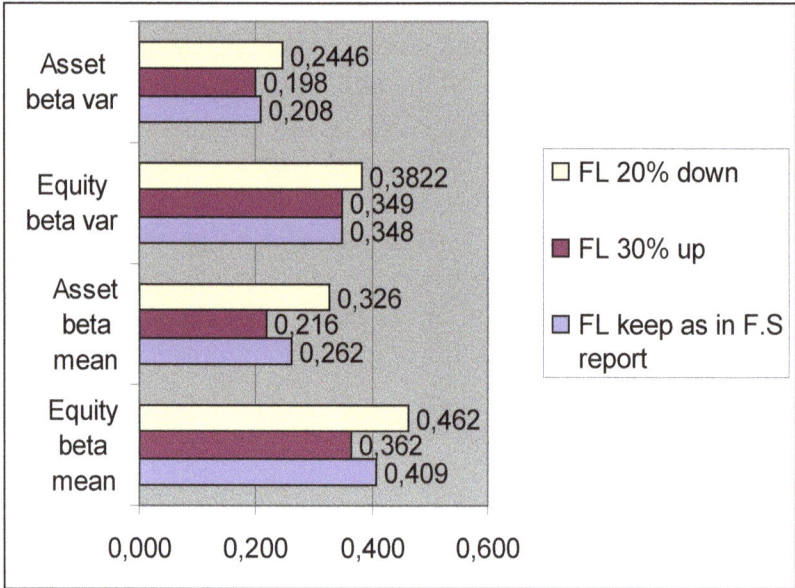

(source: Viet Nam stock exchange 2012)

E. Empirical results

In scenario 1 (current FL), asset and equity beta mean reach the medium values (0,279 and 0,477) whereas asset beta var also reaches medium (0,239), compared to the rest 2 cases.

In scenario 2 (FL 30%), asset and equity beta mean reach minimum values (0,208 and 0,385) whereas equity beta var reaches minimum (0,412), compared to the rest 2 cases.

And finally, in scenario 3 (FL down 20%), asset and equity beta mean reach maximum values while asset beta var reaches maximum value also (0,271), compared to the rest 2 cases.

4.2 Digital technology has impacts on marketing activities of HOTEL corporation

First, Firoiu and Croitoru (2015) specified Although the implications of the globalization phenomenon on tourism are extremely diverse and profound, sometimes difficult to commensurate, the evolution of the information and communication technology is currently outlining the main directions of the global economy through the accelerated pace of innovation. The hospitality industry requires a high level of adaptability to the demands of the tourist market, and the information and communication technology represents an efficient tool for increasing the degree of correlation between tourist supply and clients' demands, thus turning into a real progress bond. Improving the efficiency of this sector's activity becomes one of the primary issues on an increasingly dynamic global market, the changes regarding the distribution channel, the marketing services and the customer relationship management representing the key elements in this respect. In this context, the hotel market in Romania acquires new dimensions, its performance depending on the strong influence that the implementation of the newest informational technologies has on it, determining important changes at both the management and the operational level.

Beside, Zsarnoczky (2018) stated Digitalization is among the most important changes in our rapidly evolving world. Digital innovations and technological novelties are engines of development and show their impact everywhere, especially in the field of manufacturing, ICT and other service industries. Given the fact that tourism is based on the cooperation between a wide range of services and products, the benefits of the digital revolution in the sector are quite obvious. With the arrival of Google, which was able to rank the sites' appearance in internet searches, a fierce competition begun between blogs, tourism recommendation sites and price-comparing OTA systems. The bidirectional communication started with the use of cookies 2.0; since then, consumers have become an integral part of the business models, because businesses who seek to be successful in the long run, need to know their customers' demands in detail. The development of digital services require the identification of the user, information on their individual preferences and a decision-based calibration (by AI).

Then, Carlisle (2021) aims to present the findings from a European study on the digital skills gaps in tourism and hospitality companies. And study found The most important future digital skills include online marketing and communication skills, social media skills, MS Office skills, operating systems use skills and skills to monitor online reviews. The largest gaps between the current and the future skill levels were identified for artificial intelligence and robotics skills and augmented reality and virtual reality skills, but these skills, together with computer programming skills, were considered also as the least important digital skills.

5. Conclusion and policy suggestion

2020-2021 years have been difficult years for the tourism industry due to the impact of the COVID-19 epidemic causing many hotels to temporarily close. However, by the end of 2021 to 2022 end, the tourism industry has shown positive signs. Even so, domestic tourists will still be the main driver of the recovery in 2022.

In our study we pointed out there is potential market risk since early years before economic recession due to covid 19. In the current context we need to encourage vaccine prevention and have a step by step opening hotel industry first for domestic tourists.

For marketing strategy post covid 19 we can refer to :

Ayyildiz (2020) stated in Turkey, there are some suggestions as:

-The criteria of hygiene and necessary measures, which are the main expectations of the guests, should be maintained, and great attention should be paid to this issue.

- Hotel enterprises should turn their faces towards the smart applications that require less contact. The importance of digitalization should be acknowledged better and budget should be allocated for this.

- It should be ensured that social media is used more actively.

Figure 5- Hotels in HaLong Bay Vietnam

(source: internet)

Limitation of research

We can expand our research model for every regions of Vietnam.

ACKNOWLEDGEMENTS

Authors would like to take this opportunity to express my warm thanks to Board of Editors and Colleagues and friends to assist this publishing.

References

[1] Ayyildiz, A.Y. (2020). MARKETING STRATEGIES OF THE HOTELS IN COVID-19 PANDEMIC PROCESS: KUŞADASI SAMPLE, Business & Management Studies: An International Journal, 8(3)

[2] Chen RR, Chidambaran NK, Imerman MB, Sopranzetti BJ, Liquidity, Leverage, and Lehman: A Structural Analysis of Financial Institutions in Crisis, *Fordham School of Business Research Paper No.2279686,* 2013.

[3] Carlisle, S., Ivanov, S. and Dijkmans, C. (2021). The digital skills divide: evidence from the European tourism industry, *Journal of Tourism Futures*, 3. https://doi.org/10.1108/JTF-07-2020-0114

[4] Dimitrov V, Jain PC, The Value Relevance of Changes in Financial Leverage, *SSRN Working Paper,* 2006.

[5] Eugene FF, French KR, The Capital Asset Pricing Model: Theory and Evidence, *Journal of Economic Perspectives,* 2004.

[6] Flifel, Kaouther, Financial Markets between Efficiency and Persistence : Empirical Evidence on Daily Data, *Asian Journal of Finance and Accounting, Vol.4, No.2, pp.379-400,* 2012.

[7] Firoiu,D., & Croitoru, A.G. (2015). THE INFORMATION AND COMMUNICATION TECHNOLOGY – IMPACT ON THE HOSPITALITY INDUSTRY IN ROMANIA, Ecoforum, 4(1).

[8] Gunaratha V, The Degree of Financial Leverage as a Determinant of Financial Risk: An Empirical Study of Colombo Stock Exchange in Sri Lanka, *2nd International Conference on Management and Economics Paper,* 2013.

[9] Hac, L. D., Huy, D. T. N., Thach, N. N., Chuyen, B. M., Nhung, P. T. H., Tran, D. T., & Tran, T. A. (2021). Enhancing risk management culture for sustainable growth of Asia commercial bank-ACB in Vietnam under mixed effects of macro factors. *Entrepreneurship and Sustainability Issues, 8(3),* 291.

[10] Hang, N. T., & Huy, D. T. N. (2021). Better Risk Management of Banks and Sustainability-A Case Study in Vietnam. *Revista Geintec-Gestao Inovacao e Tecnologias*, *11*(2), 481-490.

[11] Hang, T. T. B., Nhung, D. T. H., Huy, D. T. N., Hung, N. M., & Pham, M. D. (2020). Where Beta is going–case of Viet Nam hotel, airlines and tourism company groups after the low inflation period. *Entrepreneurship and Sustainability Issues*, *7*(3), 2282.

[12] Hanh, H.T., Huy, D.T.N., Phuong, N.T.T., Nga, L.T.V., Anh, P.T (2020) Impact of Macro Economic Factors and Financial Development on Energy Projects - Case in ASEAN Countries, Management 24(2). DOI:10.2478/manment-2019-0051

[13] Hang, T.T.B., Nhung, D.T.H., Hung, N.M., Huy, D.T.N., Dat, P.M (2020) Where Beta is going–case of Viet Nam hotel, airlines and tourism company groups after the low inflation period, *Entrepreneurship and Sustainability Issues* 7(3), 2282-2298.

[14] Hanh, H.T., Chuyen, B.M., Huy, D.T.N., Phuong, N.T.T., Phuong, H.T.L., Nuong, L.N. (2020) Challenges and Opportunities from Impacts of FDI and Income on Environment Pollution: Role of Financial Accounting Transparency in FDI Firms, Journal of Security and Sustainability Issues 10(20), 643–654. https://doi.org/10.9770/jssi.2020.10.2(22)

[15] Huy, D.T.N (2015) The Critical Analysis of Limited South Asian Corporate Governance Standards After Financial Crisis, International Journal for Quality Research 9(4), 741-764.

[16] Ha, T.T.H, Khoa, N.B., Huy, D.T.N., Nhan, V.K., Nhung, D.H., Anh, P.T., Duy, P.K (2020) Modern Corporate Governance Standards and Role of Auditing-Cases in Some Western European Countries After Financial Crisis, Corporate Scandals and Manipulation, International Journal of Entrepreneurship 23(1S).

[17] Huy, D.T.N (2012) Estimating Beta of Viet Nam listed construction companies groups during the crisis, *Journal of Integration and Development* 15 (1), 57-71

[18] Huy, D. T.N., Loan, B. T., and Anh, P. T (2020) Impact of selected factors on stock price: a case study of Vietcombank in

Vietnam, *Entrepreneurship and Sustainability Issues, 7(4)*, 2715-2730. https://doi.org/10.9770/jesi.2020.7.4(10)

[19] Huy, D. T.N., Dat, P. M., và Anh, P. T (2020) Building and econometric model of selected factors' impact on stock price: a case study, *Journal of Security and Sustainability Issues 9*(M), 77-93. https://doi.org/10.9770/jssi.2020.9.M(7)

[20] Huy D.T.N., Nhan V.K., Bich N.T.N., Hong N.T.P., Chung N.T., Huy P.Q (2021) Impacts of Internal and External Macroeconomic Factors on Firm Stock Price in an Expansion Econometric model—A Case in Vietnam Real Estate Industry, *Data Science for Financial Econometrics-Studies in Computational Intelligence* 898, Springer. http://doi-org-443.webvpn.fjmu.edu.cn/10.1007/978-3-030-48853-6_14

[21] Hoang, N. T., & Huy, D. T. N. (2021). Determining factors for educating students for choosing to work for foreign units: Absence of self-efficacy. *JETT, 12*(2), 11-19.

[22] Huy, D. T. N. (2015). The critical analysis of limited south Asian corporate governance standards after financial crisis. *International Journal for Quality Research*, *9*(4),741-764.

[23] Huy, D. T. N., & Hang, N. T. (2021). Factors that affect Stock Price and Beta CAPM of Vietnam Banks and Enhancing Management Information System–Case of Asia Commercial Bank. *REVISTA Geintec-Gestao Inovacao E Tecnologias*, *11*(2), 302-308.

[24] Huy, D. T. N., Hanh, N. T. T., Hang, N. T., Nhung, P. T. H., Thao, N. T. P., Han, L. T., & Sang, D. T. (2021). General Solutions for Enhancing Quality of Teachers During Globalization in Emerging Markets Including Vietnam-and Some Pedagogy Psychological Issues. *Psychology and Education Journal*, *58*(4), 2343-2349.

[25] Huy, D. T. N., Van, P. N., & Ha, N. T. T. (2021). Education and computer skill enhancing for Vietnam laborers under industry 4.0 and evfta agreement. *Ilkogretim Online*, *20*(4), 1033-1038.

[26] Kulathunga, K. (2015). Macroeconomic Factors and Stock Market Development: With Special Reference to Colombo

Stock Exchange, International Journal of Scientific and Research Publications, 5(8), 1-7.

[27] Ihsan, H., Ahmad, E., Muhamad, I.H., & Sadia, H. (2015). International Journal of Scientific and Research Publications, 5(8)

[28] Jarrah, M., & Salim, N. (2016). The Impact of Macroeconomic Factors on Saudi Stock Market (Tadawul) Prices, Int'l Conf. on Advances in Big Data Analytics.

[29] Luthra, M., & Mahajan, S. (2014). Impact of Macro factors on BSE Bankex, International Journal of Current Research and Academic Review, 2(2), 179-186.

[30] Natocheeva,N. et al. (2020). DIGITAL TECHNOLOGIES AS A DRIVER FOR THE DEVELOPMENT OF THE TOURISM INDUSTRY. E3S Web of Conferences 159.https://doi.org/10.1051/e3sconf/202015904002

[31] Ndlovu, M., Faisal, F., Nil, G.R., & Tursoy, T. (2018).The Impact of Macroeconomic Variables on Stock Returns: A Case of the Johannesburg Stock Exchange, Romanian Statistical Review, 2, 88-104.

[32] Pan, Q., & Pan, M. (2014). The Impact of Macro Factors on the Profitability of China's Commercial Banks in the Decade after WTO Accession, Open Journal of Social Sciences, 2, 64-69.

[33] Quy, V.T., & Loi, D.T.N. (2016). Macroeconomic factors and Stock Price – A Case Of Real Estate Stocks on Ho Chi Minh Stock Exchange, Journal of Science Ho Chi Minh City Open University, 2(18), 63-75.

[34] Saeed, S., & Akhter, N. (2012). Impact of Macroeconomic Factors on Banking Index in Pakistan, Interdisciplinary Journal of Contemporary Research in Business, 4(6), 1200-1218.

[35] Thi Hang, N., Thi Tinh, D., Ngoc Huy, D. T., & Hong Nhung, P. T. (2021). Educating and training labor force Under Covid 19; Impacts to Meet Market Demand in Vietnam during Globalization and Integration Era. *Journal for Educators, Teachers and Trainers, 12*(1), 179-184. doi: 10.47750/jett.2021.12.01.023

[36] Thi Hoa, N., Hang, N. T., Giang, N. T., & Huy, D. T. N. (2021). Human resource for schools of politics and for international relation during globalization and EVFTA. *Ilkogretim Online*, *20*(4), 1386-96.

[37] Van Tuan, P., Huy, D. T. N., & Duy, P. K. (2021). Impacts of Competitor Selection Strategy on Firm Risk-Case in Vietnam Investment and Finance Industry. *Revista Geintec-Gestao Inovacao E Tecnologias*, *11*(3), 127-135.

[38] Zsarnozky, M. (2018). The Digital Future of the Tourism & Hospitality Industry. Retrieved from https://www.researchgate.net/publication/325989297_The_Digital_Future_of_the_Tourism_Hospitality_Industry

[39] https://www.sbv.gov.vn

[40] https://nif.mof.gov.vn

CASE NO. 5

DATE

7 Jan 2022

DIGITAL MARKETING APPLICATIONS IN TOURISM INDUSTRY VIA A CASE STUDY OF MTC - MY TRA COMPANY IN VIETNAM

Nguyen Tien Dung, PhD

Hanoi University of Science and Technology, Vietnam

Dung.nguyentien3@hust.edu.vn

Dinh Tran Ngoc Huy MBA, (corresponding)

Banking University of Ho Chi Minh city, Viet Nam – GSIM International University of Japan, Japan

Dtnhuy2010@gmail.com

Nguyen Thi Hoa, PhD

Thu Dau Mot University, Binh Duong Vietnam

hoant.khql@tdmu.edu.vn

Dao Thi Huong, PhD

Thai Nguyen University of Economics and Business Administration (TUEBA), *Vietnam*

dthuong2020@tueba.edu.vn

Abstract:

Currently it is necessary to suggest digital marketing plans and applications in tourism industry in Vietnam as well as emerging markets in order to support the development of this sector in coming years.

First, authors use quantitative econometric model for MyTra (MTC) travel joint stock company is listed in Vietnam stock market and find out: impacts of six (6) macroeconomic factors on stock price of a joint stock travel company, MyTra (MTC) in Vietnam in the period of 2014-2019, both positive and negative sides. The results of quantitative research, in a six factor model, show that the increase in risk free rate has a significant effect on increasing MTC stock price with the highest impact coefficient, the second is decreasing CPI, lending rate and exchange rate.

Second, this study figure out digital marketing can help MyTra company to increase tourism revenue and profits and suggest solutions for more effective marketing activities.

Last but not least, This research finding and recommended policy also can be used as reference in policy for tourism system and commercial bank and relating governmental agencies.

Keywords: digital technology, digital marketing, internet, travel company; stock price;

JEL: M21, N1

3. Introduction

Although it face difficulties from corona, MyTra (MTC) travel joint stock company in Vietnam is doing good job in:

- Restaurant, hotel business - Managing My Tra tourist area, trading in fine art goods and domestic technology products - Services: massage, karaoke, disco - Entertainment service area - Transporting passengers under contract - Business travel services and other services - Air ticket agent - Financial investment...

Digital Marketing reaches customers on different channels: Internet, TV, phone, etc. This approach can be done at any time, any space. Traditional marketing cannot do this. Online marketing can only perform 1 task of Digital Marketing.

Sometimes Internet is not required; Digital Marketing is effective on both television and radio advertising; video games; Mobile applications, etc. Digital Marketing is the most effective way of communication and promotion

It can be affirmed: Digital Marketing is the most effective marketing tool today, esp. It can be used in tourism sector.

Below pictures showing Vietnam has lots of beautiful places

Figure 1 - Mui Ne - Phan Thiet city Vietnam

Source: internet

The paper is organized as follows: after the introduction it is the research issues, literature review and methodology. Next, section 3 will cover methodology and data and section 4 presents main research findings/results. Section 5 gives us some discussion and conclusion and policy suggestion .

4. Body of manuscript

2.1 Research issues

The scope of this study will cover:

Issue 1: What are the correlation and relationship among many economic factors: MTC stock price, interest rate, exchange rate, inflation, VNIndex, S&P 500 and GDP growth?

Issue 2: What are the impacts of digital technology in marketing activities in the company as well as tourism industry?

Issue 3: What are suggested solutions regarding to tourism development in incoming period from digital marketing perspectives?

2.2 Literature review

According to Philips Kotler: "Digital marketing, or electronic marketing, is the process of planning the product, price, distribution, and promotion of products, services and ideas to meet the needs of organizations and individuals. based on electronic media and the Internet".

Social Media (Social Media) is one of the important elements of Online Marketing, understood, this is the interaction activities of the brand with the target public and customers through third-party Social platforms. . For example: Facebook, Instagram, Youtube, Forum, Twitter, etc. Social Media channels play an important role because it is flexible, capable of understanding customer needs, bringing cost-effectiveness and goals. of Digital Marketing campaign. In particular, using Social Media helps to personalize, bring the image of brands and businesses closer, connect and build relationships and trust with the public and target customers.

Manisha and Shikha (2014) stated that Exchange rate, Inflation, GDP growth rate affect banking index positively whereas Gold prices have negative impact on BSE Bankex but none of them have significant impact on Bankex. Then, Winhua and Meiling (2014) confirmed that macroeconomic do have a substantial influence to the earning power of commercial banks.

Krishna (2015) investigated the nature of the causal relationships between stock prices and the key macro economic variables in BRIC countries. The empirical evidence shows that long-run and short-run relationship exists between macro economic variables and stock prices, but this relationship was not consistent for all of the BRIC countries. And Kulathunga (2015) suggested that all macroeconomic factors influence the stock market development. More precisely, volatile inflation rate and exchange rate together with higher deposit rate have curtailed the stock market development in Sri Lanka. Moreover, positive optimism created by the economic growth and the stock market performance during the previous periods tend to enhance stock market performance. We also summarize related studies:

Table 1- Summary of previous studies

Authors	Year	Contents, results
Ahmad and Ramzan	2016	the macroeconomic factors have important concerns with stocks traded in the stock market and these factors make investors to choose the stock because investors are interested to know about the factors affecting the working of stock to manage their portfolios. Abrupt variations and unusual movements of macroeconomic variables cause the stock returns to fluctuate due to uncertainty of future gains.

Kaur	• 2017	The increasing role of digital marketing has affected the way businesses promote their offerings to existing as well as new customers. The need for digital marketing has been felt like never before in the tourism industry wherein customers have instant access to all kinds of information on the latest offers and best prices. Today digital marketing plays a critical role in the success of each business which exists in the tourism industry

Nuenen and Scarles	2021	discusses the concomitant processes of increasing familiarisation, responsiveness and responsibility that digital technology enables in the realm of tourism. We reflect on the influence of the proliferation of interactive digital platforms and solutions within tourism practice and behaviour through a range of lenses, from user generated content and associated interactive digital platforms, the emergence of gamification embedded within these, immersive mixed-reality media (such as virtual reality [VR] and augmented reality [AR]) and the changes in tourist behaviour that have paralleled these digital developments

Opute et al	• 2020	Forwarding a theoretical model that suggests a proactive approach for enhancing tourism customers service experience, and at a profit for tourism providers, this study draws the attention of tourism practitioners to the prominent role that digital technologies play in modern society, consumer socialising influence, as well as tourism customers' service experiential impact. Furthermore, this study draws from the service gaps model of service quality to explain why tourism service providers must embrace customer engagement towards ensuring that their service offerings equate, if not exceed customers' service expectations

Within the scope of this paper, we measure impacts of both internal and external macro factors on MTC stock price and suggest policies for tourism and bank system, Vietnam government, Ministry of Finance, State Bank and relevant government bodies. We also analyze data through out time series from 2014-2019.

Figure 2- Na Hang- Tuyen Quang province in Vietnam

Source: internet

3. Methodology and data

This research paper establishes correlation among macro economic factors by using an econometric model to analyze impacts of 6 macro economic factors in Vietnam such as: GDP growth, inflation, interest rate, exchange rate,… on MTC stock price.

We build a regression model with Eview software to measure impacts of factors. MTC stock price is a function with 6 variables as follows:

Y (MTC stock price) = f (x1, x2, x3, x4, x5, x6, x7) = ax1 + bx2 + cx3+dx4+ ex5 + fx6 + k

With: x1 : GDP growth rate (g), x2 : inflation, x3: VNIndex, x4: lending rate, x5: risk free rate (Rf), x6: USD/VND rate

4. Main results

4.1- General data analysis

First of all, The below chart 1 shows us that Y has a negative correlation with GDP growth:

Chart 1 – MTC stock price (Y) vs. GDP growth in Vietnam (G)

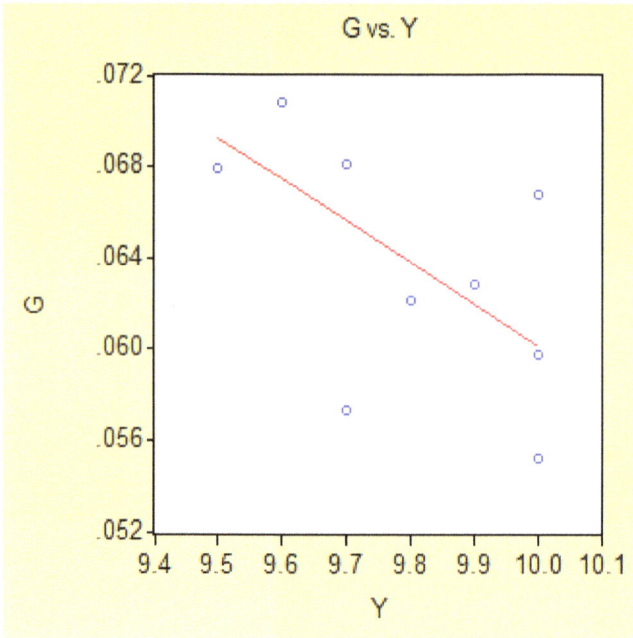

Chart 2 – CLG stock price (Y) vs. Inflation (CPI)

Next we find out that, based on the below scatter chart, Y (MTC stock price) has slightly negative correlation with inflation (CPI).

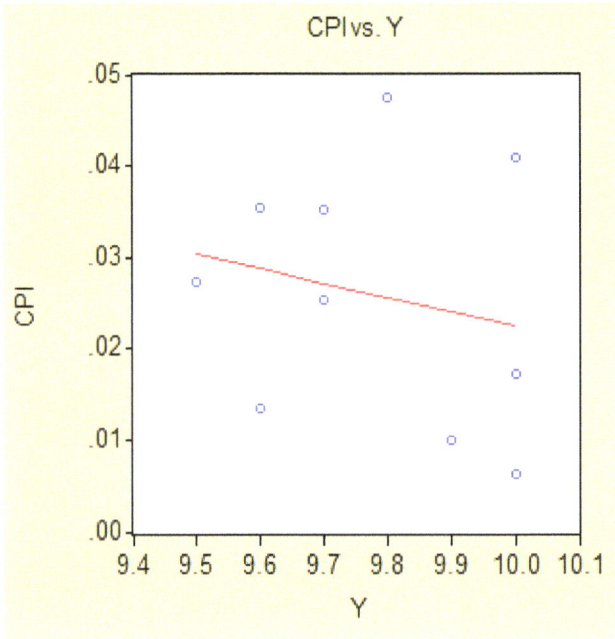

Looking at the below chart 3, we also recognize that MTC stock price (Y) and VNIndex have negative correlationship.

Chart 3 – Y vs. VNIndex

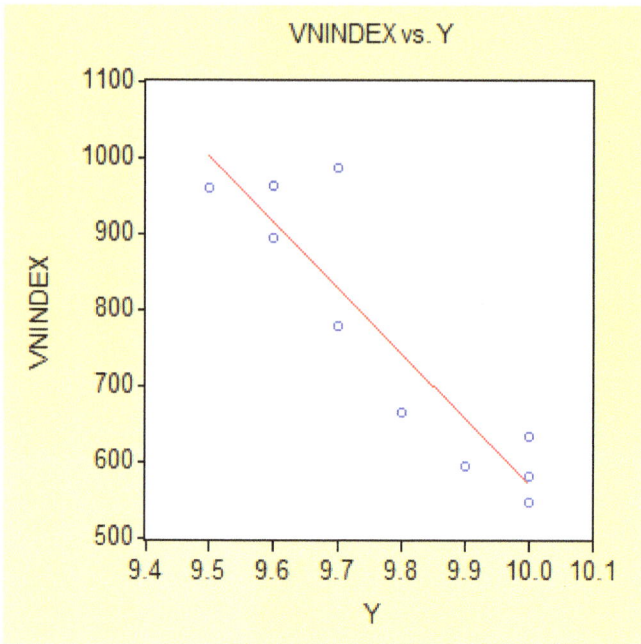

VNINDEX vs. Y

We see that, MTC stock price (Y) and lending rate have positive correlation:

Chart 4 – Y vs. Lending rate (r)

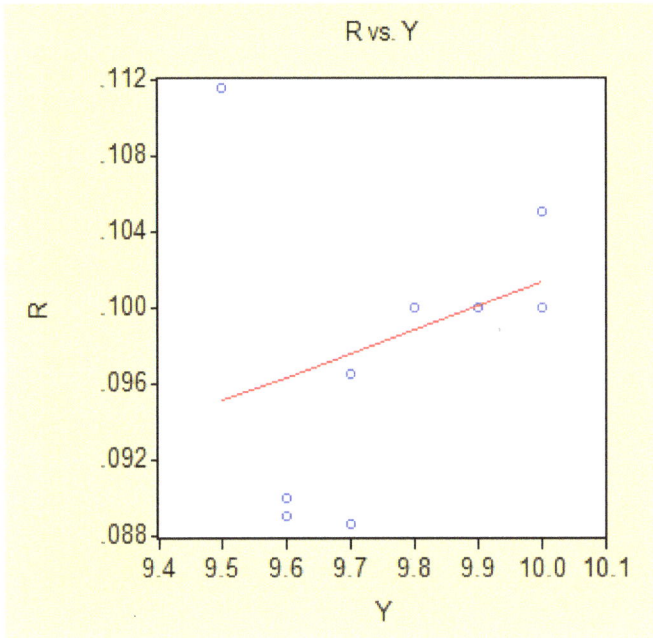

R vs. Y

In addition to, the below scatter graph shows us that MTC stock price (Y) and risk free rate (Rf) also have positive correlation.

Chart 5 – Y vs. Risk free rate (Rf)

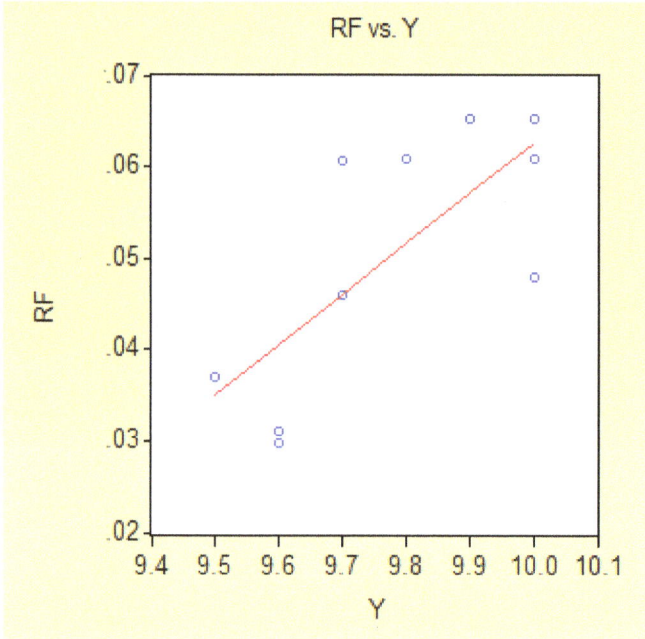

RF vs. Y

The below table 3 shows us that covariance matrix among 7 macro economic variables. MTC stock price (Y) has a positive correlation with risk free rate and lending rate but has a negative correlation with exchange rate (EX_Rate), CPI and GDP growth.

Hence, an increase in risk free rate may lead to an increase in MTC stock price.

Table 2 – Covariance matrix for 7 macro economic variables

				Covariance Matrix				
	Y	G	CPI	VNINDEX	R	RF	EX_RATE	SP500
Y	0.031600	-0.000576	-0.000501	-27.22350	0.000395	0.001756	-84.17600	-46.83340
G	-0.000576	2.77E-05	-3.50E-06	0.575578	-1.49E-05	-3.33E-05	1.720538	0.934488
CPI	-0.000501	-3.50E-06	0.000173	0.322068	-2.10E-05	-2.79E-05	0.627614	0.676458
VNINDEX	-27.22350	0.575578	0.322068	28031.78	-0.534085	-1.418033	75361.46	46087.69
R	0.000395	-1.49E-05	-2.10E-05	-0.534085	5.25E-05	2.93E-05	-0.648952	-0.758612
RF	0.001756	-3.33E-05	-2.79E-05	-1.418033	2.93E-05	0.000178	-4.028085	-2.529699
EX_RATE	-84.17600	1.720538	0.627614	75361.46	-0.648952	-4.028085	335144.0	122334.5
SP500	-46.83340	0.934488	0.676458	46087.69	-0.758612	-2.529699	122334.5	78286.05

4.2 Regression model and main findings

In this section, we will find out the relationship between eight macro economic factors and stock price.

4.2.1 Scenario 1: regression model with 6 macro variables:

Running Eviews gives us results:

Dependent Variable: Y
Method: Least Squares
Date: 02/17/20   Time: 16:55
Sample: 1 10
Included observations: 10

Variable	Coefficient	Std. Error	t-Statistic	Prob.
G	-0.871072	7.937867	-0.109736	0.9195
CPI	-1.238691	2.396971	-0.516774	0.6410
R	-2.416865	5.072054	-0.476506	0.6663
VNINDEX	-0.000645	0.000363	-1.777347	0.1736
RF	3.315625	2.919494	1.135685	0.3386
EX_RATE	-6.42E-05	8.83E-05	-0.727551	0.5195
C	11.88058	1.745252	6.807372	0.0065

R-squared	0.916073	Mean dependent var	9.780000
Adjusted R-squared	0.748220	S.D. dependent var	0.187380
S.E. of regression	0.094023	Akaike info criterion	-1.694532
Sum squared resid	0.026521	Schwarz criterion	-1.482723
Log likelihood	15.47266	F-statistic	5.457578
Durbin-Watson stat	2.440184	Prob(F-statistic)	0.095980

$Y = -0.87*G - 1.2*CPI - 2.4*R - 0.0006* VNINDEX + 3.31* Rf - 6.42E*EX\_RATE +11.8$, $R^2 = 0.91$, SER = 0.09

Therefore, we see impacts of 6 micro and macro factors, with the new variable: exchange rate USD/VND (EX_RATE), the above equation shows that MTC stock price (Y) has negative correlation with GDP growth, exchange rate, inflation, lending rate and VNIndex, whereas it has positive correlation with risk free rate. We also recognize that inflation, lending rate, then risk free rate have the highest impact on MTC stock price, while exchange rate just has a slightly impact on stock price.

5. Discussion and conclusion

Through the regression equation with above 6 micro and macroeconomic variables, this research paper used updated data from 2014-2019 to analyze the regression equation via Eview in order to show that an increase in risk free rate has a significant impact on increasing MTC stock price (Y) with the highest coefficient of impact, followed by a decrease in CPI and slight decrease in GDP growth rate, then a decrease in lending rate, a reduction in exchange rate and decrease in VNINDEX. This result was conducted based on using internet data for regression with IT software EView.

Generally speaking, managing MTC stock price depends on many factors, so the government need to use fiscal policy combined with monetary policies and socio-economic policies to reduce unemployment and stimulate economic growth, toward a good stock price management.

Recommendations for IT governance and Data Security for Risk Management

In risk management for better business performance, we need IT governance and data protection to protect intellectual properties of our firms and reduce operational risk.

Recommendations for Improving tourism activities with digital technology

- Improving digital technology applications in tourism industry, even artificial intelligence in hotels and tourism for instance, in hotel booking, hotel room management, electric lights, elevator, etc. To bring tourists a new feeling and experience when they choose Vietnam tourism destinations.

- In addition, businesses also need to apply an application model of automation technology in tourism-hotel-entertainment activities to support businesses in reducing costs, improving customer experience, helping to improve the quality of products and services for customers,domestic and international, and increasing accuracy at work.

- The push strategy in Digital Marketing is essentially: promoting customers to know about the product. Make it easy for customers to remember the product. It is important that customers have a comparison between different products (from different brands).

– Pull strategy in Digital Marketing is: to attract customers to the business. Help customers make product purchasing decisions. This is the ultimate goal of Digital Marketing.

Figure 3 - Destinations for tourists in Tuyen Quang, North of Vietnam

Source: internet

ACKNOWLEDGEMENTS
I would like to take this opportunity to express my warm thanks to Board of Editors and Colleagues, family and friends to support this publishing.

References

[1] Ahmad, N., & Ramzan, M. (2016). Stock Market Volatility and Macroeconomic Factor Volatility, International Journal of Research in Business Studies and Management, 3(7), 37-44.

[2] Arshad, Z., Ali, R. A., Yousaf, S., & Jamil, S. (2015). Determinants of Share Prices of listed Commercial Banks in Pakistan, IOSR Journal of Economics and Finance, 6(2), 56-64.

[3] Ayub, A., & Masih, M. (2013). Interest Rate, Exchange Rate, and Stock Prices of Islamic Banks: A Panel Data Analysis, MPRA Paper No. 58871.

[4] Cherif, R., & Hasanov, F. (2012). Public Debt Dynamics: The Effects of Austerity, Inflation, and Growth Shocks, IMF Working paper WP/12/230.

[5] Dinh Tran Ngoc Huy, Nguyen Thi Hang. (2021). Factors that affect stock price and Beta CAPM of Vietnam Banks and Enhancing Management infomation system - Case of Asia Commercial Bank, Revista geintec Inovacao E Tecnologias, 11(2).

[6] Dinh Tran Ngoc Huy, Pham Ngoc Van, Nguyen Thi Thu Ha. (2021).Education and computer skill enhancing for Vietnam laborers under industry 4.0 and evfta agreement, Elementary education online, 20(4).

[7] Dinh Thi Hien, Dinh Tran Ngoc Huy, Nguyen Thi Hoa. (2021). Ho Chi Minh Viewpoints about Marxism Moral Human Resource for State Management Level in Vietnam, Psychology and education, 58(5).

[8] Hac, L.D., Huy, D.T.N., Thach, N.N., Chuyen, B.M., Nhung, P.T.H., Thang, T.D., Anh, T.T. (2021). Enhancing risk management culture for sustainable growth of Asia commercial bank -ACB in Vietnam under mixed effects of macro factors , Entrepreneurship and Sustainability Issues, 8(3).

[9] Hang, T.T.B., Nhung, D.T.H., Hung, N.M., Huy, D.T.N., Dat,

P.M. (2020). Where Beta is going–case of Viet Nam hotel, airlines and tourism company groups after the low inflation period , Entrepreneurship and Sustainability Issues, 7(3).

[10] Huy, D.T.N. (2015). The Critical Analysis of Limited South Asian Corporate Governance Standards After Financial Crisis, International Journal for Quality Research, 9(4): 741-764.

[11] Huy, D.T.N. (2012). Estimating Beta of Viet Nam listed construction companies groups during the crisis , Journal of Integration and Development, 15 (1), 57-71

[12] Huy, D. T.N., Loan, B. T., and Anh, P. T. (2020). Impact of selected factors on stock price: a case study of Vietcombank in Vietnam, Entrepreneurship and Sustainability Issues, vol.7, no.4, pp. 2715-2730. https://doi.org/10.9770/jesi.2020.7.4(10)

[13] Huy, D. T.N., Dat, P. M., và Anh, P. T. (2020). Building and econometric model of selected factors' impact on stock price: a case study, Journal of Security and Sustainability Issues, vol.9(M), pp. 77-93. https://doi.org/10.9770/jssi.2020.9.M(7)

[14] Huy D.T.N., Nhan V.K., Bich N.T.N., Hong N.T.P., Chung N.T., Huy P.Q. (2021). Impacts of Internal and External Macroeconomic Factors on Firm Stock Price in an Expansion Econometric model—A Case in Vietnam Real Estate Industry, Data Science for Financial Econometrics-Studies in Computational Intelligence, vol.898, Springer. http://doi-org-443.webvpn.fjmu.edu.cn/10.1007/978-3-030-48853-6_14

[15] Huy, D.T.N. , An, T.T.B. , Anh, T.T.K. , Nhung, P.T.H. (2021). Banking sustainability for economic growth and socio-economic development – case in Vietnam, Turkish Journal of Computer and Mathematics Education, 12(2), pp. 2544–2553

[16] Kaur, G. (2017).THE IMPORTANCE OF DIGITAL MARKETING IN THE TOURISM INDUSTRY, International Journal of Research - GRANTHAALAYAH 5(6):72. DOI:10.5281/zenodo.815854

[17] Krishna, R.C. (2015). Macroeconomic Variables impact on Stock Prices in a BRIC Stock Markets: An Empirical Analysis, Journal of

Stock & Forex Trading, 4(2).

[18] Kulathunga, K. (2015). Macroeconomic Factors and Stock Market Development: With Special Reference to Colombo Stock Exchange, International Journal of Scientific and Research Publications, 5(8), 1-7.

[19] Opute, A.P., Irene, P.N.O., Iwu, C.G. (2020). Tourism Service and Digital Technologies: A Value Creation Perspective, African Journal of Hospitality Tourism and Leisure 9(2)

[20] Nuenen, T.V., Scarles, C. (2021). Advancements in technology and digital media in tourism, Tourist studies, 2. https://doi.org/10.1177/1468797621990410

[21] https://www.sbv.gov.vn

[22] https://nif.mof.gov.vn

CASE NO. 6

DATE

Sep 30th , 2020

(PUBLISHED in REvista Geintec-Gestao Inovacao ETecnologias, Vol.11(3), 2021)

Marketing Strategy based on Competitor Analysis - A Case in Vietnam Medicine Sector

Le Thi Thanh Huong[1]; Dinh Tran Ngoc Huy[2*]; Nguyen Thi Hang[3]; Nguyen Tien Dung[4]

[1]PhD, Dai Nam University, Vietnam.

[1]lethanhhuong@dainam.edu.vn

[2*]MBA, Banking University HCMC, Ho Chi Minh City Vietnam.

International University of Japan, Niigata, Japan.

[2*]dtnhuy2010@gmail.com

[3]PhD, Thai Nguyen University, University of Information and Communications Technology, Vietnam.

[3]nthang@ictu.edu.vn

[4]PhD, Hanoi University of Science and Technology, Vietnam.

[4]Dung.nguyentien3@hust.edu.vn

Abstract

M.Porter theory has mentioned competitors in a five-force model for analyzing business environment of a company.

We would like to make further analysis, in this study, related to marketing strategy based on competitor risk analysis in a typical case study in Vietnam medicine sector. Base on this analysis, we aim to create a resource of competitive information for marketing strategy, that what several scientists called resource -advantage marketing strategy.

In this field of marketing there are some our previous researches relating, so together with this study we could draw a theory of marketing strategy based on competitor risk analysis.

Authors through this study has found out that elements of marketing including our rivals or competitors in business environment can influence market risk from a quantitative point of view in a two factors model, and this research paper estimates the impacts of not only the size of firms' competitors, but also leverage, on the market risk of listed medicine companies in this category.

Our main findings also show that risk variation (by beta var) can be reduced and minimized in case we keep the same size of rival or competitor, approximately (with equity beta var 0,09).

At last, this paper illustrates findings show us that medicine sector need to reassess their business environment in case and the size of competitor smaller, and in the mean time, risk might reduce in case of smaller competitor size.

Our research limitation is we need to expand research model to other industries.

Keywords: Marketing Strategy, Competitor Theory, Competitive Firm Size, Market Risk, Vietnam, Medical Industry.

JEL Classification - G00, G3, G30, M21.

1. Introduction

Vietnam economy has experienced many efforts from medicine sector in past years and medicine industry now experienced participation of many private hospitals and joint stock companies. Therefore medicine firms also face competition just like other companies in the market and they have to realize competitive risks from the market economy. This study will help medical companies to recognize their challenges and risks from the rivals, with traditional beta CAPM formula and we develop it into asset and equity beta measures.

In fact, there will be several benefits from selecting the proper competitors, both in business and medicine industries, such as: helping our firm to get right direction and purposes. This will be more meaningful for our company in the market.

This paper is organized with introduction, literature review, main findings, discussion and conclusion.

2. Research Questions

In this study we will address some issues in the context there are different sizes of competitors: smaller or bigger, on Vietnam stock exchange, hence, this will affect market risk of medicine firms.

Issue 1: To what extent market risk will vary in medicine industry, under cases of changing size of competitors on Vietnam stock exchange?

Issue 2: To what extent the risk variation (beta var) in the medicine industry will change under various scenarios in which competitors changed from smaller to bigger or double?

Issue 3: What are recommendations for risk management?

3. Literature Review

There are relation between economic development and active, large previous studies or empirical literature (Goldsmith, 1969, & Shaw, 1973).

Next, potential rival force will show the vital characteristic of workable competition and evaluation of performance of market can be supported by potential entries sources as well as market games which function as welfare yardstick (Witteloostujn, 1992).

Whereas in order to create competitive edge for keeping customers with sustainability, the firms need to ensure its services and products with competitive features (Easton, 1988).

Next, Bergen and Peteraf (2002) pointed that competitor theory can be developed through awareness of competitor and the classification of competitors such a substitutors, indirect competitors, etc. Which can help managers to develop strategic opportunities and assess their significance.

Moreover, there are failures of banks, currency crises involved in finance history (Reinhart and Rogoff, 2009).

And volatility study is imperative in country such as India, where decline in global market and US real estate created worry (Mishra, 2009).

Also, there are difficulties such as data collection in short term created by problems such as equity cost estimation in emerging markets (Peirero, L.E., 2010).

Then, beta and formulas can be undermined by information lacking on stock exchange (Velez-Pareja, 2011).

Then, the relation between beta calculation and reliability to investment and valuation were considered (Marcin, Mariusz, Marek, and Karol, 2012).

In addition, higher leverage ratios are found out in companies having good corporate governance, compared to poor governance firms (Umar, 2011). And Chen et all (2013) mentioned that large risk exposure of Lehman Brothers caused by high leverage impacts and short-term funds over reliance and not enough collateral.

Alcock et all (2013) found out that we cannot rely on leverage as startegy in long term for enhancing business performance, but may work in short term for effective timing leverage.

And between financial risk and financial leverage ther is positive relationship and significant in case Sri Lanka (Gunaratha, 2013).

Last but not least, between leverage and volatility, there is a correct link (Ana and John,

2013).

And Huy, D.T.N et al (2020) mentioned market risk of Vietcombank in Vietnam affected by

multi macro variables.

4. Conceptual Theories

Beside, firm performance will be affected by business decision relating to their competitors. Then they can develop competition theory. The competition and rivals will drive our firm business strategies. And it is foundation to make strategy priority. (ebrary.net, access date 5/6/2021).

And Isoraite (2018) specified that there are many variables that affect the level of competitive advantage such as: business complexity and infrastructure, technology and innovation, training ad higher education, etc.

And it is important to analyze competitors in order to give proper responses to their strategies and to over come firms' competitors to achieve position of leadership and to conquer the market.

5. Methodology

For qualitative analysis; we use synthesis and inductive methods and explanatory methods.

For quantitative methods, we use scenario analysis of competitor size, combined with analytical research method and philosophical method Data we take from stock exchange and applied current tax rate is 25%.

6. General Data Analysis

We analyze from The chart 1 below that:

- There is low, acceptable risk (beta) shown by equity beta mean and asset beta mean (a of 0,665 and 0,406, respectively).
- Risk variation measure by beta var, shown via equity beta var of 0,71 (sample beta), and hence higher (>) than equity beta of 0,56 (entire sample), whereas the variance of asset beta is measured at 0,14 and hence lower (<) than asset beta of 0,145 (entire sample0.

According to statistics, 8 medicine firms equity beta (0,66) higher (>) than other firms in medical equipment and human resource group listed in stock exchange.

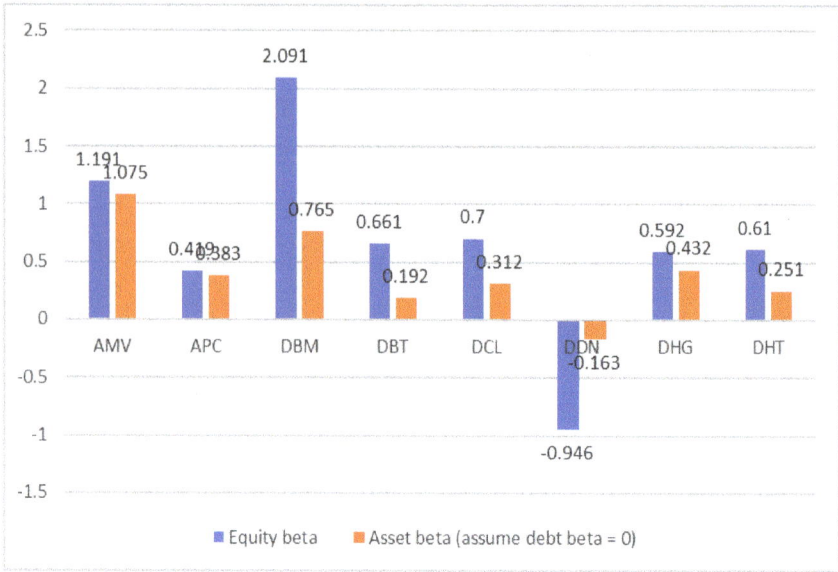

Chart 1 – 8 Listed Medicine Firm Beta Estimation

(Source: author calculation and stock exchange)

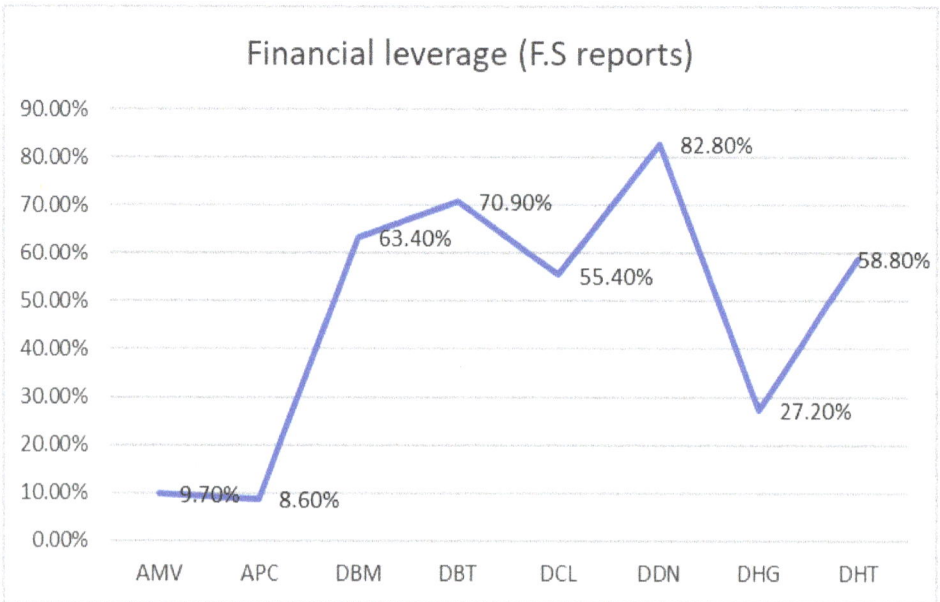

Chart 2 - Leverage of Medicine Companies

Table 1 – 8 listed Medicine Companies Statistics

Statistic re-sults	Equity beta	Asset beta (assume debt beta = 0)	Differ-ence
MAX	2,091	1,075	1,0153
MIN	-0,946	-0,163	-0,7831
MEAN	0,665	0,406	0,2589
VAR	0,7106	0,1400	0,5705
Note: Sample size : 8			

(Source: author calculation and stock exchange)

7. Empirical Research Findings and Discussion

We will change size of competitors and measure and compare market risk of 8 listed medicine firms on stock exchange. And then, leverage change is also conducted in 2 cases from 30% up to 20% down.

We model our calculation of beta in below table

Table 2 – Under 3 Cases we will Estimate Beta or Risk

	Keep leverage as current	Keep leverage up 30%	Keep leverage down 20%
Kept size of competitor or rival as current			
Kept size of competitor or rival as smaller slightly	Scenario 1	Scenario 2	Scenario 3
Kept size of competitor or rival as double			

(Source: by author)

We could hence, analyze results from below charts:

In addition, the chart 3 tell us: there is less dispersion of risk in case doubling competitor size, shown in number, if leverage down to 20%, equity beta var will go down to 0,293. On the other hand, when leverage up to 30%, equity beta var increases to 0,364 (for the case smaller size competitor)

Last but not least, the chart 4 tell us, if leverage kept with current level and there is smaller size competitors, asset beta mean value will goes down to 0,350. And for the case double size competitor, we see an increase in asset beta mean value to 0,381.

Chart 3 – What Beta Mean Change in Cases of Size of Competitor and Leverage Changing

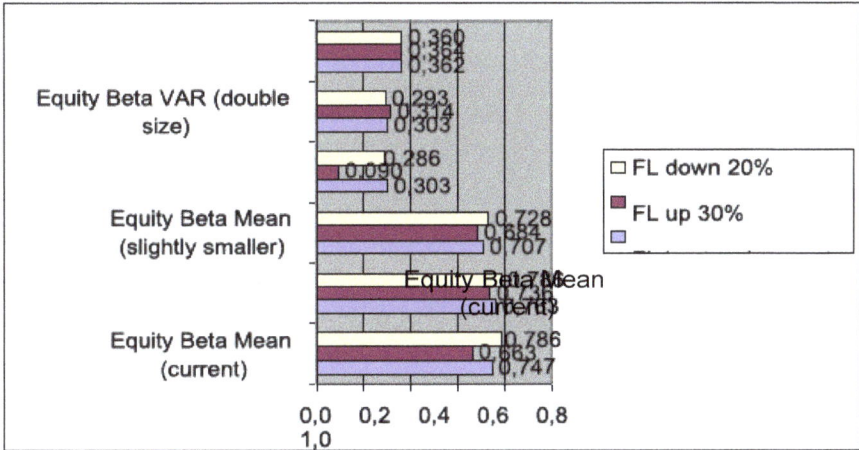

(Source: author calculation and stock exchange)

8. Conclusion and Policy Suggestion

Overall, we would see policies implications from our beta estimation as above:

•   Macro policies issued by Ministry of Finance, and State bank are need to coordinate to achieve certain goals in specific periods, for instance, fiscal policies, tax policy, etc.

Company policies:

•   Medicine firm need to build theory of competitors and risk assessment from competitors.

•   Last but not least, firm management will take note that: in case there is approximate size competitors. Max value of mean of asset beta will be measured at 0.468 and in case there is double size competitors, Min value of asset beta mean measured at 0,368.

Limitation of Research

Our research model can be expanded for other markets.

Acknowledgements

This is chance to express our warm thanks to Board of Editors, Friends and Brothers to assist this publication.

References

Alcock J, Baum A, Colley N, Steiner E. (2013). The Role of Financial Leverage in the Performance of Private Equity Real Estate Funds. *SSRN Working Paper.*

Bergen, M., & Peteraf, M.A. (2002). Competitor Identification and Competitor Analysis: A Broad- Based Managerial Approach, *Decis. Econ.,* 23: 157–169.

Chen RR, Chidambaran NK, Imerman MB, Sopranzetti BJ. (2013). Liquidity, Leverage, and Lehman: A Structural Analysis of Financial Institutions in Crisis. *Fordham School of Business Research Paper No.2279686.*

Dexheimer, John., and Haugen, Carla, (2003), Sarbanes-Oxley: Its Impact on the Venture Capital Community, *Minnesota Journal of Business Law and Entrepreneurship,* 2(1).

Dinh Tran Ngoc Huy (2015). The Critical Analysis of Limited South Asian Corporate Governance Standards After Financial Crisis, *International*

Journal for Quality Research, 15(1).

Huy, D.T.N., Loan, B.T., and Anh, P.T. (2020). Impact of selected factors on stock price: a case study of Vietcombank in Vietnam, *Entrepreneurship and Sustainability Issues, 7*(4): 2715-2730. https://doi.org/10.9770/ jesi.2020.7.4(10)

Huy, D.T.N., Dat, P.M., and Anh, P.T. (2020). Building and econometric model of selected factors' impact on stock price: a case study, *Journal of Security and Sustainability Issues, 9*(M), 77-93. https://doi.org/10.9770/ jssi.2020.9.M(7)

Huy, D.T.N., & Hien, D.T.N. (2010).The backbone of European corporate governance standards after financial crisis, corporate scandals and manipulation, *Economic and Business Review, 12*(4).

Easton, G. (1988). Competition and Marketing Strategy, *European Journal of Marketing, 22*(2).

Eugene, Fama F., and French, Kenneth R., (2004), The Capital Asset Pricing Model: Theory and Evidence, *Journal of Economic Perspectives.*

Huy, Dinh T.N., (2012), Estimating Beta of Viet Nam listed construction companies groups during the crisis, *Journal of Integration and Development, 15(1).*

Isoraite, M. (2018). The competitive advantages theoretical aspects, Ecoforum, 7-1(14).

Kale, Jayant R., Meneghetti, Costanza., and Sharur, Husayn., (2013), Contracting with Non-Financial Stakeholders and Corporate Capital Structure: The Case of Product Warantties, *Journal of Financial and Quantitative Analysis*

Pereiro, Luis E. (2010), The Beta Dilemma in Emerging Markets. *Journal of Applied Corporate Finance*

Umar. (2011). Profits, Financial Leverage and Corporate Governance. *SSRN Working Paper.*

XiYing Zhang, Ivy., (2007). Economic consequences of the Sarbanes–Oxley Act of 2002. *Journal of Accounting and Economics,* 44 (2007)

74–115.

Witteloostujn, A.V. (1992). Theories of competition and market performance, De Economist, 140. Ang, A., Chen, J., (2007), CAPM Over the Long Run: 1926-2001, *Journal of Empirical Finance*

Baker, Kent H., Singleton, Clay J., and Veit, Theodore E., (2011), Survey Research in Corporate Finance: Bridging the Gap Between Theory and Practice, *Oxford University Press.*

ADB and Viet Nam Fact Sheet, 2010. http://www.mofa.gov.vn/vi/ http://www.hsx.vn/hsx/

Exhibit

Exhibit 1- Comparison of VNIndex and other Indexes in Period of 2006-2010

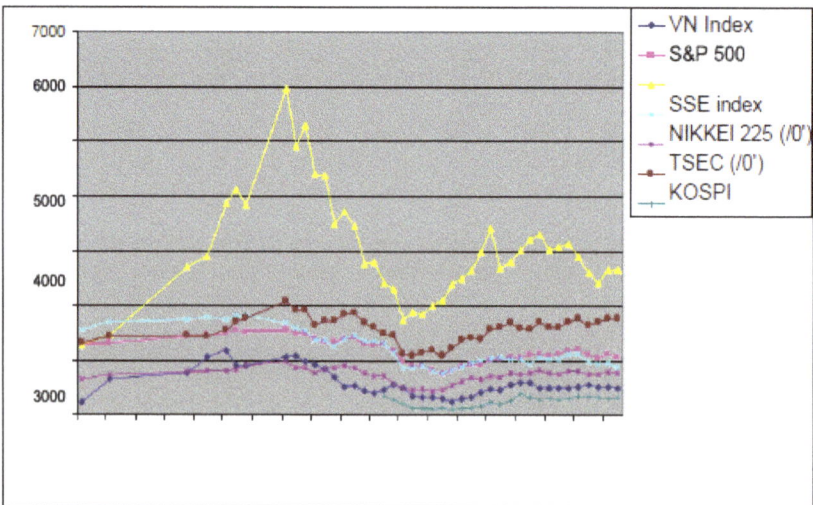

(Source: global stock exchange 2012)

CASE NO. 7

DATE

9 Jan, 2021

(Published in Revista Geintec-Gestao Inovacao E Tecnologias, 11(3), 2021)

Impacts of Competitor Selection Strategy on Firm Risk - Case in Vietnam Investment and Finance Industry

Pham Van Tuan[1*]; Dinh Tran Ngoc Huy[2]; Pham Khanh Duy[3]

[1*]PhD, National Economics University (NEU), Vietnam.

[1*]phamvantuan@neu.edu.vn [1*]ORCID: 0000-0003-0001-7331

[2]MBA, Banking University, HCMC, Ho Chi Minh City Vietnam.

Graduate School of International Management, International University of Japan, Niigata, Japan.

2dtnhuy2010@gmail.com 2ORCID: 0000-0002-2358-0699

[3]University of Economics, Ho Chi Minh City, Vietnam.

3duy_jimmy@yahoo.com 3ORCID: 0000-0003-2537-1599

Abstract

Competitor selection strategy is one of key factors that affect business strategy of our company, esp. In financial industry. We will use a single factor model in this paper to measure effects of this strategy on business risk. This paper mainly uses quantitative analysis and statistics, together with qualitative methods including synthesis, comparison and explanatory methods.

Our research findings show that in case keeping current competitor size, we can minimize the risk disperse (beta measured at 0,233). One more result is that beta CAM and competitor size there is positive relationship.

We also change size of competitors to double to measure impacts on beta CAPM. At last, we use results in order to suggest suitable policies.

Key-words: Competitor Selection Strategy, Beta CAPM, Investment and Finance Industry.

JEL: M21, G30, G32, G38.

1. Introduction

We cannot deny the truth that investment and financial industry in Vietnam has contributed so much to the development of socio-economy in recent years in the context of industry 4.0.

Therefore, this papers pay attention to effects of competitor strategy on business risks, beta CAPM in this sector.

This paper is organized with introduction, research questions, literature review, main results, discussion and conclusion.

2. Research Questions

Question 1: To what extent beta CAPM changes under effects from competitor size changing?

Question 2: What are recommendations for risk policies and competitive strategy in this sector?

3. Literature Review

We summarize previous studies as follows:

Table 1- Summary of Previous Studies

Authors	Year	Results, contents
Black	1976	Between return volatility and equity return there is negative is negative relationship
Desh-pande and Gat-ingon	1994	Provide a conceptualization of how competitive analyses can be framed by decision makers and for researching how human biases in decision making and corporate culture impact on the nature and use of competitive analysis information.
Arm-strong and Col-lopy	1996	When information about the competitor's profits was provided, over 40% of the subjects were willing to sacrifice part of their company's profits to beat or harm the competitor. Such competitor-oriented behavior occurred across a variety of treatments.

Fama and French	2004	Stock return will be affected by value and size
Kim et al	2002	In order to value product strategies effects on value of shareholders, we need to take into account competitive interaction
Daly and Hanh Phan	2013	In Asian countries, competition of bank system are much affected by economic crisis.
Ana and John	2013	Between leverage and volatility there is correct is correct connection.
Maune	2014	examine the relationship that exists between competitive intelligence and firm competitiveness through literature review. There are varying perceptions of the relationship that exists between competitive intelligence and firm competitiveness; and that there is no universally accepted model of best practice for adoption and adaption
Gupta et al	2016	Revealed that innovativeness in the marketing initiatives of the brand can be a function of the contributions made by the brand to its competitiveness.

Then, Adom et al (2016) mentioned identifying competitors and how they operate helps managers to tackle industry issues that are detrimental to their companies' health and also helps managers to learn from competitors. It also revealed that firms that pay attention to competitors' actions have been found to achieve better business performance.

Last but not last, Buehl and Melchers (2018) examined the influence of two such factors – attractiveness of the organization and competition among applicants – on the intention to fake in an interview and revealed that attractiveness influenced faking intentions. However, we found no effect for competition.

4. Conceptual Theories

Competitor Strategy Impacts on Business

Selecting proper competitors will affect business strategy through evaluating strengths and weaknesses of our firm competitors, from that we can build suitable competitive strategy to win market share.

Our firm competitors and their pricing strategy might affect our pricing plans and deliver proper responses to customers.

5. Methodology

Competitive and comparative methods are used for competitor analysis.

Tax rate is 25% in the survey and competitor size change to make a sensitivity analysis.

We use a combination of qualitative and philosophical and quantitative methods with live data from stock exchange.

We can generate policies from our analysis and results then.

6. Overall Analysis

This survey consists of 10 listed firms in RE sector, we find out that between beta CAPM and leverage there is positive correlation.

One more result from below table is that there is 30% firms with beta > 1 and 10% firms with asset beta > 1. Asset beta helped to reduce risks in many firms.

Table 2 – The number of companies in research sample with different beta values and ratio

Unit: %

	current size		double size		smaller size	
Equity Beta	No. of firms	Ratio	No. of firms	Ratio	No. of firms	Ratio
<0	0	0,0%	0	0,0%	0	0,0%
0<beta<1	6	60,0%	7	70,0%	7	70,0%
Beta > 1	4	40,0%	3	30,0%	3	30,0%
total	10	100,0%	10	100,0%	10	100,0%
	current size		double size		smaller size	
Asset Beta	No. of firms	Ratio	No. of firms	Ratio	No. of firms	Ratio
<0	0	0,0%	0	0,0%	0	0,0%
0<beta<1	9	90,0%	9	90,0%	9	90,0%
Beta > 1	1	10,0%	1	10,0%	1	10,0%
total	10	100,0%	10	100,0%	10	100,0%

(Source: VN's stock exchange 2012 and authors' calculation)

We also recognize that from above table 1: number of firms with beta >1 in 3 cases are equal (only 1 firm).

7. Empirical Research Findings and Discussion

Under cases of changing competitor size: current size, smaller and double, We estimate beta CAPM in below tables.

Table 3 – Analyzing Market Risk under Three (3) Scenarios

	FL as current
Case 1: current leverage, competitor size as current	Scenario 1
Case 2: current leverage, competitor size as doubles	Scenario 2
Case 3: current leverage, competitor size as little smaller	Scenario 3

Our results show that:

Case 1: current leverage, competitor size as current: only 40% of firms with beta higher than 1.
Case 2: current leverage, competitor size as doubles: only 1 firm with beta higher than 1.
Case 3: current leverage, competitor size as little smaller: only 1 form with beta higher than 1.

8. Comparing Statistical Results in 3 Scenarios of Changing Leverage

Table 4 - Statistical Results (FL in Case 1)

Statistic results	Equity beta	Asset beta (assume debt beta = 0)	Difference
MAX	2,159	1,592	0,5669
MIN	0,546	0,119	0,4268
MEAN	1,050	0,574	0,4767
VAR	0,2332	0,1694	0,0638
Note: Sample size : 10			

(Source: VN's stock exchange 2012 and authors' calculation. Unit of beta is a number only)

We also recognize that from above table 4: while beta mean is accepted (0,57) max equity beta still high (2,15).

Chart 1 – Statistic Results (FL in Case 2) (Source: VN Stock Exchange 2012)

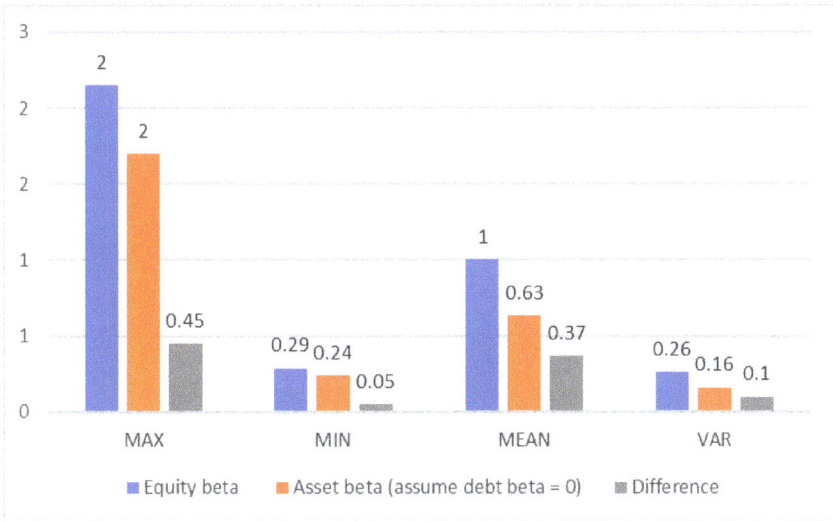

(Source: VN's stock exchange 2012 and authors' calculation. Unit of beta is a number only)

Chart 2- Statistic Results (FL in case 3) (Source: VN stock exchange 2012)

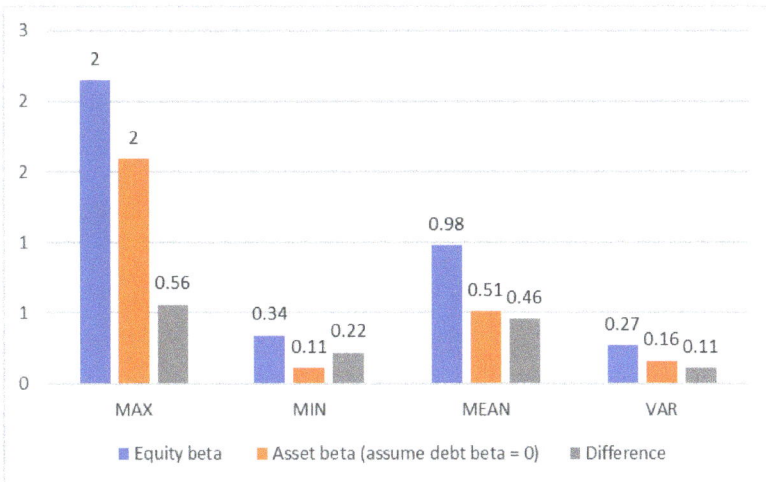

(Source: VN's stock exchange 2012 and authors' calculation. Unit of beta is a number only)

Form above tables and charts we recognize that:

If size of competitor doubles, asset beta max will increase and its value up to 1,705 from 1,592

Also below charts tell us that in case smaller size of competitor, asset beta max does not increase. Asset beta (mean) also declines to 0,517 when smaller size of competitor.

Chart 3 – Comparing Statistical Results of Equity Beta Var and Mean in Three (3) Scenarios of Changing Competitor Size (source: VN stock exchange 2012)

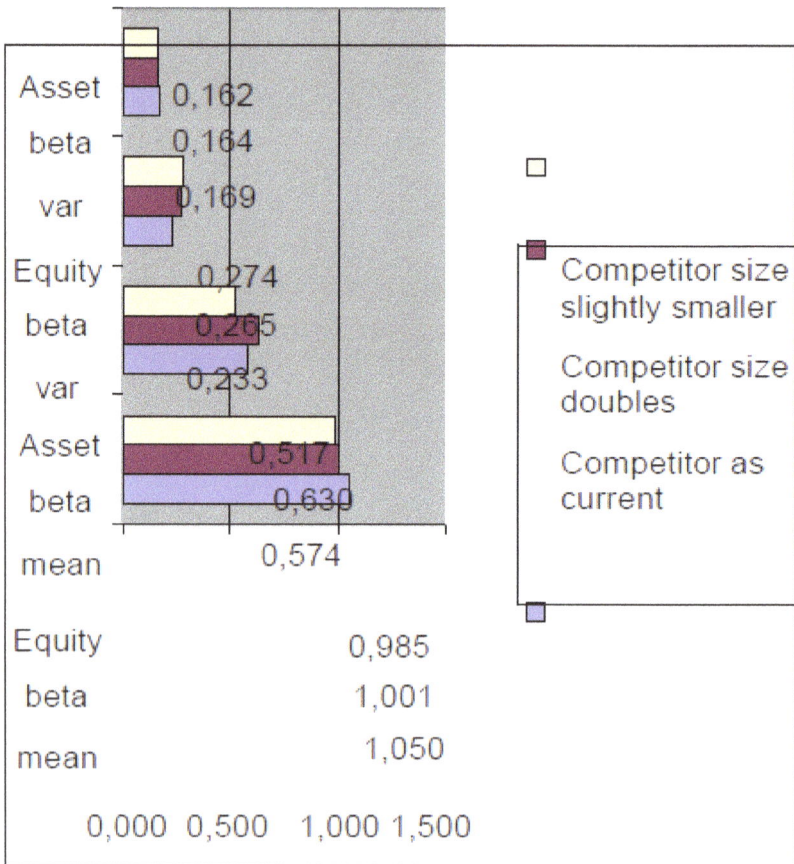

(Source: VN's stock exchange 2012 and authors' calculation. Unit of beta is a number only)

Chart 4 – Comparing Statistical Results of Equity/Asset Beta Max and

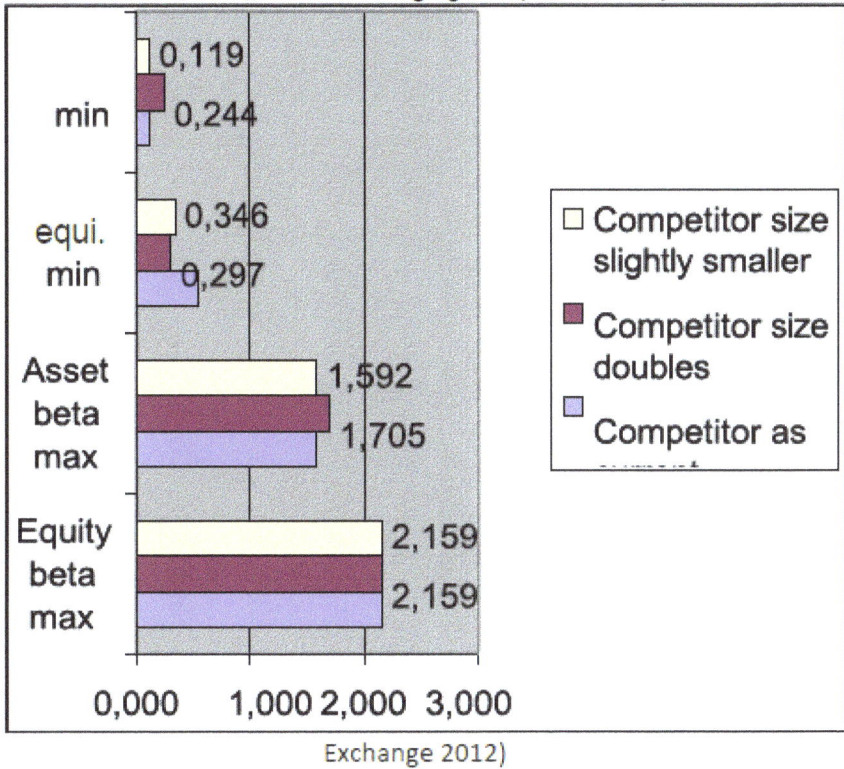

Exchange 2012)

Min in Three (3) Scenarios of Changing Competitor Size (Source: VN Stock Exchange 2012)
(Source: VN's stock exchange 2012 and authors' calculation. Unit of beta is a number only)

9. Discussion

In case smaller competitor size, we can increase number of firms with beta < 1 up to 70%, as shown in above tables.

Above charts tell us that asst beta max can increase in case doubling competitor size.

We recognize that from above table chart 3: equity beta variation in case smaller size is little higher than in case double size.

We recognize that from above table chart 4: equity beta max are the same while asset beta max is bigger in case of double size.

10. Conclusion

In conclusion, bank system need to support firms to smooth capitals flows. We note that risk can decline if in specific case in which smaller size of competitor, and then double competitor size.

We need to identify and expand competitor lists, not only current competitors presenting in the market, but also other competitors hiding and potential in the market in future.

From that, we can select proper competitors to estimate their effects on business performance and risk.

Management Implications

To achieve a competitive advantage in selling to control and gain more markets, our firms must possess a thorough knowledge of your competition and manager need to make in-depth competitive analysis including: An understanding of how your existing and potential customers win the markets; A positive identification of your competitor's strengths and weaknesses; A mechanism to develop effective competitive strategies in your target market.

Limitation of Research

We can then expand our model to other industries and markets.

Acknowledgements

I would like to take this opportunity to express my warm thanks to Board of Editors, my family, colleagues, and brother in assisting convenient conditions for my research paper.

References

Dexheimer, John., and Haugen, Carla, (2003), Sarbanes-Oxley: Its Impact on the Venture Capital Community, Minnesota Journal of Business Law and Entrepreneurship, Vol.2 No.1

Adom, A.Y., Niarko, I.K., & Som, G.N.K. (2016). Competitor Analysis in Strategic Management: Is it a Worthwhile Managerial Practice in Contemporary Times? Journal of Resources Development and Management, 24.

Armstrong, J.S., & Collopy, F. (1996). Competitor Orientation: Effects of Objectives and Information on Managerial Decisions and Profitability, Journal of Marketing Research, 4. https://doi.org/10.1177/002224379603300206

Buehl, A.K., & Melchers, K.G. (2018). Do Attractiveness and Competition Influence Faking Intentions in Selection Interviews? Journal of Personnel Psychology, 2.

Deshpande, R., & Gatingon, H. (1994). Competitive analysis, Marketing letters, 5.

Dat, P.M., Mau, N.D., Loan, B.T.T., Huy, D.T.N. (2020). Comparative China Corporate Governance standards after Financial Crisis, Corporate Scandals and Manipulation, Journal of Security and Sustainability Issues, 9(3).

Eugene, Fama F., and French, Kenneth R., (2004), The Capital Asset Pricing Model: Theory and Evidence. Journal of Economic Perspectives.

Flifel, Kaouther., (2012), Financial Markets between Efficiency and Persistence: Empirical Evidence on Daily Data. Asian Journal of Finance and Accounting.

Gunaratha V. (2013). The Degree of Financial Leverage as a Determinant of Financial Risk: An Empirical Study of Colombo Stock Exchange in Sri Lanka. 2nd International Conference on Management and Economics Paper.

Gupta, S., Malhotra, N.K., Czinkota, M., & Foroudi, P. (2016). Marketing innovation: A consequence of competitiveness, Journal of Business Research, 69(12).

Hac, L.D., Huy, D.T.N., Thach, N.N., Chuyen, B.M., Nhung, P.T.H., Thang, T.D., Anh, T.T. (2021).

Enhancing risk management culture for sustainable growth of Asia commercial bank -ACB in Vietnam under mixed effects of macro factors, Entrepreneurship and Sustainability Issues, 8(3).

Hang, T.T.B., Nhung, D.T.H., Hung, N.M., Huy, D.T.N., Dat, P.M. (2020). Where Beta is going– case of Viet Nam hotel, airlines and tourism company groups after the low inflation period, Entrepreneurship and Sustainability Issues, 7(3).

Huy, D.T.N. (2015). The Critical Analysis of Limited South Asian Corporate Governance Standards After Financial Crisis, International Journal for Quality Research, 9(4): 741-764.

Huy, Dinh T.N., (2012), Estimating Beta of Viet Nam listed construction companies groups during the crisis, Journal of Integration and Development, 15(1).

Huy, D.T.N., Loan, B.T., and Anh, P.T. (2020). 'Impact of selected factors on stock price: a case study of Vietcombank in Vietnam'. Entrepreneurship and Sustainability Issues, 7(4), 2715-2730. https://doi.org/10.9770/jesi.2020.7.4(10)

Huy, D.T.N., Dat, P.M., and Anh, P.T. (2020). 'Building and econometric model of selected factors' impact on stock price: a case study'. Journal of Security and Sustainability Issues, 9(M), 77-93. https://doi.org/10.9770/jssi.2020.9.M(7)

Huy D.T.N., Nhan V.K., Bich N.T.N., Hong N.T.P., Chung N.T., Huy P.Q. (2021). 'Impacts of Internal and External Macroeconomic Factors on Firm Stock Price in an Expansion Econometric model—A Case in Vietnam Real Estate Industry', Data Science for Financial Econometrics-Studies in Computational Intelligence, vol.898, Springer.

http://doi-org-443.webvpn.fjmu.edu.cn/10.1007/978-3-030-48853-6_14

Kale, Jayant R., Meneghetti, Costanza., and Sharur, Husayn., (2013), Contracting with Non-Financial Stakeholders and Corporate Capital Structure: The Case of Product Warantties, Journal of Financial and Quantitative Analysis

Lu, Wenling., and Whidbee, David A., (2013), Bank Structure and Failure, Journal of Financial Econoic Policy

Maune, A. (2014). Competitive intelligence and firm competitiveness: An overview, Corporate Ownership and Control 12(1): 533-542.

(Planned to PUBLIHS IN SCOPUS JOURNAL)

A One Factor Model Affect The Risk Level of Viet Nam Hardware Industry During and After The Global Crisis 2007-2011

Dinh Tran Ngoc Huy, MBA

Banking University HCMC Ho Chi Minh city, Vietnam - International University of Japan, Japan

ABSTRACT

Using a one factor model, this paperwork estimates the impacts of the size of firms' competitors in the hardware industry on the market risk level, measured by equity and asset beta, of 22 listed companies in this category.

This study identified that the risk dispersion level in this sample study could be minimized in case the competitor size doubles (measured by equity beta var of 0,678).

Beside, the empirical research findings show us that asset beta min value decreases from 0,054 to 0,030 when the size of competitor doubles.

Last but not least, most of beta values are acceptable.

Ultimately, this paper illustrates calculated results that might give proper recommendations to relevant governments and institutions in re-evaluating their policies during and after the financial crisis 2007-2011.

███████	CASE NO. 8	**DATE** Jan 23, 2020

1. Introduction

Studies reveal that competition has affected business risk and return. Eugene F., and French, Kenneth R., (2004) also indicated in the three factor model that "value" and "size" are significant components which can affect stock returns. They also mentioned that a stock's return not only depends on a market beta, but also on market capitalization beta. The market beta is used in the three factor model, developed by Fama and French, which is the successor to the CAPM model by Sharpe, Treynor and Lintner. Pagano and Mao (2007) stated that An intermediated market can therefore remain viable in the face of competition from a possibly faster, non-intermediated market as long as the specialist can generate revenue for the above services that covers his/her costs associated with asymmetric information, order processing, and inventory management. As Luis E. Peirero (2010) pointed, the task of estimating cost of equity in emerging markets is more difficult because of problems such as collecting data in short periods.

Together with financial system development and the economic growth, throughout many recent years, Viet Nam hardware industry is considered as one of active economic sectors, which has some positive effects for the economy. Additionally, financial risk and reactions has become an issue after the global crisis 2007-2009 which has some certain impacts on the whole Viet nam economy, and specifically, the Viet Nam hardware industry. Hence, this research paper analyzes market risk under a one factor model of these listed firms during this period. The purpose of this study is to find out how much market risk for this industry in changing contexts of competitors.

Therefore, this paperwork will explain not only the relationship between risk and competitor size, but also presents how much risk for the hardware industry in each competitor scenario. It finds out competition or competitor size definitely has certan effects on market risk of listed hardware firms.

This paper is organized as follow. The research issues and literature review will be covered in next sessions 2 and 3, for a short summary. Then, methodology and conceptual theories are introduced in session 4 and 5. Session 6 describes the data in empirical analysis. Session 7 presents empirical results and findings. Next, session 8 covers the analytical results. Then, session 9 will conclude with some policy suggestions. This paper also supports readers with references, exhibits and relevant web sources.

2. Research Issues

For the estimating of impacts of a one factor model: the size of competitor on beta for listed hardware industry companies in Viet Nam stock exchange, research issues will be mentioned as following:

Issue 1: Whether the risk level of hardware industry firms under the different changing scenarios of the size of competitor increase or decrease so much.

Issue 2: Whether the disperse distribution of beta values become large in the different changing scenarios of the size of competitor in the hardware industry.

3. Literature review

Black (1976) proposes the leverage effect to explain the negative correlation between equity returns and return volatilities. Diamond and Dybvig (1983) said banks can also help reduce liquidity risk and therefore enable long-term investment. Next, Kim et all (2002) noted that the nature of competitive interaction in an industry is important in assessing the effect of corporate product strategies on shareholder value. Jimenez et all (2005) pointed As market power is the primary source of franchise value, reduced competition in banking markets has been seen as promoting banking stability.

Umar (2011) found that firms which maintain good governance structures have leverage ratios that are higher (forty-seven percent) than those of firms with poor governance mechanisms per unit of profit. Daly and Hanh Phan (2013) investigated the competitive structure of the banking industries in five emerging asian countries including Viet Nam and showed that the global financial crisis affected dramatically the competition of banking system in emerging Asian countries.

Chen et all (2013) supported regulators' suspicions that over-reliance on short-term funding and insufficient collateral compounded the effects of dangerously high leverage and resulted in undercapitalization and excessive risk exposure for Lehman Brothers. The model reinforces the importance of the relationship between capital structure and risk management. Then, Alcock et all (2013) found evidence that leverage cannot be viewed as a long-term strategy to enhance performance, but in the short term, managers do seem to add significantly to fund excess returns by effectively timing leverage choices to the expected future market environment. And Gunaratha (2013) revealed that in different industries in Sri Lanka, the degree of financial leverage has a significant positive correlation with financial risk.

4. Conceptual theories

The impact of competition or the size of competitor on the economy and business

In a competitive hardware market, there are many firms offering the similar products and services and this helps customers select a variety of qualified goods that meet their demand. Competitors could affect price and customer service policies; hence, affect revenues and profits of a typical company. Sources of competition include, but not limit to, training. Increasing training can help competition raising productivity.

Different kinds of market contain various types of risks. And different organizational structure can offer various competition degree.

5. Methodology

In this study, analytical research method is used, philosophical method is used and especially, scenario analysis method is used. Analytical data is from the situation of listed hardware material industry firms in VN stock exchange and applied current tax rate is 25%.

Risk here is assumed understood as fluctuations and volatility of beta which is sometimes higher than 1 or more or lower than that. We use historical and real data on the HNX and HOSE stock exchange in the period 2007-2011 for estimating risk. This is a part of our quantitative analysis method used combined with financial analytical method.

Scenario analysis method is applied in three (3) cases of changing size of competitors under changing competitive strategy. We estimate how much risk in case the firm selects competitor with doubling size, smaller size and approximate size. And beta results can be used for CAPM model to estimate WACC or cost of capital if readers want to go to further steps. In later sessions, we will explain the relationship between competitor size and beta. When we mention the competitor selecting strategy, we stand from the point of view of firm management, although the calculated results can be used for various stakeholders including investors.

In the below table 1, 2, 3 and others, the symbols such as "VTC" will represent for stock code of each listed firm on the stock exchange.

Finally, we use the results to suggest policy for both these enterprises, relevant organizations and government.

6. General Data Analysis

The research sample has total 22 listed firms in the hardware industry market with the live data from the stock exchange.

Firstly, we estimate equity and asset beta values of these firms, as well as the risk dispersion. Secondly, we change the competitor size from aprroxiamte size to doubling size and slightly smaller size to see the sensitivity of beta values. We figure out that in 3 cases, asset beta mean values are estimated at 0,441, 0,393 and 0,430 which are negatively correlated with the size of competitors. Also in 3 scenarios, we find out equity beta mean values (0,748, 0,678 and 0,728) are also negatively correlated with the competitive firm size. Various competitors selected definitely have certain effects on asset and equity beta values.

7. Empirical Research Findings and Discussion

In the below section, data used are from total 22 listed hardware industry companies on VN stock exchange (HOSE and HNX mainly). In the scenario 1, current financial leverage degree is kept as in the 2011 financial statements which is used to calculate market risk (beta) whereas competitor size is kept as current, then changed from double size to slightly smaller size. Then, two (2) FL scenarios are changed up to 30% and down to 20%, compared to the current FL degree. In short, the below table 1 shows three scenarios used for analyzing the risk level of these listed firms.

Market risk (beta) under the impact of tax rate, includes: 1) equity beta; and 2) asset beta.

Table 1 – Analyzing market risk under three (3) scenarios (Made by Author)

	FL as current
Competitor size as current	Scenario 1
Competitor size slightly smaller	Scenario 2
Competitor size double	Scenario 3

7.1 Scenario 1: current financial leverage and competitor size kept as current

In this case, all beta values of 22 listed firms on VN hardware industry market as following:

Table 2 – Market risk of listed companies on VN hardware industry market under one factor model (case 1) (source: VN stock exchange 2012)

Order No.	Company stock code	Equity beta	Asset beta (assume debt beta = 0)	Note	Financial leverage (F.S reports)
1	CMT	0,665	0,326		51,1%
2	SVT	0,860	0,651	TLC as comparable	24,2%
3	VIE	0,283	0,054	UNI as comparable	81,0%
4	HPT	0,238	0,063	TST as comparable	73,7%
5	NIS	0,347	0,165	VTC as comparable	52,5%
6	TST	0,739	0,236		68,1%
7	ST8	0,891	0,682		23,5%
8	TAG	0,632	0,411		35,0%
9	POT	1,046	0,533		49,0%
10	CKV	0,604	0,221		63,5%
11	ONE	0,551	0,217	UNI as comparable	60,6%
12	PMT	1,234	1,056		14,4%

13	SMT	0,934	0,654	PMT as comparable	30,0%
14	UNI	1,186	0,732		38,3%
15	TLC	1,066	0,770		27,8%
16	KST	0,679	0,386	TLC as comparable	43,1%
17	VAT	1,028	0,485		52,8%
18	VTC	0,635	0,431		32,2%
19	ELC	0,200	0,100	ITD as comparable	50,0%
20	SAM	1,191	1,069		10,2%
21	LTC	1,102	0,329		70,2%
22	ITD	0,351	0,132		62,5%
				Average	46,1%

7.2. Scenario 2: competitor size double

All beta values of total 22 listed firms on VN hardware industry market as below:

Table 3 – Market risks of listed hardware industry firms under one factor model (case 2) (source: VN stock exchange 2012)

Order No.	Company stock code	Equity beta	Asset beta (assume debt beta = 0)	Note
1	CMT	0,665	0,326	
2	SVT	0,212	0,161	VIE as comparable
3	VIE	0,263	0,050	LTC as comparable
4	HPT	0,113	0,030	ITD as comparable
5	NIS	0,487	0,231	ST8 as comparable
6	TST	0,739	0,236	
7	ST8	0,891	0,682	
8	TAG	0,632	0,411	
9	POT	1,046	0,533	
10	CKV	0,604	0,221	
11	ONE	0,294	0,116	TAG as comparable
12	PMT	1,191	1,019	
13	SMT	0,369	0,258	NIS as comparable
14	UNI	1,186	0,732	
15	TLC	1,066	0,770	
16	KST	0,168	0,095	VIE as comparable
17	VAT	1,168	0,551	
18	VTC	0,635	0,431	
19	ELC	0,542	0,271	CMG as comparable
20	SAM	1,191	1,069	
21	LTC	1,102	0,329	
22	ITD	0,351	0,132	

7.3. Scenario 3: Competitor size slightly smaller

All beta values of total 22 listed firms on the hardware industry market in VN as following:

Table 4 – Market risk of listed hardware industry firms under one factor model (case 3) (source: VN stock exchange 2012)

Order No.	Company stock code	Equity beta	Asset beta (assume debt beta = 0)	Note
1	CMT	0,665	0,326	
2	SVT	0,860	0,651	TLC as comparable
3	VIE	0,131	0,025	ONE as comparable
4	HPT	0,238	0,063	TST as comparable
5	NIS	0,347	0,165	VTC as comparable
6	TST	0,739	0,236	
7	ST8	0,891	0,682	
8	TAG	0,632	0,411	
9	POT	1,046	0,533	
10	CKV	0,604	0,221	
11	ONE	0,551	0,217	UNI as comparable
12	PMT	1,191	1,019	
13	SMT	0,826	0,578	HTP as comparable
14	UNI	1,186	0,732	
15	TLC	1,066	0,770	
16	KST	0,405	0,230	VTC as comparable
17	VAT	1,168	0,551	
18	VTC	0,635	0,431	
19	ELC	0,200	0,100	ITD as comparable
20	SAM	1,191	1,069	
21	LTC	1,102	0,329	DTL as comparable
22	ITD	0,351	0,132	BVG as comparable

All three above tables and data show that values of equity and asset beta in the three cases of changing competiotor size have certain fluctuation.

8. Comparing statistical results in 3 scenarios of changing leverage:

Table 5 - Statistical results (FL in case 1) (source: VN stock exchange 2012)

Statistic results	Equity beta	Asset beta (assume debt beta = 0)	Difference
MAX	1,234	1,069	0,165
MIN	0,200	0,054	0,147
MEAN	0,748	0,441	0,307
VAR	0,1085	0,0893	0,019
Note: Samle size 22 firms			

Table 6 – Statistical results (FL in case 2) (source: VN stock exchange 2012)

Statistic results	Equity beta	Asset beta (assume debt beta = 0)	Difference
MAX	1,191	1,069	0,1217
MIN	0,113	0,030	0,0833
MEAN	0,678	0,393	0,2846
VAR	0,1392	0,0903	0,0489
Note: Sample size : 22			

Table 7- Statistical results (FL in case 3) (source: VN stock exchange 2012)

Statistic results	Equity beta	Asset beta (assume debt beta = 0)	Difference
MAX	1,191	1,069	0,1217
MIN	0,131	0,025	0,1064
MEAN	0,728	0,430	0,2980
VAR	0,1226	0,0894	0,0332
Note: Sample size : 22			

Based on the calculated results, we find out:

First of all, Equity beta mean values in all 3 scenarios are acceptable (< 0,8) and asset beta mean values are also small (< 0,5). In the case of reported leverage in 2011, equity beta max is 1,234 which is somewhat acceptable. If competitor size doubles, equity beta min decreases from 0,200 to 0,113. Finally, when competitor size is slightly smaller, asset beta min decreases from 0,054 to 0,025.

The below chart 1 shows us : when competitive firm size decreases slightly, average equity beta value decrease slightly (0,728) compared to that at the initial selected competitor (0,748). Next, average asset beta decreases little (to 0,430). However, in case the competitor size doubles, the risk level of the selected firms decreases little more (0,393). Last but not least, the fluctuation of equity beta value (0,139) in the case of doubling size competitors is higher than (>) the results in the rest 2 cases. And we could note that in the case competitor size slightly smaller, the risk is less dispersed (0,089).

Chart 1 – Comparing statistical results of equity beta var and mean in three (3) scenarios of changing competitor size (source: VN stock exchange 2012)

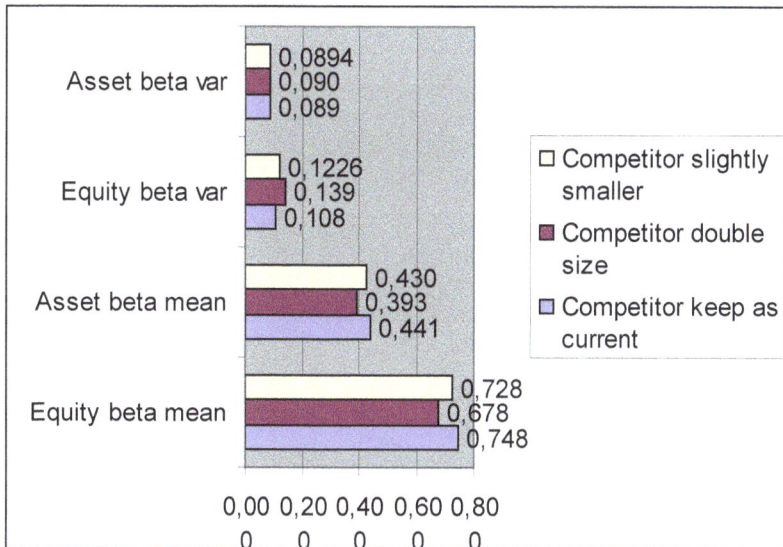

9. Conclusion and Policy suggestion

In conclusion, the government has to consider the impacts on the mobility of capital in the markets when it changes the macro policies and the legal system and regulation for developing the hardware market. The Ministry of Finance continues to increase the effectiveness of fiscal policies and tax policies which are needed to combine with other macro policies at the same time. The State Bank of Viet Nam continues to increase the effectiveness of capital providing channels for hardware companies as we could note that in this study when competitive firm size doubles, the risk level decreases (equity beta mean value is estimated at: 0,678), and the equity beta var value (0,139) is little higher than that in case competitor size as current (0,108).

Furthermore, the entire efforts among many different government bodies need to be coordinated.

Finally, this paper suggests implications for further research and policy suggestion for the Viet Nam government and relevant organizations, economists and investors from current market conditions (for example, they can do research on tax effects on the market risk of these firms).

ACKNOWLEDGEMENTS

I would like to take this opportunity to express my warm thanks to Board of Editors and Colleagues at Citibank –HCMC, SCB and BIDV-HCMC, Dr. Chen and Dr. Yu Hai-Chin at Chung Yuan Christian University for class lectures, also Dr Chet Borucki, Dr Jay and my ex-Corporate Governance sensei, Dr. Shingo Takahashi at International University of Japan. My sincere thanks are for the editorial office, for their work during my research. Also, my warm thanks are for Dr. Ngo Huong, Dr. Ho Dieu, Dr. Ly H. Anh, Dr Nguyen V. Phuc and my lecturers at Banking University – HCMC, Viet Nam for their help.

Lastly, thank you very much for my family, colleagues, and brother in assisting convenient conditions for my research paper.

REFERENCES

Chen RR, Chidambaran NK, Imerman MB, Sopranzetti BJ. (2013). Liquidity, Leverage, and Lehman: A Structural Analysis of Financial Institutions in Crisis. Fordham School of Business Research Paper No.2279686.

Dexheimer, John., & Haugen, Carla. (2003). Sarbanes-Oxley: Its Impact on the Venture Capital Community, Minnesota Journal of Business Law and Entrepreneurship, Vol.2(1).

Eugene, Fama F., and French, Kenneth R. (2004). The Capital Asset Pricing Model: Theory and Evidence. Journal of Economic Perspectives.

Flifel, Kaouther. (2012). Financial Markets between Efficiency and Persistence : Empirical Evidence on Daily Data. Asian Journal of Finance and Accounting, Vol.4, No.2, pp.379-400

Gunaratha V. (2013). The Degree of Financial Leverage as a Determinant of Financial Risk: An Empirical Study of Colombo Stock Exchange in Sri Lanka. 2nd International Conference on Management and Economics Paper.

Huy DTN. (2013). Estimating Beta of Viet Nam Listed Public Utilities, Natural Gas and Oil Company Groups During and After The Financial Crisis 2007-2011. Economic and Business Review, (15)1 : 57-71

Litvak, Kate. (2008). Defensive Management: Does the Sarbanes-Oxley Act Discourage Corporate Risk-Taking?, Law and Economics Research Paper, No. 108.

Ling, Amy. (2013), Tax Issues Relating to Intangibles, Asia-Pacific Tax Bulletin.

Mamun MAA. (2013). Performance Evaluation of Prime Bank Limited in Terms of Capital Adequacy. Global Journal of Management and Business Research. (13)9: 26-29.

Ovat OO. (2013). Liquidity Constraints and Entrepreneurial Financing in Nigeria: The Fate of Fresh Graduate Entrepreneurs. Global Journal of Management and Business Research, (13)9 : 49-57.

XiYing Zhang, Ivy. (2007). Economic consequences of the Sarbanes–Oxley Act of 2002. Journal of Accounting and Economics, 44 (2007) 74–115

Research

Ang, A., Chen, J., (2007), CAPM Over the Long Run: 1926-2001, Journal of Empirical Finance

Baker, Kent H., Singleton, Clay J., and Veit, Theodore E., (2011), Survey Research in Corporate Finance: Bridging The Gap Between Theory and Practice, Oxford University Press

ADB and Viet Nam Fact Sheet, 2010

Other web sources

http://www.mofa.gov.vn/vi/

http://www.hsx.vn/hsx/

www.tuoitre.com.vn;

www.saigontimes.com.vn;

www.mof.gov.vn ;

Exhibit

Exhibit 1 – Inflation, GDP growth and macroeconomics factors

(source: Viet Nam commercial banks and economic statistical bureau)

Year	Inflation	GDP	USD/VND rate
2011	18%	5,89%	20.670
2010	11,75% (Estimated at Dec 2010)	6,5% (expected)	19.495
2009	6,88%	5,2%	17.000
2008	22%	6,23%	17.700
2007 12,63% 8,44% 16.132			
2006	6,6%	8,17%	
2005	8,4%		
Note	approximately		

Exhibit 2 – Comparing statistical results of equity beta var and mean in three (3) scenarios of changing competitor size in the commercial electric industry

(source: VN stock exchange 2012)

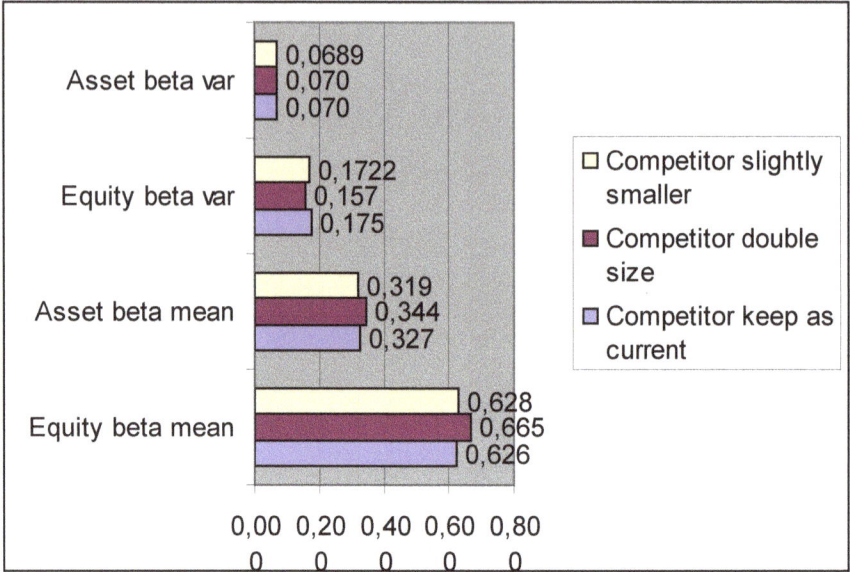

CASE NO. 9

DATE

Oct 1st, 2020

Various Industrial Competitors Affect The Risk Level of Viet Nam Non-Banking Investment and Financial Service Industry During The Economic Crisis 2007-2009

Dinh Tran Ngoc Huy, MBA[1*]

[1*] *Banking University, Ho Chi Minh city Viet Nam*
MBA, Graduate School of International Management, International University of Japan, Niigata, Japan
[*]E-mail: dtnhuy2010@gmail.com

ABSTRACT

Using a one factor model, this paperwork estimates the impacts of the size of firms' competitors in the natural gas and oil industry on the market risk level, measured by equity and asset beta, of 15 listed companies in this category.

This study identified that the risk dispersion level in this sample study could be minimized in case the competitor size kept as current approximate size (measured by equity beta var of 0,129).

Beside, the empirical research findings show us that asset beta min value decreases from 0,107 to 0,034 when the size of competitor doubles.

Last but not least, most of beta values are acceptable except a few exceptional cases.

Ultimately, this paper illustrates calculated results that might give proper recommendations to relevant governments and institutions in re-evaluating their policies during and after the financial crisis 2007-2011.

KEYWORDS : *risk management, competitive firm size, market risk, asset and equity beta, natural gas and oil industry*

JEL CLASSIFICATION : *G00, G3, G30*

---

1. Introduction

Together with financial system development and the economic growth, throughout many recent years, Viet Nam natural gas and oil industry is considered as one of active economic sectors, which has some positive effects for the economy. Additionally, financial risk and reactions has become an issue after the global crisis 2007-2009 which has some certain impacts on the whole Viet nam economy, and specifically, the Viet Nam natural gas and oil industry. Hence, this research paper analyzes market risk under a one factor model of these listed firms during this period.

This paper is organized as follow. The research issues and literature review will be covered in next sessions 2 and 3, for a short summary. Then, methodology and conceptual theories are introduced in session 4 and 5. Session 6 describes the data in empirical analysis. Session 7 presents empirical results and findings. Next, session 8 covers the analytical results. Then, session 9 presents risk analysis and session 10 covers discussion. Session 11 will conclude with some policy suggestions. This paper also supports readers with references, exhibits and relevant web sources.

2. Research Issues

For the estimating of impacts of a one factor model: the size of competitor on beta for listed natural gas and oil industry companies in Viet Nam stock exchange, research issues will be mentioned as following:

Issue 1: Whether the risk level of natural gas and oil industry firms under the different changing scenarios of the size of competitor increase or decrease so much.

Issue 2: Whether the disperse distribution of beta values become large in the different changing scenarios of the size of competitor in the natural gas and oil industry.

3. Literature review

Sharpe, Treynor, Lintner (1965) and Mossin (1966), based on diversification and modern portfolio theories of Markowitz, Sharpe and Miller, built CAPM model to estimate appropriate expected rate of return on an underlying asset which shows the sensitivity of asset return on non-diversifiable risk, beta. Moreover, Cohen (1985) and Handa (1989) identified that, for stocks riskier /

less risky than the market index, estimates of betas increase/decrease as the return interval increases. And Kothari, Shanken, and Sloan (1995) show that beta significantly explains the cross-sectional variation in average returns. Fama, Eugene F., and French, Kenneth R., (2004) also indicated in the three factor model that "value" and "size" are significant components which can affect stock returns. They also mentioned that a stock's return not only depends on a market beta, but also on market capitalization beta. The market beta is used in the three factor model, developed by Fama and French, which is the successor to the CAPM model by Sharpe, Treynor and Lintner.

Next, Kim et all (2002) noted that the nature of competitive interaction in an industry is important in assessing the effect of corporate product strategies on shareholder value. Pagano and Mao (2007) stated that An intermediated market can therefore remain viable in the face of competition from a possibly faster, non-intermediated market as long as the specialist can generate revenue for the above services that covers his/her costs associated with asymmetric information, order processing, and inventory management. Daly and Hanh Phan (2013) investigated the competitive structure of the banking industries in five emerging asian countries including Viet Nam and showed that the global financial crisis affected dramatically the competition of banking system in emerging Asian countries.

Last but not least, Ana and John (2013) Binomial Leverage – Volatility theorem provides a precise link between leverage and volatility.

4. Conceptual theories

The impact of competition or the size of competitor on the economy and business

In a specific industry such as natural gas and oil industry, there are many firms offering the similar products and services and this helps customers select a variety of qualified goods that meet their demand. Competitors could affect price and customer service policies; hence, affect revenues and profits of a typical company. The competition could drive down profits that firms can earn. Sources of competition include, but not limit to, training. Increasing training can help competition raising productivity.

Two or more diefferent firms offer various products or services to the same group of customer and the same need. This is called indirect competition.

5. Methodology

In this research, analytical research method is used, philosophical method is used and specially, scenario analysis method is used. Analytical data is from the situation of listed natural gas and oil industry firms in VN stock exchange and applied current tax rate is 25%.

Finally, we use the results to suggest policy for both these enterprises, relevant organizations and government.

6. General Data Analysis

The research sample has total 10 listed firms in the natural gas and oil industry market with the live data from the stock exchange.

Firstly, we estimate equity and asset beta values of these firms, as well as the risk dispersion. Secondly, we change the competitor size from aprroxiamte size to doubling size and slightly smaller size to see the sensitivity of beta values. We figure out that in 3 cases, asset beta mean values are estimated at 0,377, 0,323 and 0,371 which are decreasing more if the size of competitors is bigger. Also in 3 scenarios, we find out equity beta mean values (0,826, 0,728 and 0,792) are also decreasing. Various competitors selected definitely have certain effects on asset and equity beta values.

Table 1 – The number of companies in research sample with different beta values and ratio

Equity Beta	current size No. of firms	Ratio	double size No. of firms	Ratio	smaller size No. of firms	Ratio
<0	0	0,0%	2	20,0%	0	0,0%
0<beta<1	6	60,0%	4	40,0%	6	60,0%
Beta > 1	4	40,0%	4	40,0%	4	40,0%
total	10	100,0%	10	100,0%	10	100,0%
Asset Beta	current size No. of firms	Ratio	double size No. of firms	Ratio	smaller size No. of firms	Ratio
<0	0	0,0%	2	20,0%	0	0,0%
0<beta<1	9	90,0%	7	70,0%	9	90,0%
Beta > 1	1	10,0%	1	10,0%	1	10,0%
total	10	100,0%	10	100,0%	10	100,0%

7. Empirical Research Findings and Discussion

In the below section, data used are from total 10 listed natural gas and oil industry companies on VN stock exchange (HOSE and HNX mainly). In the three scenarios, current financial leverage degree is kept as in the 2011 financial statements which is used to calculate market risk (beta) whereas competitor size is kept as current, then changed from double size to slightly smaller size. In short, the below table 1 shows three scenarios used for analyzing the risk level of these listed firms.

Market risk (beta) under the impact of tax rate, includes: 1) equity beta; and 2) asset beta.

Table 2 – Analyzing market risk under three (3) scenarios (Made by Author)

	FL as current
Competitor size as current	Scenario 1
Competitor size slightly smaller	Scenario 2
Competitor size double	Scenario 3

7.1 Scenario 1: current financial leverage and competitor size kept as current

In this case, beta values of 10 listed firms on VN natural gas and oil industry market as:

(refer to exhibit 2)

There is no listed firms with both equity and asset beta values < 0, whereas there are 4 listed firms with equity beta values > 1, or 26% of firms. However there is no listed firms with asset beta > 1.

7.2. Scenario 2: competitor size double

Beta values of total 10 listed firms on VN natural gas and oil industry market as:

(refer to exhibit 3).

There is no listed firms with both equity and asset beta values < 0, whereas there are 4 listed firm with equity beta value > 1, or 26% of firms.

7.3. Scenario 3: Competitor size slightly smaller

Beta values of total 10 listed firms on the natural gas and oil industry market in VN as:

(refer to exhibit 4).

There is no listed firms with both equity and asset beta values < 0 and there is 4 listed firms with beta values > 1 (or 26%).

All three above tables and data show that values of equity and asset beta in the three cases of changing competiotor size have certain fluctuation.

8. Comparing statistical results in 3 scenarios of changing leverage:

Table 3 - Statistical results (FL in case 1) (source: VN stock exchange 2012)

Statistic results	Equity beta	Asset beta (assume debt beta = 0)	Difference
MAX	2,111	1,478	0,6330
MIN	0,281	0,056	0,2251
MEAN	0,813	0,407	0,4059
VAR	0,3748	0,1945	0,1803
Note: Sample size : 10			

Table 4 – Statistical results (FL in case 2) (source: VN stock exchange 2012)

Statistic results	Equity beta	Asset beta (assume debt beta = 0)	Difference
MAX	2,111	1,478	0,6330
MIN	-1,313	-1,172	-0,1407
MEAN	0,385	0,130	0,2547
VAR	1,2317	0,5979	0,6339
Note: Sample size : 10			

Table 5- Statistical results (FL in case 3) (source: VN stock exchange 2012)

Statistic results	Equity beta	Asset beta (assume debt beta = 0)	Difference
MAX	2,111	1,478	0,6330
MIN	0,234	0,029	0,2050
MEAN	0,810	0,406	0,4038
VAR	0,3954	0,1952	0,2002
Note: Sample size : 10			

Based on the calculated results, we find out:

First of all, Equity beta mean values in all 3 scenarios are acceptable (< 0,9) and asset beta mean values are also small (< 0,4). In the case of reported leverage in 2011, equity beta max is 1,617 which is little high in a few exceptional cases. If competitor size doubles, asset beta min decreases from 0,107 to 0,034. Finally, when competitor size is slightly smaller, asset beta min reduces more to the value of 0,028.

The below chart 1 shows us : when competitive firm size decreases slightly, average equity beta value decrease more (0,792) compared to that at the initial selected competitor (0,602). Next, average asset beta decreases little (to 0,371). However, in case the competitor size doubles, the risk level of the selected firms decreases more (0,728). Last but not least, the fluctuation of equity beta value (0,235) in the case of doubling size competitors is higher than (>) the results in the rest 2 cases. And we could note that in the case competitor size slightly smaller, the risk is less dispersed (0,037 compared to 0,051).

Chart 1 – Comparing statistical results of equity beta var and mean in three (3) scenarios of changing competitor size , 2007-09 (source: VN stock exchange 2012)

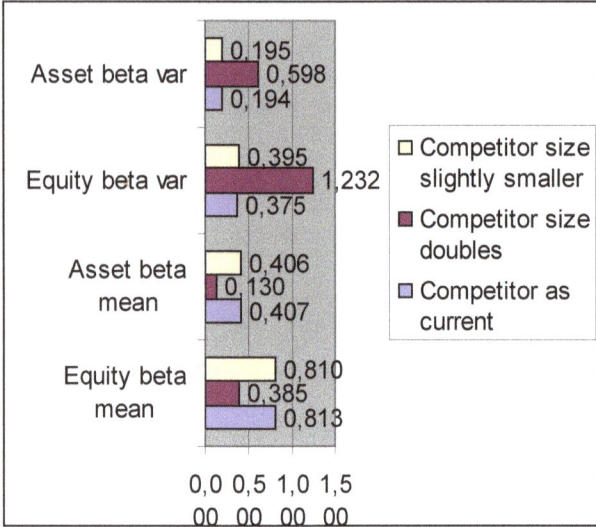

Chart 1 – Comparing statistical results of equity beta var and mean in three (3) scenarios of changing competitor size (source: VN stock exchange 2012)

Chart 2 – Comparing statistical results of equity/asset beta max and min in three (3) scenarios of changing competitor size, 2007-09 (source: VN stock exchange 2012)

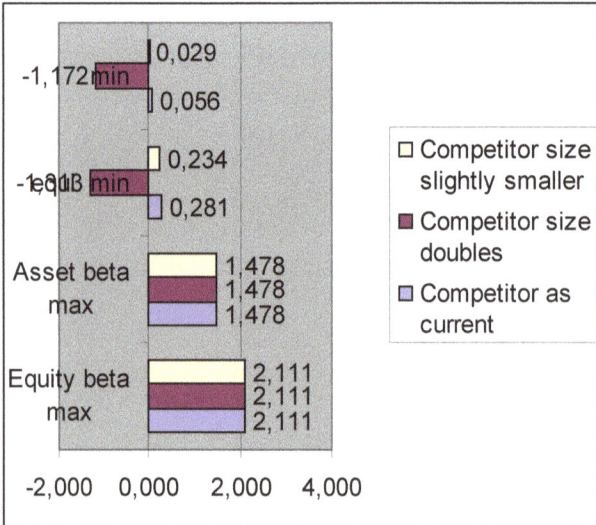

Chart 2 – Comparing statistical results of equity/asset beta max and min in three (3) scenarios of changing competitor size (source: VN stock exchange 2012)

9. Risk analysis

Generally speaking, during the financial crisis 2007-2011, esp. the period 2007-2009, the water industry can survive well and maintain the development and profits, although these firms have to face other kinds of risks: materials or water or electric prices increasing. These risks can affect the operating cash flow of these companies.

10. Discussion

Table 1 shows us there are 73%, 73% of firms having acceptable beta values (0 < beta < 1) in cases : current or doubling sizet competitors. If competitor size is smaller, this number is maintained at 73%. Moreover, chart 2 tells us that equity and asset beta min values decrease (0,067 and 0,034) in case doubling size competitors.

Looking at exhibit 5, it is noted that comparing to beta results of electronic and electrical industry in the period 2007-2011, asset beta mean of natural gas and oil industry group during 2007-2011 is higher in current situation (0,377). And the risk dispersion in natural gas and oil industry when competitor size is smaller during 2007-2011 (shown by asset beta var of 0,03) is also smaller than that in electronic and electrical industries (0,07).

11. Conclusion and Policy suggestion

In conclusion, the government has to consider the impacts on the mobility of capital in the markets when it changes the macro policies and the legal system and regulation for developing the natural gas and oil market. The Ministry of Finance continues to increase the effectiveness of fiscal policies and tax policies which are needed to combine with other macro policies at the same time. The State Bank of Viet Nam continues to increase the effectiveness of capital providing channels for natural gas and oil companies as we could note that in this study when competitive firm size doubles, the risk level decreases (equity beta mean value is estimated at: 0,728), and the equity beta var value (0,235) is little higher than that in case competitor size as current (0,129).

Furthermore, the entire efforts among many different government bodies need to be coordinated.

Finally, this paper suggests implications for further research and policy suggestion for the Viet Nam government and relevant organizations, economists and investors from current market conditions.

ACKNOWLEDGEMENTS

I would like to take this opportunity to express my warm thanks to Board of Editors and Colleagues at Citibank –HCMC, SCB and BIDV-HCMC, Dr. Chen and Dr. Yu Hai-Chin at Chung Yuan Christian University for class lectures, also Dr Chet Borucki, Dr Jay and my ex-Corporate Governance sensei, Dr. Shingo Takahashi at International University of Japan. My sincere thanks are for the editorial office, for their work during my research. Also, my warm thanks are for Dr. Ngo Huong, Dr. Ho Dieu, Dr. Ly H. Anh, Dr Nguyen V. Phuc and my lecturers at Banking University – HCMC, Viet Nam for their help.

Lastly, thank you very much for my family, colleagues, and brother in assisting convenient conditions for my research paper.

REFERENCES

Dexheimer, John., and Haugen, Carla, (2003), Sarbanes-Oxley: Its Impact on the Venture Capital Community, Minnesota Journal of Business Law and Entrepreneurship, Vol.2 No.1

Eugene, Fama F., and French, Kenneth R., (2004), The Capital Asset Pricing Model: Theory and Evidence, Journal of Economic Perspectives

Flifel, Kaouther., (2012), Financial Markets between Efficiency and Persistence : Empirical Evidence on Daily Data, Asian Journal of Finance and Accounting

Gunaratha V. (2013). The Degree of Financial Leverage as a Determinant of Financial Risk: An Empirical Study of Colombo Stock Exchange in Sri Lanka. 2nd International Conference on Management and Economics Paper.

Gao, Huasheng., Harford, Jarrad., and Li, Kai., (2013), Determinants of Corporate Cash Policy: Insights from Private Firms, Journal of Financial Economics

Huy, Dinh T.N., (2012), Estimating Beta of Viet Nam listed construction companies groups during the crisis, Journal of Integration and Development

Kale, Jayant R., Meneghetti, Costanza., and Sharur, Husayn., (2013), Contracting With Non-Financial Stakeholders and Corporate Capital Structure: The Case of Product Warantties, Journal of Financial and Quantitative Analysis

Litvak, Kate., (2008), Defensive Management: Does the Sarbanes-Oxley Act Discourage Corporate Risk-Taking?, Law and Economics Research Paper, No. 108

Ling, Amy., (2013), Tax Issues Relating to Intangibles, Asia-Pacific Tax Bulletin

Lu, Wenling., and Whidbee, David A., (2013), Bank Structure and Failure, Journal of Financial Econoic Policy

Mukerjee, Kaushik., (2013), Customer-Oriented Organizations: A Framework for Innovation, Journal of Business Strategy

Pereiro, Luis E.,(2010), The Beta Dilemma in Emerging Markets, Journal of Applied Corporate Finance

Research

Ang, A., Chen, J., (2007), CAPM Over the Long Run: 1926-2001, Journal of Empirical Finance

Baker, Kent H., Singleton, Clay J., and Veit, Theodore E., (2011), Survey Research in Corporate Finance: Bridging The Gap Between Theory and Practice, Oxford University Press

ADB and Viet Nam Fact Sheet, 2010

Other web sources

http://www.mofa.gov.vn/vi/

http://www.hsx.vn/hsx/

www.tuoitre.com.vn;

www.saigontimes.com.vn;

www.mof.gov.vn ;

Exhibit

Exhibit 1 – Inflation, GDP growth and macroeconomics factors

(source: Viet Nam commercial banks and economic statistical bureau)

Year	Inflation	GDP	USD/VND rate
2011	18%	5,89%	20.670
2010	11,75% (Estimated at Dec 2010)	6,5% (expected)	19.495
2009	6,88%	5,2%	17.000
2008	22%	6,23%	17.700
2007	12,63%	8,44%	16.132
2006	6,6%	8,17%	
2005	8,4%		
Note		approximately	

Exhibit 2 – Market risk of listed companies on VN natural gas and oil industry market under one factor model (case 1) (source: VN stock exchange 2012)

Order No.	Company stock code	Equity beta	Asset beta (assume debt beta = 0)	Note	Financial leverage
1	AGR	0,597	0,074		77,2%
2	APG	0,334	0,305	CLS as comparable	2,8%
3	APS	0,372	0,202		57,4%
4	AVS	0,281	0,205	CLS as comparable	22,1%
5	BSI	0,491	0,056	AGR as comparable	22,4%
6	BVS	2,111	1,478		26,3%
7	CLS	0,341	0,174		50,0%
8	CTS	1,073	0,703		32,8%
9	PVF	1,523	0,179		91,3%
10	VNR	1,002	0,692		43,0%

Exhibit 3 - Market risks of listed natural gas and oil industry firms under one factor model (case 2) (source: VN stock exchange 2012)

Order No.	Company stock code	Equity beta	Asset beta (assume debt beta = 0)	Note
1	AGR	0,006	0,001	NVB as comparable
2	APG	-1,286	-1,172	AVS as comparable
3	APS	0,372	0,202	
4	AVS	-1,313	-0,956	ABI as comparable
5	BSI	0,019	0,002	NVB as comparable
6	BVS	2,111	1,478	

7	CLS	0,341	0,174	
8	CTS	1,073	0,703	
9	PVF	1,523	0,179	
10	VNR	1,002	0,692	

Exhibit 4 – Market risk of listed natural gas and oil industry firms under one factor model (case 3) (source: VN stock exchange 2012)

Order No.	Company stock code	Equity beta	Asset beta (assume debt beta = 0)	Note
1	AGR	0,234	0,029	BSI as comparable
2	APG	0,334	0,305	CLS as comparable
3	APS	0,372	0,202	
4	AVS	0,281	0,205	CLS as comparable
5	BSI	0,827	0,095	PVI as comparable
6	BVS	2,111	1,478	
7	CLS	0,341	0,174	
8	CTS	1,073	0,703	
9	PVF	1,523	0,179	
10	VNR	1,002	0,692	

Exhibit 5 – Comparing statistical results of equity beta var and mean in three (3) scenarios of changing competitor size in 18 listed commercial electric firms 2007-2011 (source: VN stock exchange 2012)

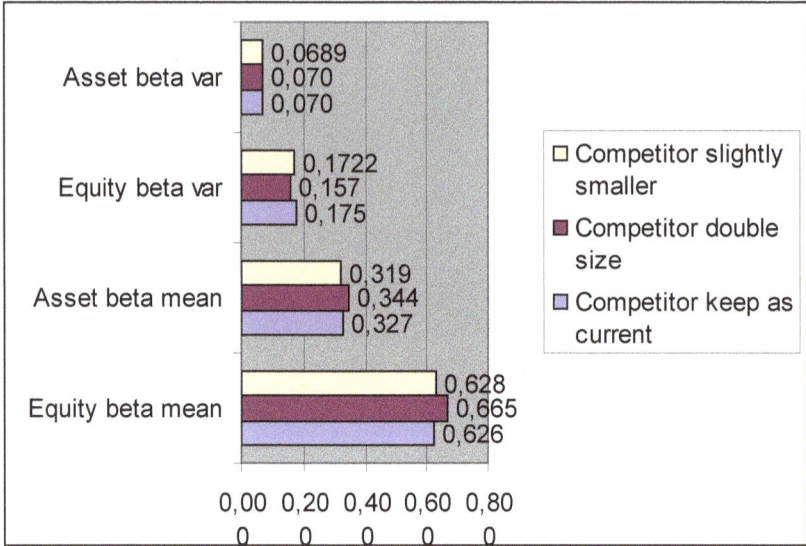

Asset beta var
0,0689
0,070
0,070

Equity beta var
0,1722
0,157
0,175

Asset beta mean
0,319
0,344
0,327

Equity beta mean
0,628
0,665
0,626

0,00 0,20 0,40 0,60 0,80
0   0   0   0   0

□ Competitor slightly smaller
■ Competitor double size
□ Competitor keep as current

	DATE
CASE NO. 10	Oct 1st , 2020

(Planned to be Published in Q3 Scopus Journal)

A Two Factors Model On The Risk Level of Viet Nam Electric Power Industry During and After The Global Crisis 2007-2011

Dinh Tran Ngoc Huy, MBA[1*]

[1*] *Banking University, Ho Chi Minh city Viet Nam*
MBA, Graduate School of International Management, International University of Japan, Niigata, Japan
[*]E-mail: dtnhuy2010@gmail.com

ABSTRACT

This research paper aims to find out the risk level of listed electric power firms increasing or decreasing during the crisis 2007-2011. The significance of this paper is to provide these firms with financing information based on risk level. Using a two (2) factors model, this research paper analyzes the impacts of both financial leverage and the size of firms' competitors in the electric power industry on the market risk level of 20 listed companies in this category.

This paper founds out that the risk dispersion can be reduced to 0,039 (asset beta var) if leverage is up to 30%.

Beside, the empirical research findings show us that the market risk level measured by asset beta mean is also reduced to 0,131 when financial leverage increases 30%.

Last but not least, this paper illustrates calculated results that might give proper recommendations to relevant governments and institutions in re-evaluating their policies after the financial crisis 2007-2011.

KEYWORDS : *risk management, market risk, asset beta, electric power industry*

JEL CLASSIFICATION : *G00, G3, G30*

1. Introduction

Financial development has positive effect for the economic growth, throughout many recent years, Viet Nam electric power industry is considered as one of active economic sectors, which has some positive effects for the economy (source: http://icon.com.vn/vn-s83-125717-641/40-nam-nhung-dau-an-phat-trien.aspx).

This paper is organized as follow. The research issues and literature review will be covered in next sessions 2 and 3, for a short summary. Then, methodology and conceptual theories are introduced in session 4 and 5. Session 6 describes the data in empirical analysis. Session 7 presents empirical results and findings. Next, session 8 covers the analytical results. Then, session 9 presents analysis of risk. Lastly, session 10 will conclude with some policy suggestions. This paper also supports readers with references, exhibits and relevant web sources.

2. Research Issues

We mention some issues on the estimating of impacts of external financing on beta for listed electric power industry companies in Viet Nam stock exchange as following:

Issue 1: Whether the risk level of electric power industry firms under the different changing scenarios of leverage increase or decrease so much.

Issue 2: Whether the disperse distribution of beta values become large in the different changing scenarios of leverage estimated in the electric power industry.

3. Literature review

Goldsmith (1969), Mc Kinnon (1973) and Shaw (1973) pointed a large and active theoretical and empirical literature has related financial development to the economic growth process.

Black (1976) proposes the leverage effect to explain the negative correlation between equity returns and return volatilities. Diamond and Dybvig (1983) said banks can also help reduce liquidity risk and therefore enable long-term investment.

Fama, Eugene F., and French, Kenneth R., (2004) also indicated in the three factor model that "value" and "size" are significant components which can affect stock returns. They also mentioned that a stock's return not only depends on a market beta, but also on market capitalization beta. The market beta is used in the three factor model, developed by Fama and French, which is the successor to the CAPM model by Sharpe, Treynor and Lintner. Next, Peter and Liuren (2007) mentions equity volatility increases proportionally with the level of financial leverage, the variation of which is dictated by managerial decisions on a company's capital structure based on economic conditions. And for a company with a fixed amount of debt, its financial leverage increases when the market price of its stock declines.

Reinhart and Rogoff (2009) pointed the history of finance is full of boom-and-bust cycles, bank failures, and systemic bank and currency crises. Adrian and Shin (2010) stated a company can also proactively vary its financial leverage based on variations on market conditions.

Then, as Luis E. Peirero (2010) pointed, the task of estimating cost of equity in emerging markets is more difficult because of problems such as collecting data in short periods.

Next, Umar (2011) found that firms which maintain good governance structures have leverage ratios that are higher (forty-seven percent) than those of firms with poor governance mechanisms per unit of profit. Flifel (2012) stated today, the assumption of efficient capital markets is very controversial, especially in these times of crisis, and is challenged by research showing that the pricing was distorted by detection of long memory. Finally, Chen et all (2013) supports suspicions that over-reliance on short-term funding and insufficient collateral compounded the effects of dangerously high leverage and resulted in undercapitalization and excessive risk exposure for Lehman Brothers.

In general, financial leverage can be considered as one among many factors that affect business risk of natural gas and oil firms.

Last but not least, financial leverage can be considered as one among many factors that affect business risk of consumer good firms.

Hence, we see that no researches done on figuring out the relationship among risk level and financial leverage and competitor size.

4. Conceptual theories

The impact of financial leverage on the economy

A sound and effective financial system has positive effect on the development and growth of the economy. Financial institutions and markets can enable corporations to solve liquidity needs and enhance long-term investments. This system include many channels for a firm who wants to use financial leverage or FL (for example, companies can use different kinds of loans or issuing corporate bonds), which refers to debt or to the borrowing of funds to finance company's assets.

In a specific industry such as electric power industry, on the one hand, using leverage with a decrease or increase in certain periods could affect tax obligations, revenues, profit after tax and technology innovation and compensation and jobs of the industry.

During and after financial crises such as the 2007-2009 crisis, there raises concerns about the role of financial leverage of many countries, in both developed and developing markets. On the one hand, lending programs and packages might support the business sectors. On the other hand, it might create more risks for the business and economy.

When firms use leverage, it encounters risk. The higher the leverage, the riskier they take. During the crisis period, lending rates might increase, so firms receive more risk.

5. Methodology

For estimating systemic risk results and leverage impacts, in this study, we use the live data during the crisis period 2007-2011 from the stock exchange market in Viet Nam (HOSE and HNX and UPCOM).

In this research, analytical research method is used, philosophical method is used and specially, leverage scenario analysis method is used. Analytical data is from the situation of listed electric power industry firms in VN stock exchange and current tax rate is 25%.

Analytical method is used to describe the calculated data and number in the context of the crisis. Philosophical method means the study done based on the observation of several factors fluctuating including leverage changes, competitor size changes. Leverage scenario analysis is used to support for analysis part.

Finally, we use the results to suggest policy for both these enterprises, relevant organizations and government.

6. General Data Analysis

The research sample has total 20 listed firms in the electric power industry market with the live data from the stock exchange (the sample size equals the population as on the stock exchange).

Firstly, we estimate equity beta values of these firms and use financial leverage to estimate asset beta values of them. Secondly, we change the leverage from what reported in F.S 2011 to increasing 30% and reducing 20% to see the sensitivity of beta values. We found out that in 3 cases, asset beta mean values are estimated at 0,471, 0,389 and 0,539 which are negatively correlated with the leverage. Also in 3 scenarios, we find out equity beta mean values (0,602, 0,512 and 0,664) are also negatively correlated with the leverage. Leverage degree changes definitely has certain effects on asset and equity beta values.

7. Empirical Research Findings and Discussion

In the below section, data used are from total 20 listed electric power industry companies on VN stock exchange (HOSE and HNX mainly). In the scenario 1, current financial leverage degree is kept as in the 2011 financial statements which is used to calculate market risk (beta). Then, two (2) FL scenarios are changed up to 30% and down to 20%, compared to the current FL degree.

Market risk (beta) under the impact of tax rate, includes: 1) equity beta; and 2) asset beta.

	FL as current	FL up 30%	FL down 20%
Competitor size As current	Scenario 1	Scenario 2	Scenario 3
Competitor size twice smaller			
Competitor size double			

7.1 Scenario 1: current financial leverage (FL) as in financial reports 2011 and competitor size kept as current, twice smaller and double

In this case, all beta values of 20 listed firms on VN electric power industry market as following:

Table 1 – Market risk of listed companies on VN electric power industry market

Order No.	Company stock code	Equity beta	Asset beta (assume debt beta = 0)	Note	Financial leverage (F.S reports)
1	BTP	0,840	0,357		57,5%
2	CHP	0,407	0,168	BTP as comparable	58,7%
3	DNC	-0,865	-0,270		68,8%
4	DRL	0,473	0,388	NLC as comparable	17,9%
5	DTV	0,527	0,499	NLC as comparable	5,4%
6	GHC	0,359	0,117	NBP as comparable	67,3%
7	HJS	0,699	0,200		71,3%
8	KHP	0,615	0,308		50,0%
9	NBP	0,914	0,604		33,9%
10	ND2	0,180	0,043	TBC as comparable	76,2%
11	NLC	0,550	0,510		7,2%
12	NT2	0,639	0,137		78,6%
13	PPC	0,811	0,232		71,3%
14	RHC	0,361	0,200		44,7%
15	SBA	0,177	0,062	SJD as comparable	64,8%
16	SEB	0,427	0,194		54,5%
17	SHP	0,485	0,245	BTP as comparable	49,4%
18	SJD	0,420	0,221		47,4%
19	TBC	0,612	0,568		7,3%
20	TIC	0,351	0,343		2,2%
				Average	46,72%

7.2. Scenario 2: financial leverage increases up to 30% and competitor size kept as current, twice smaller and double

If leverage increases up to 30%, all beta values of total 20 listed firms on VN electric power industry market as below:

Table 2 – Market risks of listed electric power industry firms (case 2)

Order No.	Company stock code	Equity beta	Asset beta (assume debt beta = 0)	Note	Financial leverage (30% up)
1	BTP	0,840	0,212		74,8%
2	CHP	0,246	0,059	BTP as comparable	76,2%
3	DNC	-0,865	-0,092		89,4%
4	DRL	0,448	0,344	NLC as comparable	23,2%
5	DTV	0,520	0,484	NLC as comparable	7,0%
6	GHC	0,146	0,018	NBP as comparable	87,5%
7	HJS	0,699	0,051		92,7%
8	KHP	0,615	0,215		65,0%
9	NBP	0,914	0,511		44,0%
10	ND2	0,007	0,000	TBC as comparable	99,1%
11	NLC	0,550	0,498		9,4%
12	NT2	0,639	-0,014		102,2%
13	PPC	0,811	0,059		92,7%
14	RHC	0,361	0,151		58,1%
15	SBA	0,084	0,013	SJD as comparable	84,2%
16	SEB	0,427	0,124		70,9%
17	SHP	0,358	0,128	BTP as comparable	64,2%
18	SJD	0,420	0,161		61,6%
19	TBC	0,612	0,554		9,5%
20	TIC	0,351	0,341		2,9%
				Average	60,73%

7.3. Scenario 3: leverage decreases down to 20% and competitor size kept as current, twice smaller and double

If leverage decreases down to 20%, all beta values of total 20 listed firms on the electric power industry market in VN as following:

Table 3 – Market risk of listed electric power industry firms (case 3)

Order No.	Company stock code	Equity beta	Asset beta (assume debt beta = 0)	Note	Financial leverage (20% down)
1	BTP	0,840	0,453		46,0%
2	CHP	0,505	0,268	BTP as comparable	46,9%
3	DNC	-0,865	-0,389		55,0%
4	DRL	0,489	0,419	NLC as comparable	14,3%
5	DTV	0,532	0,509	NLC as comparable	4,3%
6	GHC	0,487	0,225	NBP as comparable	53,9%
7	HJS	0,699	0,300		57,1%
8	KHP	0,615	0,369		40,0%
9	NBP	0,914	0,666		27,1%
10	ND2	0,282	0,110	TBC as comparable	61,0%
11	NLC	0,550	0,518		5,8%
12	NT2	0,639	0,237		62,9%
13	PPC	0,811	0,348		57,1%
14	RHC	0,361	0,232		35,7%
15	SBA	0,233	0,112	SJD as comparable	51,8%
16	SEB	0,427	0,241		43,6%
17	SHP	0,563	0,341	BTP as comparable	39,5%
18	SJD	0,420	0,261		37,9%
19	TBC	0,612	0,577		5,8%
20	TIC	0,351	0,345		1,8%
				Average	37,37%

All three above tables and data show that values of equity and asset beta in the case of increasing leverage up to 30% or decreasing leverage degree down to 20% have certain fluctuation.

8. Comparing statistical results in 3 scenarios of changing leverage:

Table 4 - Statistical results (FL in case 1)

Statistic results	Equity beta	Asset beta (assume debt beta = 0)	Difference
MAX	0,914	0,604	0,3094

MIN	-0,865	-0,270	-0,5946
MEAN	0,449	0,256	0,1927
VAR	0,1353	0,0417	0,0936
Note: Sample size : 20			

Table 5 – Statistical results (FL in case 2)

Statistic results	Equity beta	Asset beta (assume debt beta = 0)	Difference
MAX	0,914	0,554	0,3594
MIN	-0,865	-0,092	-0,7730
MEAN	0,409	0,191	0,2182
VAR	0,1500	0,0393	0,1107
Note: Sample size : 20			

Table 6- Statistical results (FL in case 3)

Statistic results	Equity beta	Asset beta (assume debt beta = 0)	Difference
MAX	0,914	0,666	0,2475
MIN	-0,865	-0,389	-0,4757
MEAN	0,473	0,307	0,1661
VAR	0,1314	0,0482	0,0832
Note: Sample size : 20			

Based on the above results, we find out:

Equity beta mean values in all 3 scenarios are low (< 0,5) and asset beta mean values are also small (< 0,4) and max equity beta values are lower than (<) 1. In the case of reported leverage in 2011, equity beta value fluctuates in an acceptable range from -0,865 (min) up to 0,914 (max) and asset beta fluctuates from -0,270 (min) up to 0,604 (max). If leverage increases to 30%, equity beta moves in an unchanged range and asset beta moves from -0,092 (min) up to 0,554 (max). Hence, we note that there is an increase in asset beta min value if leverage increases. When leverage decreases down to 20%, equity beta value moves in an unchanged range and asset beta changes from -0,389 (min) up to 0,666 (max). So, there is a small increase in equity beta min value and small decrease in asset beta min when leverage decreases in scenario 3.

Beside, Exhibit 5 informs us that in the case 30% leverage up, average equity beta value of 20 listed firms decreases down to 0,040 while average asset beta value of these 20 firms decreases little less to 0,065. Then, when leverage reduces to 20%, average equity beta value of 20 listed firms goes up to 0,024 and average asset beta value of 20 firms up to 0,051.

The below chart 1 shows us : when leverage degree decreases down to 20%, average equity and asset beta values increase slightly (0,473 and 0,307) compared to those at the initial reported leverage (0,449 and 0,256). Then, when leverage degree increases up to 30%, average equity beta decreases little more and average asset beta value also decreases more (to 0,409 and 0,191). However, the fluctuation of equity beta value (0,150) in the case of 30% leverage up is higher than (>) the results in the rest 2 leverage cases. And we could note that the using of leverage in the case of 30% leverage up causes a decrease in asset beta var down to 0,039.

Chart 1 – Comparing statistical results of three (3) scenarios of changing FL

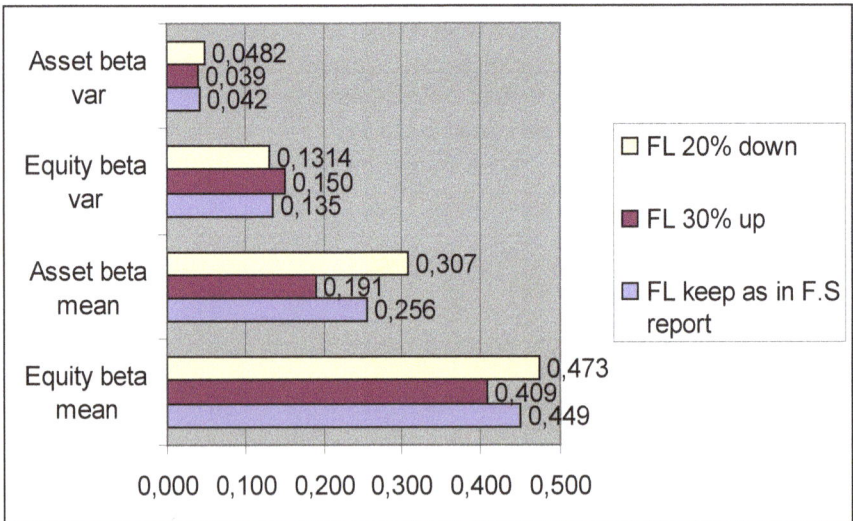

9. Risk analysis

In short, the using of financial leverage could have both negatively or positively impacts on the financial results or return on equity of a company. The more debt the firm uses, the more risk it takes. Beside, the increasing interest on loans might drive the earning per share (EPS) lower.

On the other hand, in the case of increasing leverage, the company will expect to get more returns. The financial leverage becomes worthwhile if the cost of additional financial leverage is lower than the additional earnings before taxes and interests (EBIT). Considering risk vs. return, FL becomes a decisional variable for managers.

In addition, chart 1 shows that the risk dispersion (asset beta var) decreases if leverage increases 30% and increases if financial leverage decreases 20%.

10. Conclusion and Policy suggestion

In general, the government has to consider the impacts on the mobility of capital in the markets when it changes the macro policies. Beside, it continues to increase the effectiveness of building the legal system and regulation supporting the plan of developing electric power market. The Ministry of Finance continues to increase the effectiveness of fiscal policies and tax policies which are needed to combine with other macro policies at the same time. The State Bank of Viet Nam continues to increase the effectiveness of capital providing channels for electric power companies as we could note that in this study when leverage is going to increase up to 30%, the risk level decreases much as well as the asset beta var, compared to the case it is going to decrease down to 20%.

Furthermore, the entire efforts among many different government bodies need to be coordinated.

Finally, this paper suggests implications for further research and policy suggestion for the Viet Nam government and relevant organizations, economists and investors from current market conditions.

ACKNOWLEDGEMENTS

I would like to take this opportunity to express my warm thanks to Board of Editors and Colleagues at Citibank –HCMC, SCB and BIDV-HCMC, Dr. Yea-Mow Chen and Dr. Yu Hai-Chin at Chung Yuan Christian University for class lectures, also Dr Chet Borucki, Dr Jay and my ex-Corporate Governance sensei, Dr. Shingo Takahashi at International University of Japan. My sincere thanks are for the editorial office, for their work during my research. Also, my warm thanks are for Dr. Ngo Huong, Dr. Ho Dieu, Dr. Ly H. Anh, Dr Nguyen V. Phuc and my lecturers at Banking University – Ho Chi Minh, Viet Nam for their help.

Lastly, thank you very much for my family, colleagues, and brother in assisting convenient conditions for my research paper.

REFERENCES

Carr, Peter., and Wu, Liuren., (2007), Leverage Effect, Volatility Feedback, and Self-Exciting Market Disruptions, SSRN Working Paper

Chen RR, Chidambaran NK, Imerman MB, Sopranzetti BJ (2013), Liquidity, Leverage, and Lehman: A Structural Analysis of Financial Institutions in Crisis, Fordham School of Business Research Paper No.2279686

Chen, Zhihong, Huang Yuan., and Wei, John, K.C (2013), Executive Pay Disparity and The Cost of Equity Capital, Journal of Financial and Quantitative Analysis

Eugene, Fama F., and French, Kenneth R., (2004), The Capital Asset Pricing Model: Theory and Evidence, Journal of Economic Perspectives

Flifel, Kaouther (2012), Financial Markets between Efficiency and Persistence : Empirical Evidence on Daily Data, Asian Journal of Finance and Accounting

Tran Ngoc Huy, Dinh., (2010), A Set of Limited Asian Pacific Corporate Governance Standards After Financial Crisis, Corporate Scandals and Market Manipulation, SSRN Working Paper Series

Pereiro, Luis E.,(2010), The Beta Dilemma in Emerging Markets, Journal of Applied Corporate Finance

Umar (2011), Profits, Financial Leverage and Corporate Governance, SSRN Working Paper.

OECD Corporate Governance Guidelines, OECD, 1999

The Emergency Economic Stabilization Act of 2008

Research

13. Clarke, Thomas., (2003), International Corporate Governance: A Comparative Perspective, Routledge

14. Baker, Roger M., (2010), Corporate Governance, Competition and Political Parties: Explaining Corporate Governance Change in Europe, Oxford University Press, USA

Other web sources

15. www.ecgi.org/codes

16. http://www.itgovernance.co.uk/corpgov_us.aspx

17. http://corporatelawandgovernance.blogspot.com/2010/07/

18. http://www.sec.gov/news/speech/2008/spch062708psa-eng.htm

19. http://www.iadb.org/research/projects_detail.cfm?id=81

20. http://info.worldbank.org/etools/docs/library/

CASE NO. 11

DATE

9 Jan , 2022

(Planned to be Published in Q3 Scopus Journal)

Selecting Various Industrial Competitors Affect The Risk Level of Viet Nam Water Industry During and After The Global Crisis 2007-2011

Dinh Tran Ngoc Huy, MBA[1*]

[1*] Banking University, Ho Chi Minh city Viet Nam
MBA, Graduate School of International Management, International University of Japan, Niigata, Japan
*E-mail: dtnhuy2010@gmail.com

ABSTRACT

Using a one factor model, this paperwork estimates the impacts of the size of firms' competitors in the water industry on the market risk level, measured by equity and asset beta, of 10 listed companies in this category.

This study identified that the risk dispersion level in this sample study could be minimized in case the competitor size slightly smaller (measured by equity beta var of 0,285).

Beside, the empirical research findings show us that asset beta max value decreases from 0,998 to 0,869 when the size of competitor doubles.

Last but not least, most of beta values are acceptable except a few exceptional cases.

Ultimately, this paper illustrates calculated results that might give proper recommendations to relevant governments and institutions in re-evaluating their policies during and after the financial crisis 2007-2011.

KEYWORDS : *risk management, competitive firm size, market risk, asset and equity beta, water industry*

JEL CLASSIFICATION : *G00, G3, G30*

1. Introduction

Together with financial system development and the economic growth, throughout many recent years, Viet Nam water industry is considered as one of active economic sectors, which has some positive effects for the economy. Additionally, financial risk and reactions has become an issue after the global crisis 2007-2009 which has some certain impacts on the whole Viet nam economy, and specifically, the Viet Nam water industry. Hence, this research paper analyzes market risk under a one factor model of these listed firms during this period.

This paper is organized as follow. The research issues and literature review will be covered in next sessions 2 and 3, for a short summary. Then, methodology and conceptual theories are introduced in session 4 and 5. Session 6 describes the data in empirical analysis. Session 7 presents empirical results and findings. Next, session 8 covers the analytical results. Then, session 9 presents risk analysis and session 10 covers discussion. Session 11 will conclude with some policy suggestions. This paper also supports readers with references, exhibits and relevant web sources.

2. Research Issues

For the estimating of impacts of a one factor model: the size of competitor on beta for listed water industry companies in Viet Nam stock exchange, research issues will be mentioned as following:

Issue 1: Whether the risk level of water industry firms under the different changing scenarios of the size of competitor increase or decrease so much.

Issue 2: Whether the disperse distribution of beta values become large in the different changing scenarios of the size of competitor in the water industry.

3. Literature review

Black (1976) proposes the leverage effect to explain the negative correlation between equity returns and return volatilities. Diamond and Dybvig (1983) said banks can also help reduce liquidity risk and therefore enable long-term investment. Fama, Eugene F., and French, Kenneth R., (2004) also indicated in the three factor model that "value" and "size" are significant components which can affect stock returns. They also mentioned that a stock's return not only depends on a market beta, but also on market capitalization beta. The market beta is used in the three factor model, developed by Fama and French, which is the successor to the CAPM model by Sharpe, Treynor and Lintner.

Next, Kim et all (2002) noted that the nature of competitive interaction in an industry is important in assessing the effect of corporate product strategies on shareholder value. Pagano and Mao (2007) stated that An intermediated market can therefore remain viable in the face of competition from a possibly faster, non-intermediated market as long as the specialist can generate revenue for the above services that covers his/her costs associated with asymmetric information, order processing, and inventory management. Daly and Hanh Phan (2013) investigated the competitive structure of the banking industries in five emerging asian countries including Viet Nam and showed that the global financial crisis affected dramatically the competition of banking system in emerging Asian countries.

Last but not least, Ana and John (2013) Binomial Leverage – Volatility theorem provides a precise link between leverage and volatility.

4. Conceptual theories

The impact of competition or the size of competitor on the economy and business

In a specific industry such as water industry, there are many firms offering the similar products and services and this helps customers select a variety of qualified goods that meet their demand. Competitors could affect price and customer service policies; hence, affect revenues and profits of a typical company. The competition could drive down profits that firms can earn. Sources of competition include, but not limit to, training. Increasing training can help competition raising productivity.

Two or more diefferent firms offer various products or services to the same group of customer and the same need. This is called indirect competition.

5. Methodology

In this research, analytical research method is used, philosophical method is used and specially, scenario analysis method is used. Analytical data is from the situation of listed water industry firms in VN stock exchange and applied current tax rate is 25%.

Finally, we use the results to suggest policy for both these enterprises, relevant organizations and government.

6. General Data Analysis

The research sample has total 10 listed firms in the water industry market with the live data from the stock exchange.

Firstly, we estimate equity and asset beta values of these firms, as well as the risk dispersion. Secondly, we change the competitor size from aprroxiamte size to doubling size and slightly smaller size to see the sensitivity of beta values. We figure out that in 3 cases, asset beta mean values are estimated at 0,471, 0,310 and 0,231 which are decreasing more if the size of competitors is smaller. Also in 3 scenarios, we find out equity beta mean values (0,602, 0,444 and 0,285) are also decreasing. Various competitors selected definitely have certain effects on asset and equity beta values.

Table 1 – The number of companies in research sample with different beta values and ratio

Equity Beta	current size		double size		smaller size	
	No. of firms	Ratio	No. of firms	Ratio	No. of firms	Ratio
<0	1	10,0%	0	0,0%	0	0,0%
0<beta<1	7	70,0%	9	90,0%	10	100,0%
Beta > 1	2	20,0%	1	10,0%	0	0,0%
total	10	100,0%	10	100,0%	10	100,0%
Asset Beta	current size		double size		smaller size	
	No. of firms	Ratio	No. of firms	Ratio	No. of firms	Ratio
<0	1	10,0%	0	0,0%	0	0,0%
0<beta<1	9	90,0%	10	100,0%	10	100,0%
Beta > 1	0	0,0%	0	0,0%	0	0,0%
total	10	100,0%	10	100,0%	10	100,0%

7. Empirical Research Findings and Discussion

In the below section, data used are from total 10 listed water industry companies on VN stock exchange (HOSE and HNX mainly). In the three scenarios, current financial leverage degree is kept as in the 2011 financial statements which is used to calculate market risk (beta) whereas competitor size is kept as current, then changed from double size to slightly smaller size. In short, the below table 1 shows three scenarios used for analyzing the risk level of these listed firms.

Market risk (beta) under the impact of tax rate, includes: 1) equity beta; and 2) asset beta.

Table 2 – Analyzing market risk under three (3) scenarios (Made by Author)

	FL as current
Competitor size as current	Scenario 1
Competitor size slightly smaller	Scenario 2
Competitor size double	Scenario 3

7.1 Scenario 1: current financial leverage and competitor size kept as current

In this case, beta values of 10 listed firms on VN water industry market as:

(refer to exhibit 2)

There are only 1 listed firms with both equity and asset beta values < 0, or 10% of listed firms whereas there are 2 listed firms with equity beta values > 1, or 20% of firms.

7.2. Scenario 2: competitor size double

Beta values of total 10 listed firms on VN water industry market as:

(refer to exhibit 3).

There is no listed firms with both equity and asset beta values < 0, whereas there is 1 listed firm with equity beta value > 1, or 10% of firms. However, there is no listed firm with asset beta > 1. Competitor size increase has reduced the number of firms with equity beta value > 1.

7.3. Scenario 3: Competitor size slightly smaller

Beta values of total 10 listed firms on the water industry market in VN as:

(refer to exhibit 4).

There is no listed firms with both equity and asset beta values < 0 and there is no listed firms with beta values > 1.

All three above tables and data show that values of equity and asset beta in the three cases of changing competiotor size have certain fluctuation.

8. Comparing statistical results in 3 scenarios of changing leverage:

Table 3 - Statistical results (FL in case 1) (source: VN stock exchange 2012)

Statistic results	Equity beta	Asset beta (assume debt beta = 0)	Difference
MAX	1,170	0,998	0,1726
MIN	0,057	0,021	0,0361
MEAN	0,602	0,471	0,1310
VAR	0,1230	0,1015	0,0215
Note: Sample size : 10			

Table 4 – Statistical results (FL in case 2) (source: VN stock exchange 2012)

Statistic results	Equity beta	Asset beta (assume debt beta = 0)	Difference
MAX	1,269	0,869	0,3996
MIN	0,126	0,023	0,1035
MEAN	0,444	0,310	0,1344
VAR	0,1770	0,0944	0,0825
Note: Sample size : 10			

Table 5- Statistical results (FL in case 3) (source: VN stock exchange 2012)

Statistic results	Equity beta	Asset beta (assume debt beta = 0)	Difference
MAX	0,531	0,462	0,0692
MIN	0,012	0,005	0,0078
MEAN	0,285	0,231	0,0536
VAR	0,0351	0,0295	0,0056
Note: Sample size : 10			

Based on the calculated results, we find out:

First of all, Equity beta mean values in all 3 scenarios are acceptable (< 0,7) and asset beta mean values are also small (< 0,5). In the case of reported leverage in 2011, equity beta max is 1,170 which is little high in a few exceptional cases. If competitor size doubles, asset beta max decreases from 0,998 to

0,869. Finally, when competitor size is slightly smaller, asset beta max reduces more to the value of 0,462.

The below chart 1 shows us : when competitive firm size decreases slightly, average equity beta value decrease more (0,285) compared to that at the initial selected competitor (0,602). Next, average asset beta decreases little (to 0,231). However, in case the competitor size doubles, the risk level of the selected firms decreases little (0,310). Last but not least, the fluctuation of equity beta value (0,177) in the case of doubling size competitors is higher than (>) the results in the rest 2 cases. And we could note that in the case competitor size slightly smaller, the risk is less dispersed (0,03).

Chart 1 – Comparing statistical results of equity beta var and mean in three (3) scenarios of changing competitor size (source: VN stock exchange 2012)

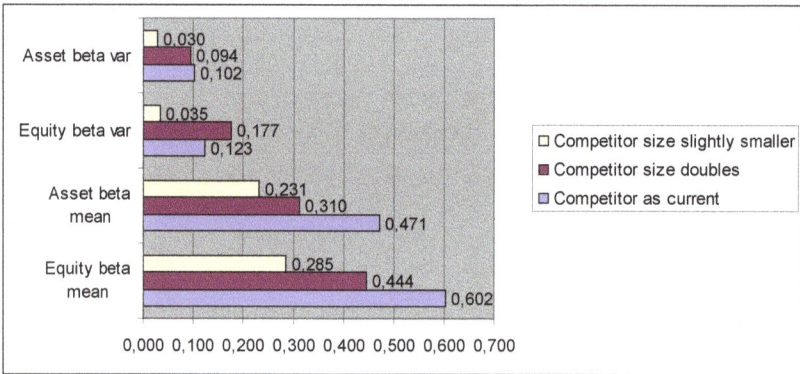

Chart 2 – Comparing statistical results of equity/asset beta max and min in three (3) scenarios of changing competitor size (source: VN stock exchange 2012)

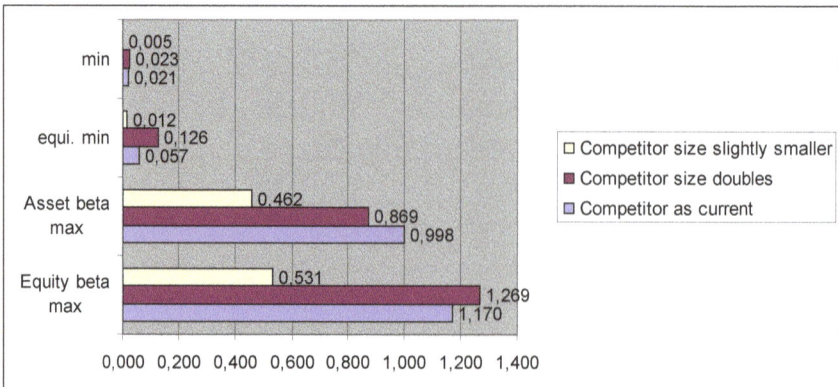

9. Risk analysis

Generally speaking, during the financial crisis 2007-2011, esp. the period 2007-2009, the water industry can survive well and maintain the development and profits, although these firms have to face other kinds of risks: materials or water or electric prices increasing. These risks can affect the operating cash flow of these companies.

10. Discussion

Table 1 shows us there are 70%, 90% of firms having acceptable beta values (0 < beta < 1) in cases : current or doubling size competitors. If competitor size is smaller, this number is increases to 100%. Moreover, chart 2 tells us that equity and asset beta min values increase (0,126 and 0,023) in case doubling size competitors.

Looking at exhibit 5, it is noted that comparing to beta results of electronic and electrical industry in the period 2007-2011, asset beta mean ofwater industry group during 2007-2011 is higher in current situation (0,471). And the risk dispersion in water industry when competitor size is smaller during 2007-2011 (shown by asset beta var of 0,03) is also smaller than that in electronic and electrical industries (0,06).

11. Conclusion and Policy suggestion

In conclusion, the government has to consider the impacts on the mobility of capital in the markets when it changes the macro policies and the legal system and regulation for developing the water market. The Ministry of Finance continues to increase the effectiveness of fiscal policies and tax policies which are needed to combine with other macro policies at the same time. The State Bank of Viet Nam continues to increase the effectiveness of capital providing channels for water companies as we could note that in this study when competitive firm size doubles, the risk level increases (equity beta mean value is estimated at: 0,444), and the equity beta var value (0,177) is little higher than that in case competitor size as current (0,123).

Furthermore, the entire efforts among many different government bodies need to be coordinated.

Finally, this paper suggests implications for further research and policy suggestion for the Viet Nam government and relevant organizations, economists and investors from current market conditions.

ACKNOWLEDGEMENTS

I would like to take this opportunity to express my warm thanks to Board of Editors and Colleagues at Citibank –HCMC, SCB and BIDV-HCMC, Dr. Chen and Dr. Yu Hai-Chin at Chung Yuan Christian University for class lectures, also Dr Chet Borucki, Dr Jay and my ex-Corporate Governance sensei, Dr. Shingo Takahashi at International University of Japan. My sincere thanks are for the editorial office, for their work during my research. Also, my warm thanks are for Dr. Ngo Huong, Dr. Ho Dieu, Dr. Ly H. Anh, Dr Nguyen V. Phuc and my lecturers at Banking University – HCMC, Viet Nam for their help.

Lastly, thank you very much for my family, colleagues, and brother in assisting convenient conditions for my research paper.

REFERENCES

Dexheimer, John., and Haugen, Carla, (2003), Sarbanes-Oxley: Its Impact on the Venture Capital Community, Minnesota Journal of Business Law and Entrepreneurship, Vol.2 No.1

Eugene, Fama F., and French, Kenneth R., (2004), The Capital Asset Pricing Model: Theory and Evidence, Journal of Economic Perspectives

Flifel, Kaouther., (2012), Financial Markets between Efficiency and Persistence : Empirical Evidence on Daily Data, Asian Journal of Finance and Accounting

Gunaratha V. (2013). The Degree of Financial Leverage as a Determinant of Financial Risk: An Empirical Study of Colombo Stock Exchange in Sri Lanka. 2nd International Conference on Management and Economics Paper.

Gao, Huasheng., Harford, Jarrad., and Li, Kai., (2013), Determinants of Corporate Cash Policy: Insights from Private Firms, Journal of Financial Economics

Huy, Dinh T.N., (2012), Estimating Beta of Viet Nam listed construction companies groups during the crisis, Journal of Integration and Development

Kale, Jayant R., Meneghetti, Costanza., and Sharur, Husayn., (2013), Contracting With Non-Financial Stakeholders and Corporate Capital Structure: The Case of Product Warantties, Journal of Financial and Quantitative Analysis

Litvak, Kate., (2008), Defensive Management: Does the Sarbanes-Oxley Act Discourage Corporate Risk-Taking?, Law and Economics Research Paper, No. 108

Ling, Amy., (2013), Tax Issues Relating to Intangibles, Asia-Pacific Tax Bulletin

Lu, Wenling., and Whidbee, David A., (2013), Bank Structure and Failure,Journal of Financial Econoic Policy

Mukerjee, Kaushik., (2013), Customer-Oriented Organizations: A Framework for Innovation, Journal of Business Strategy

Pereiro, Luis E.,(2010), The Beta Dilemma in Emerging Markets, Journal of Applied Corporate Finance

Shi, Mingtao., (2013), Capturing Strategic Competencies :Cloud Security as a Case Study, Journal of Business Strategy

Young, L., (2011), Market Orientation Processes, Australasian Marketing Journal

Research

Ang, A., Chen, J., (2007), CAPM Over the Long Run: 1926-2001, Journal of Empirical Finance

Baker, Kent H., Singleton, Clay J., and Veit, Theodore E., (2011), Survey Research in Corporate Finance: Bridging The Gap Between Theory and Practice, Oxford University Press

ADB and Viet Nam Fact Sheet, 2010

Other web sources

http://www.mofa.gov.vn/vi/

http://www.hsx.vn/hsx/

www.tuoitre.com.vn;

www.saigontimes.com.vn;

www.mof.gov.vn ;

Exhibit

Exhibit 1 – Inflation, GDP growth and macroeconomics factors

(source: Viet Nam commercial banks and economic statistical bureau)

Year	Inflation	GDP	USD/VND rate
2011	18%	5,89%	20.670
2010	11,75% (Estimated at Dec 2010)	6,5% (expected)	19.495
2009	6,88%	5,2%	17.000
2008	22%	6,23%	17.700
2007 12,63% 8,44% 16.132			
2006	6,6%	8,17%	
2005	8,4%		
Note	approximately		

Exhibit 2 – Market risk of listed companies on VN water industry market under one factor model (case 1) (source: VN stock exchange 2012)

Order No.	Company stock code	Equity beta	Asset beta (assume debt beta = 0)	Note	Financial leverage (F.S reports)
1	BTW	1,042	0,895	PJS as comparable	14,1%
2	BWA	0,551	0,509	LKW as comparable	7,6%
3	CLW	0,430	0,279	NBW as comparable	35,0%
4	GDW	0,790	0,555	BTW as comparable	29,8%
5	LKW	0,585	0,501	NTW as comparable	14,3%
6	NBW	0,603	0,413	SFC as comparable	31,5%
7	NNT	0,131	0,021	PCG as comparable	84,0%
8	NTW	0,658 0,516		HFC as comparable	21,6%
9	PJS	1,170	0,998	VMG as comparable	14,7%
10	TDW	0,057	0,021	NNT as comparable	63,3%
				Average	31,60%

Exhibit 3 - Market risks of listed electric power industry firms under one factor model (case 2) (source: VN stock exchange 2012)

Order No.	Company stock code	Equity beta	Asset beta (assume debt beta = 0)	Note
1	BTW	0,126	0,108	NNT as comparable

2	BWA	0,180	0,166	NTW as comparable
3	CLW	0,969	0,630	SD3 as comparable
4	GDW	0,231	0,162	TDW as comparable
5	LKW	0,170	0,146	NTW as comparable
6	NBW	1,269	0,869	S96 as comparable
7	NNT	0,142	0,023	HJS as comparable
8	NTW	0,191	0,150	GDW as comparable
9	PJS	0,858	0,731	CLW as comparable
10	TDW	0,304	0,112	HJS as comparable

Exhibit 4 – Market risk of listed water industry firms under one factor model (case 3) (source: VN stock exchange 2012)

Order No.	Company stock code	Equity beta	Asset beta (assume debt beta = 0)	Note
1	BTW	0,347	0,298	PJS as comparable
2	BWA	0,501	0,462	LKW as comparable
3	CLW	0,139	0,091	NBW as comparable
4	GDW	0,263	0,185	BTW as comparable
5	LKW	0,531	0,456	VE3 as comparable

6	NBW	0,196	0,134	GDW as comparable
7	NNT	0,028	0,005	CLW as comparable
8	NTW	0,440	0,345	LKW as comparable
9	PJS	0,390	0,332	NTW as comparable
10	TDW	0,012	0,005	NNT as comparable

Exhibit 5 – Comparing statistical results of equity beta var and mean in three (3) scenarios of changing competitor size in 18 listed commercial electric firms 2007-2011 (source: VN stock exchange 2012)

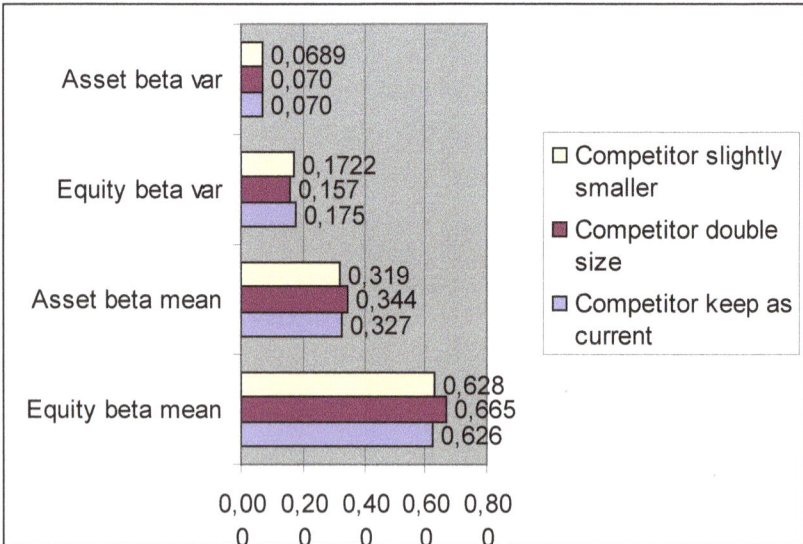

Part Three

Recommendations for Marketing in Banking and Other Industries:
Commerce-Investment-Finance-Tourism-Airlines-Hotels-Manufacturing-
Hardware-Medicine-Agriculture-Electric-Gas & Oil and Other **Industries**

The contents are presented in the following order:

Chapter One

Marketing principles and standards

(written by Dinh Tran Ngoc Huy, Pham Minh Dat, Pham Van Tuan, Nguyen Thi Phuong Thanh, Nguyen Thuy Dung, Do Thu Huong, Phan Anh, Pham Van Hong)

1. Conclusion
2. General Principles and Qualified Standards in Marketing

Chapter Two

Recommendations for Improving Marketing in Various Industries

(written by Main Author Dinh Tran Ngoc Huy, Dr Esra Sipahi, Do Thu Huong, Pham Van Tuan and Dinh Tran Ngoc Hien)

Chapter Three

Lessons from The US, European And Asia in Marketing

(written by Dinh Tran Ngoc Huy, Dr Esra Sipahi, ...)

Chapter Four

E-commerce, IT and Digital Technology Suggestions to Improve Marketing

(written by Dinh Tran Ngoc Huy, Nguyen Thi Phuong Thanh, Nguyen Thi Hang, Dr Esra Sipahi, Nguyen Thuy Dung)

Chapter One

Marketing principles and standards

(written by Dinh Tran Ngoc Huy, Tran Thi Thanh Nga, Nguyen Thi Hang, Dinh Thien Phuc, Dinh Tran Ngoc Hien, Pham Van Tuan, Pham Minh Dat)

Conclusion

Generally speaking, we identified that digital marketing (online marketing) has been becoming more popular and help companies/clients save cost, more speed and return. Our book has proposed that modern marketing will research on many aspects such as economic-politics-culture-sports-social sciences, etc. and will identify new demand of clients.

With this book proposal, we expect not only new marketing theories and concepts but also practical marketing models and concepts which can be applied in daily business in developing countries (including Vietnam, Asian Pacific, Middle East, Latin America and Africa, etc.), as well as in developed nations.

Proposed Ten (12) Principles of Marketing and 22 marketing quality standards

Within the scope of this book (part I), we aims to build Twenty two (22) Marketing standards for listed and unlisted companies as below, a system with impacts on business operation and governance that we think it still can be developed through time.

Table 4 - Twenty two (22) components of the 1st comparative marketing standards for listed and unlisted companies

Factor No.	Subjects or parties	Main quality factors	Sub quality factors
1	Leadership	Proper actions and plans in marketing;	Consider both bad and good sides;
2	Marketing strategy model	Identify gap between our products and those of competitors;	Contribute to Build process to control risks; Implement suitable forms;

3	Competitor risk	Implement suitable forms;	Analysis of substitutes and competitors products or services;
4	CRO and Risk officer (R.O)	Guidelines for Risk, RM analysis;	Contribute to Build and Implement process to control risk;
5	CFO/Chief accountant	Approve suitable processes and standards, principles for setting minim marketing budget	Understand risks and uncertainties of business, plans to avoid or mitigate them;
6	Online and digital marketing	Has certain goals (increasing traffics, sales, or more followers and brand awareness)	Provide sound information even before client need;
7	Email marketing	Segmenting list of email;	Write friendly way and good content; email to offer discounts;
8	Compliance officer	Update and deliver relevant regulations and standards; share experiences on cases failures;	Identify legal risks if any;
9	Board of Directors and strategic planning	Daily management of business operation; cooperate and support CMO;	Follow and Apply Plan Do Check Action (PDCA cycle) in marketing;
10	Marketing KPIs	Lead conversion rate (opportunities/leads); customer lifetime value (initial cost-revenue earned from a client); web traffics to marketing leads;	ROI, sale over marketing cost, Return on marketing investment;
11	Customer service	Help marketing to retain clients;	Resolve client complaints well; make client feel special and unique via email, phone or in person;
12	Selling process	Transparency ,easy to train;	Easy to read and train new employees;
13	Chairman	Functions separated from CEO;	Pay attention to business goals, Good collaboration with stakeholders

14	Supply chain management	Balance between price and quality; transfer data analytics to expertise in supply chain;	Implement relationship marketing for enhancing multiple relations in supply chain; integrate suppliers in your team;
15	Technology innovation	Apply green technology;	Carefully planned with business strategies;
16	Advertising	Into selected effective projects with good client network;	clear and consistent with business statement; single message;
17	Information Technology	Apply digital technology and IT in marketing;	Manage cybersecurity risk well;
18	Human Resource Management	Find suitable persons for CMO and marketing/sale team;	Prepare compensation
19	CMOs	build and execute integrated field campaigns that involve email marketing, direct mail marketing, and other channels	Clear duties and advise for CEO; good cooperation with sale team;
20	Marketing and sale team	Various actions: advertising, direct marketing, branding, packaging, your online presence, printed materials, PR activities, sales presentations, sponsorships, trade show appearances, etc.	Under training program to know marketing and sale tactics;
21	Marketing communication	Create sustain demand and shorten sale cycle;	Try to create preferences for long term brand positioning;
22	Physical display	Make sure environment fresh, clean, or green, natural conditions (atmosphere,land,…) are good, reduced pollution; provide added values to clients;	Ensure good conditions of business facilities, design, equipment and transportation;

Next, not only we suggest to implement a marketing strategy form in Appendix for the above 20 elements of marketing quality standards, but we also continue to propose 12 principles of a so-called good marketing management which can be used in most of companies, from small to medium to big size, esp. in developing countries including Vietnam as following:

Principle 1 – The company needs to choose a suitable marketing model and implement marketing strategy form as suggested in this book, for ex.

Principle 2 – The firm needs to perform cost vs. Benefit analysis for its marketing plans.

Principle 3 – The company need to coordinates related functions: advertising, customer service, sales, brand management with marketing function.

Principle 4 – Marketing standards are vital, so that top management set up private minimum budgets for them

Principle 5 – The company ensures a designated person to take care of marketing principles and qualified standards in this book, for marketing practice

Principle 6 – Marketing reports better to be supported with IT software solutions to be part of effective MIS and read by top management

Principle 7 – The corporation understands capital sources needed for environment protection and CSR.

Principle 8 – The firm needs to evaluate marketing efforts in relation to improving better leadership and corporate governance, at least from qualitative approach

Principle 9 – Corporation need to apply 4P, 7P, 5M and PENCILS in marketing and advertising to retain and keep client loyalty

Principle 10 – Corporate management needs to delegate tasks rationally and properly for CMOs and marketing, sale team and compensate them accordingly.

Principle 11 – Corporation need to pay attention to quality then follows quantity target and evaluate which one will create more wastes for firm.

Principle 12 – Corporate need to allocate a person in charge for implementing SWOT analysis and forms attached at the end of this book.

Hence, we recommend management to use two (2) implementation forms attached in the appendix section to be used flexibly in various companies and organizations in most of industries. The person in charge can be a marketing/ sale officer or CMO, or designated person, etc.

Chapter Two

Recommendations for Improving Marketing in Various Industries

(written by Main Author Dinh Tran Ngoc Huy, Dr Esra Sipahi, Do Thu Huong, Pham Van Tuan and Dinh Tran Ngoc Hien)

First, not only we have a clear business plan, but we might also need to have marketing strategy, for example see below figure:

Figure 19- Shaping marketing strategy

Marketing Strategy

(source: Neil A. Morgan et al., 2018)

Second, marketing has certain established goals. These goals are often associated with sales volume, market share and profitability, so the assessment of volume often has to be conducted in two ways:

- Sale Prediction: is the prediction of the market's reaction to the strategy. It is the result of using a hypothetical strategy. To predict people use some main methods as follows:

Using econometric models

+ Assume the responses of market certainty through the model explaining individual behavior.

+ Experiments and experimental markets.

- Budget forecasting: predicting the certain profitability of the proposed strategy. To calculate that, it is necessary to predict investment and exploitation budgets close to the activities that the strategy intends. Detail:

+ Calculate investment capital, fixed costs and variable costs incurred in the process of production, circulation, advertising...

+ Predict sales with reliability and accuracy.

+ Assume the responses of market certainty through the model explaining individual behavior.

Third solution is increasing your presence in front of clients/consumers, it will help to fasten sale processes and approaches to small group of potential clients.

Fourth solution is focusing more on quality rather than quantity. This will win favor of potential clients. It will be more wasteful if we focus on quantity instead.

Fifth solution is the application of Philip Kotler concept of 5M when firms conduct marketing and advertising including: Mission - Message - Media - Money (or Budget)- Measurement.

Six solution we mentioned is still Philip Kotler concept of Public relation factors including: PENCILS consisting of: Publication – Events – News – Community affairs – Identify media – Lobbying – Social Investments.

Seventh solution is from Marketing guru Seth Godin: Godin asserts that the only way to spread an idea or attract attention is to stand out. Godin also introduced the concept of "permissive marketing", which means that a business offers a product of value to consumers but only conducts marketing after receiving a nod from them.

Last but not least, the marketing literature broadly indicates that a firm's marketing efforts impact its marketplace and economic performance through the formulation and implementation of specific patterns of resource deployments designed to achieve marketing objectives in a target market (e.g., Katsikeas et al. 2016; Morgan 2012). This formulation-implementation dichotomy perspective suggests that goal-setting and marketing strategy development systems are used as future-oriented decision-making frameworks to define desired goals and identify and select marketing strategy options that may enable these goals to be accomplished, followed by a period of enactment in which firms seek to operationalize the intended marketing strategy decisions to achieve the desired goals (e.g., Morgan et al. 2012; Noble & Mokwa 1999; Piercy 1998).

And also, we look at below figure to see marketing communication mix components which is needed to develop in implementing an effective marketing strategy (Marketing communication will consist of advertising, direct marketing, branding, packaging, your online presence, printed materials, PR activities, sales presentations, sponsorships, trade show appearances, etc.). Establishing effective marketing communication for supply chain or audiences based on each group of target audiences (classified by The countries/areas that potential clients live in, Their age group, Gender, Educational background, Marital status, Family status, Occupation,Their interests).

:

Figure 20 - Marketing communication mix components

(source: https://businessjargons.com/marketing-communication.html, access date 15/1/2021)

Last but not least, we would suggest Marketing management team and firm leaders to consider to apply Plan-Do -Check-Action (PDCA cycle) in marketing as below:

Table 5 - PDCA cycle application in marketing

PLAN	DO
Convert client process of buying: *Awareness-> Interest ->* *Consideration -> Intent -> Buy*	*Digital or online marketing tools;* *Marketing techniques, push and pull strategies;*
CHECK	ACTION
- Measuring plans and goals; KPIs measurables; *- Marketing plan checklist;* *- Market segmentation for target audience*	*- Resolve clients complaints; retain customers;* *- Develop channels of marketing;* *- Create library marketing content;*

(source: author analysis)

Finally, Actions of competitors and our firm responses can be shown in below table:

Table 6- Actions of our competitors

Competitor marketing strategy	Competitor actions	Our firm responses
Market penetration	Offer products to more customers and expand current client database	Enhance clients experience; Increase clients loyalty
Market development for existing products	Offer products to new markets (Asia, Europe,…), new clients (businesses, students,…)	Increase advertising; Competitor-based pricing

New product development	Provide new products with new features or new technology	Improve marketing mix;
Product diversification	Offer various new products to new markets	Improve promotion and place; Improve customer service;
Competitor marketing strategy characteristics	**Competitor actions**	**Our firm responses**
Calm	- no or slow to responses - trust client loyalty	- selected responses not wasteful
No interested	- consider their competitors not dangerous and not harmful	- identify their strengths and weaknesses (to exploit) and attack/ expand markets
Aggressive	- quick and aggressive response to their competitors	- smart strategies to enter markets and less resources consuming
Smart	- unexpected and flexible strategies, attract clients	- learn from their strategies to enter markets

(source: author synthesis and analysis)

The above responses are our suggestions, therefore you can make suggestions in your own firm case. For instance, we could make evaluation to recognize strengths and weaknesses of our competitors, then we set up our marketing strategies to respond (see our 3 implementation forms suggested in appendix).

And in addition, Pham Van Tuan (2022) proposed the theoretical model, tested hypotheses, corrected scales to create new scales for Vietnam's fashion, quantifying the intensity of the impact of moderator variable of purchase involvement on the relationship between satisfaction and loyalty. Noticeably, the word of mouth has been the most impacted (0.638) by satisfaction rather than trust and commitment. The affirmative finding in this paper is that satisfaction has the greatest influence on loyalty through word of mouth, which means that the more satisfied customers are, the more the customers will spread their satisfaction to customers and potential customers. This is the important focus paid high attention to by marketers for fashion products in general and fashion shirts in particular.

Customers with a broad knowledge tend to make better purchasing decisions in the future, significantly expand efforts to find and process information, which increases their satisfaction. Firstly, customers with ego involvement shall endeavor to avoid dissatisfaction after purchasing important products in life. Secondly, in high-risk situations, the high-involvement purchase takes customers much time and effort to make wise decisions after the careful consideration, investigation, and to bring about motivation of stronger satisfaction. Customers with high-involvement purchase tend to make better decisions and gain more satisfaction. The easy access to information provided by manufacturers can increase customer satisfaction. Customers with high level of involvement are specially promoted to experience the satisfaction with provided products.

Chen and Tsai (2008) have also studied the impact of involvement, as a moderator variable, on the relationship between satisfaction and loyalty in China, a developing country with considerable similarities in consumer behavior and characteristics with Vietnam. The study has demonstrated that customers with high involvement tend to require more information than ones with low involvement do.

In general, the impact by satisfaction on loyalty is positive and proportional, but not all relationships are strong enough. This implies that the purchase behaviors in the fashion market are extremely complex, requiring proper marketing strategies and tactics. The paper provides references for administrators to know how to increase customer loyalty. Results of commitment, trust and word of mouth in this paper suggest administrators develop marketing plans and programs with the central focus on word of mouth for viral marketing to target customers. This is proper and appropriate in Vietnam market in which consumers have the "mob" mentality with a large proportion.

To further clarify the relationship between satisfaction and loyalty, the research results also show that the influence of the moderator variable on customers' purchase involvement is positive. The paper recommends that sale programs should be publicly announced and attached with "commitment" to attractive promotions to increase the loyalty (behavior loyalty), which significantly improves purchase behavior. This is considered as the false loyalty, which is explained that customers' purchase behavior only occurs at promotion programs. It is also quite true to the real situation in Vietnam when the income per capita is still modest.

Firstly, the involvement is a very important and interesting subject in customer behavior research. This paper has just emphasized on purchase involvement, and not mentioned ego-involvement which aimed at further researches.

Secondly, this paper has focused only three factors of loyalty (including commitment, trust, and word of mouth) and purchase involvement to test relationships with satisfaction. The further researches may survey other factors of loyalty to more understand the researched relationships.

Last but not least, the word of mouth is referred to positive and advantageous communications and satisfaction hereof is general and overall satisfaction. Negative and disadvantageous word-of-mouth communications and partial satisfaction with each stage of sales processes has not been demonstrated in this paper and this is a direction for further research.

Chapter Three

Lessons from The US, European And Asia in Marketing

(written by Main author Dinh Tran Ngoc Huy, Dr Esra Sipahi, Dr Phan Anh)

Firstly, we see a nice example of Starbucks. Starbucks is a good example of making good use of social media in its famous marketing strategies. They exploit what their fans want. They have a hugely successful Facebook, Twitter and Instagram accounts.

Figure 21- Starbuck marketing

(source: internet)

Among the reasons why Starbucks is so successful is:

+Connecting the same topic on different Social media

+Share your campaign on social media

+Contact with customers

+Advertise discounted products

+Organize events with artists

+Use images, videos very delicately

Secondly, we see another example of Colgate. They provide information and videos on proper oral hygiene. They share valuable information to users about how to brush their teeth, keep their teeth healthy, how to floss effectively, how to prevent tooth decay, etc. Consumers receive useful and free information. costs, they learn, apply to their lives and those around them. A brand that helps users solve problems in their lives increases the likelihood of future orders as well as word of mouth about your brand. Colgate spends millions of dollars marketing budget to invest in extremely attractive videos, images, and content that meet the needs of users.

Thirdly, we analyze Channel example. The first is product strategy. They build a product line with their own style, elegance, courtesy, not following any trends. Channel's somewhat conservative product strategy has set them apart in the luxury market.

The channel is particularly oblivious to competitors such as Louis Vuitton or Gucci. Regardless of whether the competitor has a product or media move, the Channel still does its job well and there is no change in relation to the opponent. Unlike other brands, Channel says no to discounts, they don't need to promote sales or please customers by seasonal promotions, events... To promote revenue, Channel chooses a development strategy more affordable products so that some customer segments can own the product at a price that suits their pocket.

Figure22 - Chanel marketing strategy

(source: internet)

Another good example is success of KFC and Amazon in China market where they offer values to clients.

Next is discount policy, for instance, in special events such as Black Friday or In Vietnam, Lazada or Tiki offer discounts tickets on purchases.

Figure 23- Lazada program

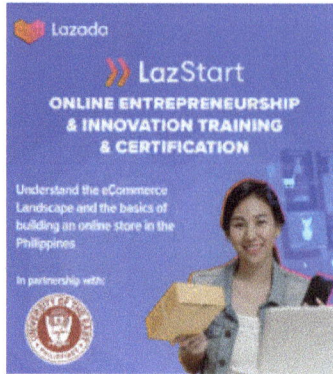

(source: internet)

Last but not least we take Dove-Unilever as a nice example. Dove launched "Dove Campaign for True Beauty" (Real Beauty) which is a great success in creating a common brand positioning for Unilever's health and beauty care product group. On websites, TV commercials or street banners, Unilever's Dove brand offers health advice or compliments to clients, but doesn't say why you should use Dove products. Dove is following the criteria: win customers by enhancing their value and providing them with useful information.

Figure 24- Dove advertisement

(source: internet)

And lastly, Zappos is a US-based company and an online shoe and clothing retailer with 10 years of history, revenue of $4.3 billion in 2008. Zappos has just been acquired by Amazon for about $900 million. With 3C strategy:

clothing, customer service and company culture are the "golden keys" to help Zappos constantly grow and reach the success it is today. Zappos leaders see corporate culture as a differentiator to create a competitive advantage for the company. It used Blog an Twitter successfully.

Zappos has a policy of hiring only happy and optimistic people to work, and always tries to create a friendly and sociable environment for all employees. Zappos's motto is: "You can't keep customers happy without happy employees, and you can't have happy employees if your company culture isn't engaging and inspiring for employee".

Looking at below figure we see differences among countries in branding initiatives:

Figure 25- Asian branding

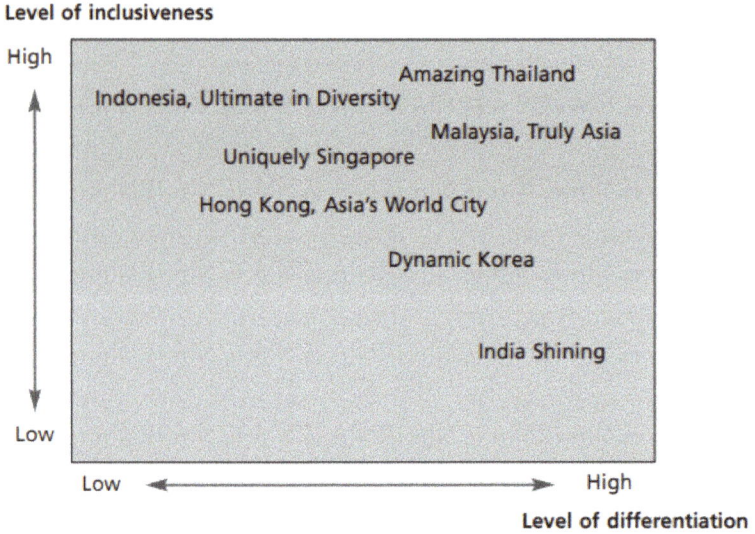

Level of inclusiveness

High

Amazing Thailand
Indonesia, Ultimate in Diversity

Malaysia, Truly Asia
Uniquely Singapore

Hong Kong, Asia's World City

Dynamic Korea

India Shining

Low

Low ⟶ High

Level of differentiation

(source: VentureRepublic)

In era of industry 4.0, Next solutions will be: firms need to continue to use Google marketing with SEO (help to optimize clients search with quality contents) and Google Ads while they still take advantage of social media such as Facebook, Zalo, Viber, Youtube, Tiktok, Twitter, Linkedin, Snapchat, Pinterest, Periscope, Tumblr, and Instagram. Among them top video platforms in Vietnam are : Youtube, TikTok , Facebook, Instagram.

Moreover, Honda give us a nice example. It has 4 business segments: automobile, motorcycle, financial services and power and distributed over a network of 700 retail dealers in Japan; 1,300 dealers in the US; 1,500 dealers in Asia (excluding Japan); and 1,100 dealers in Europe. Honda motorbikes has 6,500+ outlets in Japan. The firm used TV advertisements to a large extent. Honda has released ads with different themes to attract customers. Online ad campaigns have also helped the brand establish its competitive edge. The brand also proactively engages with its users on social media websites like Facebook, Instagram etc.

Figure 26- Honda plan

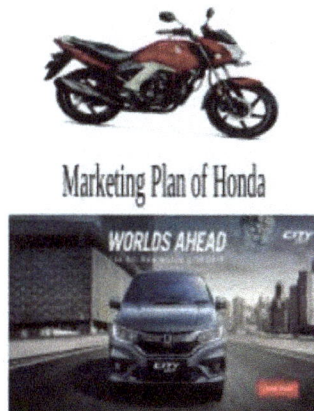

Marketing Plan of Honda

(source: internet)

And here is an example of Toyota. Toyota was founded in 1937 as a local company and became a leading global automobile corp. Its marketing mix strategy: various products (for luxury - Prius and Lexus cars, for the elderly, and people with disabilities; place: with dealership and retailers, promotion via: PR, personal selling, advertising, sale promotion, direct selling and advertising via TV, newspapers, and websites; price: combination between market-based pricing (market and competitors) and value-based pricing (product perceived value).

Figure 27 - Toyota advertising

(source: internet)

We see another example of Samsung, a success of cutting edge technology. And another story of Nike that has transferred Western values in Asia. The company also launched Nike App in Asia for its journey of digital transformation.

Figure 28 - Samsung media

(source: internet)

We still remember examples of Kodak and Nokia ho are failed in competition game with more aggressive competitors. To avoid failures, our firms need to have suitable responses to competitor risks at least with our suggestions and recommendations in this book.

And Last but not least, we look at below figure:

Figure 29- Sales Funnel

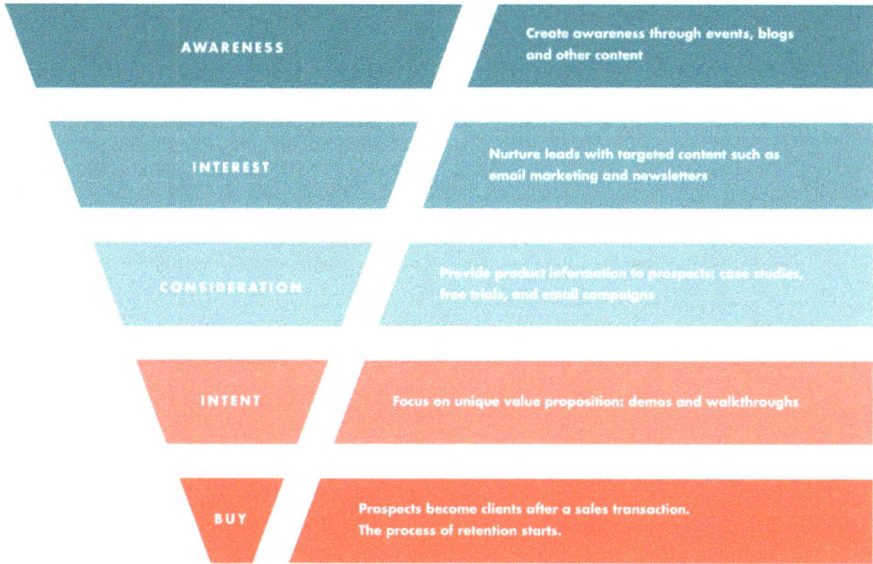

(source: reliablesoft.net, access date 17/1/2022)

Chapter Four

E-commerce, IT and Digital Technology Suggestions to Improve Marketing

(written by Main author Dinh Tran Ngoc Huy, Nguyen Thi Phuong Thanh, Co-Main author Dr Esra Sipahi Dongul, Nguyen Thuy Dung, Dr Sylwia G.)

Among reasons for competitor risk might include: technological change and lack of management experience, or changes in consumer preferences, etc. Hence, we can see innovation and technology solutions are needed for marketing.

Next point is the combination of E-commerce and Digital technology in marketing has helped many firms to boost revenues and increase client network. E-commerce platforms has played vital roles in digital advertising and online content marketing and in customers' purchasing process as well.

In banking, finance, tourism, hotel, medicine, retail and other sectors, digital technology and e-commerce together will help them to enhance their digital presence and advertise values for community.

So the process will be: IT & AI & machine learning -> digital marketing tools -> e-commerce -> digital transformation -> digital presence -> client interaction and connectivity -> data and automation -> marketing control and checking -> Allow Actions and PDCA cycle

There are opportunities and challenges as presented below:

Opportunities:

- E-commerce platform development to develop online business operation and online order

- Promote online advertising and social media

- Enhance digital presence and customer connectivity

- E-commerce and IT and AI platforms (or better combination) will allow our business to move from local to global marketing.

- E-commerce will help not only B2B but also and esp., B2C or C2C marketing channels (or individual marketing), digital marketing communication and personal sales will have more room to develop

- For tourism and hotel and airlines sector, both mobile marketing, advertising and digital media will have more chance to grow

- Client network will be expanded because digital clients will share experience and satisfaction and became loyal consumers

- Marketing team will have more chance to practice digital content marketing in which quality of information and content will be highly evaluated

- There are opportunities for enhancing marketing team capabilities in the industry 4.0 and globalization

Challenges:

- There is challenge for marketing strategy, planning, implementation and control. Marketing control is a new concept in which we suggest marketing management team to follow our 22 marketing standards and 12 marketing principles as recommended in above section.

- There is cybersecurity risk to be managed

- There is barriers to be managed because of several reasons such as conflicts of interest, etc.

- Challenge for SMEs to take advantage of digital marketing tools to increase sales and profits

Marketing with IT applications:

Not only helping at the general level, when applying information technology in marketing will help a content marketer in other details. Specifically, technology is an effective arm for content marketing to perform tasks such as designing videos, websites, presentation materials, blog posts... Plus with great support from SEO and SEM, your work will be Optimize time, impress customers.

Performing well SEO will increase the number of visitors to the website, this is the opportunity for firms to create interest and love for the website and the business itself, the results is to increase awareness and promote corporate brand. This result is also the basis of helping businesses increase sales.

To effectively implement this tool, businesses need a website designed professionally, the business can then implement or use the services of professional SEO providers.

Paying search engines so that ads can appear is a form of buying key words on Google or Google Adwords Ads, a form of online marketing advertising on Google's search engine and other engines such as Yahoo, Bing, ...

The business will pay Google for one or more keywords related to the product or services that the business is doing. When a user searches the web with key words such as business keywords registered with Google, then your website will be displayed.

It can be said that ICT plays a key role in the transformation of marketing from traditional to modern. Currently, most of the marketing activities of enterprises are associated with information technology. In particular, Digital Marketing including SEO, SEM, Email Marketing, advertising on website, social network, ... has grown tremendously. This makes it easier for businesses to access, exchange and transmit information to their customers than ever before.

Beside, there are some marketing and innovation issues:

Innovation such as Cloud technology is considered to use in medium to big companies in Vietnam including commercial banks. The cloud technology will help Vietnam banks to increase speed and productivity as they can process thousands of data in a second, i.e faster ; however, what if any risk in cloud technology and transactions stop, Vietnam banks also need to manage these risky scenes. Application of internal technology in the banking sector in Vietnam has been developed over the years with internal applications payments, electronic money and more recently, applications such as cloud computing, artificial intelligence ... (source: Dinh Tran Ngoc Huy et al, 2021). Therefore, these factors will influence marketing strategy.

Last but not least we need to take care of cybersecurity risk: Enhance network security solutions; Ensuring information security is not only the responsibility of the technical team, therefore, service businesses will need to upgrade equipment, software, tools related to the network system and website; building a comprehensive security policy for the company and customers in both present and future.

Lastly, we see in below figure:

Figure 30- Integrated Lifecycle marketing

	1. Initial	2. Managed	3. Defined	4. Quantified	5. Optimised
Plan *Creating a strategic roadmap*	No strategy. Unclear goals or prioritisation.	Prioritised activities. Goals not modelled or aligned. Martech adoption ad-hoc.	Multichannel marketing plan in place. Revenue-based funnel acquisition model.	Retention and LTV model. 90 day planning. Martech roadmap and structured evaluation.	Digital transformation implemented. Structured testing and optimisation programme.
Reach *Build awareness Drive visits*	Limited ad hoc use of paid media. No outreach. SEO not proactive.	Search target keywords defined. Simple use of AdWords/online media.	Structured approach to paid, owned and earned media to agreed targets.	Programmatic. Regular improvements to media. New media review ad hoc.	Media fully optimised based on attribution and evaluation of new options.
InterAct *Experience, flow and content*	No insight on personas and customer journeys. No content strategy.	Some hero content and CTAs for lead generation and profiling.	Content marketing and personalised journeys to encourage leads/sales.	Personalisation optimised. Ad hoc AB testing of site sections.	Multivariate testing. High quality content marketing. Structured testing.
Convert *Build multichannel sales*	No paid retargeting. No email welcome or nurture.	Initial media retargeting. Targeted newsletter. Simple welcome emails.	Re-targeting optimised Welcome and abandon emails. Personalisation.	Segmented lifecycle emails, personalisation & paid media retargeting	Retargeting and personalisation optimised across touchpoints.
Engage *Customer loyalty and retention*	Limited experience research. Email newsletter and social media.	No loyalty programme Targeted newsletter. No personalisation	Customer research informs site improvement. E-mail re-engagement	Loyalty programme. NPS. RFM-based email and personalisation	Retargeting and personalisation optimised. Machine Learning applied.
Brand *Building emotional connection*	Basic brand identity, but brand benefits not communicated.	Brand values defined, but not clear on-site. Customer reviews.	Online value prop defined Blog and social media develop brand.	Brand personality and defects researched and acted on promptly.	Fully integrated brand reputation management including PR.
Governance *Managing growth approach*	Analytics in place, not reviewed. No social media governance. Skills gap.	Analytics reviewed ad-hoc. Regular performance reviews. Social listening.	Dashboard performance reviews. Social governance. Digital Skills.	Value-based KPIs 90-day planning review. Skills improvement.	Lifetime value KPIs Structured defect reduction problem
	"Basic Lifecycle Marketing"	"Improving Lifecycle marketing"	"Planned Lifecycle marketing"	"Managed Lifecycle marketing"	"Optimised Lifecycle marketing"

(source: https://www.smartinsights.com/tag/race-planning-system/, access date 15/1/2021)

Last but not least, marketing management team need to create unique selling point (UPS) in marketing strategy, to differentiate our products and services from competitors, as well as make our offer special so that we can win competition game. No need to spend more money, try using less expensive way for marketing, improving website and refresh our images.

In addition we would like to address cybersecurity risk management involved in client database management as below:

According to Dinh Tran Ngoc Huy, Gwoździewicz S. et al (2021):

When we accept technology innovation adoption in banking activities, for instance, cloud technology, banks need to make assessment on risks of cloud and of transactions stopped and security of loosing important data. Banks need risk management plans for that.

Also when banks increase online transactions via digital technology, there will be higher risk of hackers and viruses, so they need to prevent and handle risks happening.

In Korea, from 2010 up to now the government has shifted from a perspective that encourages cooperation between ICT (Information and Communication Technology) and other major industries such as automotive, shipbuilding, construction and textiles, to a perspective that it is good to provide tax incentives to companies that invest in products related to digital security. 90% of Korean businesses use information security products and 41% use information security services. Small and medium-sized businesses are most in need of government assistance. It is in the Korea that Internet banks such as K Bank, Toss Bank,... operated under both Banking Act and The Internet Only Bank Act in 2018 and became the most effective Fintech businesses in the country.

In the US, there is Blockchain regulations and in Europe, cryptocurrencies businesses have to register with authorized financial agencies. Cryptocurrencies taxation is another matter taking into account. In Japan, in April 2017, cryptocurrencies are under Payment Service Act, market will adjust itself and some cryptocurrencies exchange businesses will be suspended if people loss much money (see an example of Coincheck lost 400 m USD in tokens).

In summary, in some emerging markets, digital currency might be considered by central banks and needs regulations.

In Europe, to make it safer and higher security, The Delegated Regulation on strong customer authentication (EU) 2018/389) which will enter into force on 14 September 2019 will require online payment and internet banking with credit cards having 3 components: knowledge (password or PIN), possession (token or mobile) or inherence (fingerprint or voice or facial features to identify payers).

The European Parliament resolution of 26 May 2016 on virtual currencies (2016/2007 (INI) emphasizes the importance of commensurate regulatory approaches at European Union level in order not to block innovation or burden it with unnecessary costs at an early stage, and at the same time seriously Address the regulatory challenges that the widespread use of virtual currencies and DLT can pose. Dated on 10/4/2018, A Declaration for establishing a European Blockchain Services Infrastructure (EBSI) signed by Norway and 21 State Members, that will support the cross-border digital public services, security and privacy highest standards (Gwoździewicz S., Huy, D.T.N. et.al., 2, 2020.

The End

Finally, not only in this book we clarify again the relationship between marketing, sale and customer service, but we also propose some suggestions for companies, government agencies and bank system to establish effective marketing management policies in better governance and risk management based on below analysis and consideration, and also, there are many factors that affect quality of marketing activities of companies including, but not limited to:

- The speed of technology 4.0 and technology revolution, IT and digital technology and technology innovations which can enable online shopping and purchasing , shipping and delivery goods to clients, etc.

- Financial innovations, such as Fintech platforms

- Firms, banks, medical firms and government-related bodies need to coordinate to issue green financing and harmonizing environmental and community health, social benefits with profit maximization goal.

- Last but not least, as we analyze competitor risks -> risk management -> competitive advantage. This shows effects of and indicated competitor risks as a source of firm competitive advantage, via a medium stage: risk management. For these risk management tools, we also wrote and published 2 books on that topic (for instance, companies might choose: Preventing/Reducing the probabilities of risks, Mitigating the impact of risks, Reducing the sensitivity of the organization to risks through flexibility and agility, and Firms ability to quickly recover from a realized risk).

- Finally, not only relationship between marketing and corporate governance and risk management, but also marketing control and applying PDCA in marketing will be new concepts in this book we would like to introduce to global audience and Vietnamese readers; hence, firms may want to apply 3 implementation forms (see appendix) and 22 marketing standards as well as 12 principles we suggested in the book.

Based on the above recommendations and contents of this book, we propose realistic marketing models, principles, activities and standards and policy implications. We also present concepts of competitor risks and effects and leave risk management part for readers with our 2 risk management books published before.

Welcome readers around the world send feedback to main author's email: dtnhuy2010@gmail.com ! Visit me on: www.dinhtranngochuy.com !

References

1. Allen, Franklin., Gale, Douglas., (2002), A Comparative Theory of Corporate Governance, Wharton Financial Institutions Center

2. Allen, F., and Gale, D., (1992), Stock Price Manipulation, Review of Financial Studies

3. Allen, F., and Gorton, G., (1992), Stock Price Manipulation, Market Microstructure and Asymmetric Information, European Economic Review

4. Armenakis, Achilles A., and Bedeian, Arthur G., (1999), Organizational Change: A Review of theory and Research in 1990s, Journal of Management, Vol.25, No.3

5. Bailey, W., and Ng., E., (1991), Default Premiums in Commodity Markets: Theories and Evidence, Journal of Finance

6. Becht, Marco., Bolton, Patrick., and Roel, Ailsa., (2005), Corporate Governance and Control, ECGI Working series paper

7. Bernd W. Wirtz, & Peter Daiser. (2018).Business Model Development: A Customer-Oriented Perspective,Journal of Business Models, 6(3)

8. Blume, Brian D., Ford, Kevin J., Baldwin Timothy T., and Huang, Jason L., (2010), Transfer of Training: A Meta Analytic Review, Journal of Management, Vol.36, No.4

9. Bruner, Christopher M., (2011), Corporate Governance Reform in a Time of Crisis, Journal of Corporation Law, Vol. 36, No. 2

10. Charreaux, Gerars., and Desbrieres, Philippe., (2001), Corporate Governance: Stakeholder Value Versus Shareholder Value, Journal of Management & Governance, Vol.5, No.2

11. Chatterjea, Arkadev., Jerian, Joseph A., and Jarrow, Robert A.,

(2001), Market Manipulation and Corporate Finance: A new Perspectives, 1994 Annual Meeting Review, SouthWestern Finance Association, Texas, USA.

12. Cheung, Stephen Y.L., Chan, Bob Y., (2004), Corporate Governance in Asia, Asia-Pacific Development Journal, Vol.11, No.2

13. Code of Proper Practice for Corporate Directors, Institute of Corporate Directors, Philippines, 2000

14. Coffee, John C., Jr., (2005), A Theory of Corporate Scandals: Why The US and Europe differ, Working Paper no.274, The Center for Law and Economics Studies, NY, USA

15. Coffee, John C., (2006), Gatekeepers: The Professions and Corporate Governance, Oxford University Press

16. Conreras, F.L., & Ramos, M.L.Z. (2015). What is Marketing? A Study on Marketing Managers' Perception of the Definition of Marketing, FÓRUM EMPRESARIAL, 21(1).

17. Commission Decision (of 5 July 2016) on the signing of a contractual arrangement on a public-private partnership for cybersecurity industrial research and innovation between the European Union, represented by the Commission, and the stakeholder organisation C(2016)4400), 2016.

18. Digital Transformation Innovation. Gartner, Germany 2020

19. Directive (EU) 2016/1148 of the European Parliament and of the Council of 6 July 2016 concerning measures for a high common level of security of network and information systems across the Union

20. Deloitte, Global Risk Management Survey, 8th, 2019.

21. Diệp Bình, Cách mạng 4.0: Nhiều cơ hội và rủi ro tiềm ẩn cho ngành ngân hàng, truy cập tại http://doisongtieudung.vn/cach-mang-40-nhieu-co-hoi-va-rui-ro-tiem-an-cho-nganh-ngan-hang-538662.html

22. Donker, Han., and Zahir, Saif., (2008), Takeovers, Corporate control, and return to target sharehodelrs, Intl. Journal of Corporate

Governance, Vol.1, No.1

23. MohsenEjrami, M., Salehi, N., Admadian, S. (2016). The Effect of Marketing Capabilities on Competitive Advantage and Performance with Moderating Role of Risk Management in Importation Companies, Procedia Economics and Finance, 36. https://doi.org/10.1016/S2212-5671(16)30012-0

24. Eryigit, C. (2017). Marketing Models: A Review of the Literature, International Journal of Market Research 59(3):355. DOI:10.2501/IJMR-2017-028

25. E&Y and the State Securities Commission, Survey Report on the practical situation of risk management activities in Vietnamese enterprises (2012, 2013), Hanoi.

26. Erkens, David., Hung, Mingyi., and Matos, Pedro P., (2010), Corporate Governance in the 2007-2008 Financial Crisis: Evidence from Financial Institutions Worldwide, ECGI Finance Working Paper, No.249/2009

27. Filip, Andrei., Vito, Jackie Di., (2009), Financial reporting quality revisited: interactions between earnings management and the value relevance of accounting information, Intl. Journal of Corporate Governance, Vol.1, No.3

28. Fulghieri, P. and D. Lukin, (2001), Information Production, Dilution Costs, and Optimal Security Design, Journal of Financial Economics

29. Gilson, Ronald J., Milhaupt, Curtis J., (2004), Choice as Regulatory Term, EGCI Law working paper, No.22/2004

30. *General Statistics Office, annual socio-economic situation report;*

31. Gimpel, H., Rau, D., & Roglinger, M (2016), Fintech – Geschaftsmodelle im Visier. Wirtschaftsinfornatik & Management, Vol.8 (3) p.38-47.

32. Goldstein, I. and A. Guembel, 2008, Manipulation and the Allocational Role of Prices, Review of Economic Studies

33. *Government (2020), Resolution No. 42 / NQ-CP dated April 9, 2020*

on measures to support people in difficulty due to the COVID-19 pandemic;

34. Gwoździewicz S. Prokopowicz S., 2016, The Internet banking security and conditions of electronic data transfer in BIG DATA technology in Poland, Pravo Ekonomija Menadžment I. Međunarodni naučni zbornik, Srbske Rozvojove Združenie, Bački Petrovac, Srbija 2016.

35. Hopt, Klaus J., (2011), Comparative Corporate Governance: The State of the Art and International Regulation, American Journal of Comparative Law, Vol.59

36. Hubert Gatignon, Erin Anderson, Kristiaan Helsen. (1989). Competitive Reactions to Market Entry: Explaining Interfirm Differences, Journal of Marketing research 3. https://doi. org/10.1177/002224378902600104

37. Hùng Cường, Cách mạng công nghiệp 4.0, Việt Nam có thể đi đầu và bắt kịp công nghệ tiên tiến, truy cập tại https://www.most.gov.vn/ vn/tin-tuc/11682/cach-mang-cong-nghiep-4-0--viet-nam-co-the-di-dau-va-bat-kip-cong-nghe-tien-tien-.aspx

38. IFRs and US GAPP, Deloitte, 2007.

39. Industry 4.0 Cybersecurity. Challenges & Recommendations, European Union Agency for Network and Information Security, ENISA, May 2019.

40. Jokipii, Annukka., (2009), Determinants and consequences of internal control in firms: a contingency theory based analysis, Journal of Management & Governance, Vol.14, No.2

41. Jong, Abe De., (2009), Irrational executives and corporate governance, Intl. Journal of Corporate Governance, Vol.1, No.3

42. Judge, William., Filatotchev, Igor., and Aguilera, Ruth., (2010), Comparative Corporate governance & International Business Research, Corporate Governance: An Intl. Review, Vol.18, Issue 3

43. Khwaja, Asim Ijaz., Mian, Atif., (2005), Unchecked intermediaries:Price manipulation in an emerging stock market,

Journal of Financial Economics 78 (2005) 243-241

44. Klaus Schwab 2016: The Fourth Industrial Revolution: what it means, how to respond, access at https://www.weforum.org/agenda/2016/01/the-fourth-industrial-revolution-what-it-means-and-how-to-respond/

45. Kotler, P., & Armstrong, G. (2013).Principles of marketing .Edinburgh Gate: Pearson Education Limited.

46. Korea Code of Best Practices for Corporate Governance, Committee on Corporate Governance, 2003

47. Kosiński, J., 2015, Cybercrime paradigms, Warsaw.

48. Kotler, P., & Keller, K. L. (2012). Marketing management. Upper Saddle River, NJ: Pearson Prentice Hall.

49. Krush, M. T., Sohi, R. S., & Saini, A. (2015). Dispersion of marketing capabilities: Impact on marketing's influence and business unit outcomes. Journal of the Academy of Marketing Science, 43, 32-51.

50. Lynn, R.A. (1987), ANTICIPATING COMPETITIVE REACTION: MARKETING STRATEGY IN THE 1980s, Journal of Consumer Marketing, Vol. 4 No. 1, pp. 5 -12 . https://doi.org/10.1108/eb008184

51. Martin Roll. (2006). Asian Brand Strategy - HOW ASIA BUILDS STRONG BRANDS, PALGRAVE MACMILLAN, ISBN-13: 978–1–4039–9279–6

52. McCarthy, E. J. (1960). Basic Marketing: A managerial approach. Homewood, IL:

53. Richard D. Irwin. McDonald, M. (2009). The future of marketing: Brightest star in the firmament, or a fading meteor? Some hypotheses and a research agenda. Journal of Marketing Management, 25(5/6), 431-450.

54. Morgan, F. W. (1984). Punitive damages awards for flagrant mismarketing of products. Journal of Public Policy & Marketing, 3, 113.

55. Neil A. Morgan, Kimberly A. Whitler, Hui Feng & Simos Chari.

(2018). Research in marketing strategy, Journal of the Academy of Marketing Science, 3. https://doi.org/10.1007/s11747-018-0598-1

56. Neuendorf, K. A. (2002). The content analysis guidebook. Thousand Oaks, CA: Sage.

57. Suris, O. (1993). Advertising: Ads aim to sell hush puppies to new yuppies. Wall Street Journal, pp. 84-86.

58. Verhoef, P. C., & Leeflang, P. S. (2009). Understanding the marketing departments influence within the firm. Journal of Marketing, 73(2), 14-37.

59. Verhoef, P. C., & Leeflang, P. S. (2010). Getting marketing back into the boardroom: The influence of the marketing department in companies today. GFK-Marketing Intelligence Review, 1(2), 34- 41.

60. Malin, Chris., (2008), Institutional Shareholers: their role in the shaping of corporate goevrnance, Intl. Journal of Corporate Governance, Vol.1, No.1

61. Libuda, Ł., 2016, Era Big Data - risk management, Bank. Miesięcznik Finansowy, 6 (278).

62. Litvak, Kate., (2008), Defensive Management: Does the Sarbanes-Oxley Act Discourage Corporate Risk-Taking?, Law and Economics Research Paper, No. 108

63. Lukas Y. Setia-Atmaja, (2009), Governance mechanisms, simultaneity and firm value in Australia, Intl. Journal of Corporate Governance, Vol.1, No.3

64. McNulty, Terry., Pettigrew, Andrew., Jobome, Greg., and Morris, Claire., (2009), The role, power and influence of companychairs, Journal of Management & Governance, Vol.15, No.1

65. Manz, Charles C., Stewart, Greg L., and Courtright, Stephen H., (2011), Self-Leadership: A Multilever Review, Journal of Management, Vol.37, No.1

66. Mahbub, T. (2021). The Implication of COVID-19 Pandemic on Banks Marketing Preferences. Retrieved from: https://ssrn.com/

abstract=3912742

67. Mulbert, Peter O., (2010), Corporate Governance of Banks after the Financial Crisis - Theory, Evidence, Reforms, ECGI Law Working Paper, No. 130/2009

68. Nätti, S., and I. Lähteenmäki. (2016). The evolution of market orientation in Finnish retail banking–from regulation to value creation. Management and Organizational History 11 (1): 28–47.

69. Ngân hàng Nhà nước Việt Nam, 2016, Báo cáo đánh giá tác động của cuộc cách mạng công nghiệp lần thứ tư và một số định hướng hoạt động của ngành Ngân hàng Việt Nam, Kỷ yếu hội thảo OECD;

70. *Ngân hàng Nhà nước Việt Nam, 2016: Báo cáo đánh giá tác động của cuộc cách mạng công nghiệp lần thứ tư và một số định hướng hoạt động của ngành Ngân hàng Việt Nam, Kỷ yếu hội thảo OECD (2016);*

71. Nguyễn Thị Hiền, ThS Đỗ Thị Bích Hồng – Viện chiến lược ngân hàng, 2017, Tác động của cách mạng công nghiệp lần thứ 4 tới lĩnh vực tài chính – ngân hàng, Tạp chí tài chính

72. Nghiêm Xuân Thành, 2017, "Cách mạng công nghiệp lần thứ 4 và sự chuẩn bị của ngành ngân hàng Việt Nam", tạp chí Tài chính kỳ 2- tháng 02/2017.

73. Parmigiani, Anne., Klassen, Robert D., and Russon, Michael V., (2011), Efficiency Meet Accountability: Performance Implications of Supply Chain Configuration, Control, and Capabilities, Journal of Operation Management, Vol.29, Issue 3

74. Priporas, Constantinos-Vasilios, Kamenidou, Irene, Nguyen, Nga and Shams, Riad (2020) *The impact of the macro-environment on consumer scepticism towards cause-related marketing: insights from an economic crisis setting.* International Marketing Review, 37 (5) . pp. 841-861.

75. *Prime Minister (2020), Directive No. 11 / CT-TTg dated 04/03/2020 on urgent tasks and solutions to remove difficulties for production and business, ensuring social security. deal with translation*

COVID-19;

76. Regulation (EU) 2019/881 of the European Parliament and of the Council of 17 April 2019 on ENISA (the European Union Agency for Cybersecurity) and on information and communications technology cybersecurity certification and repealing Regulation (EU) No 526/2013 (Cybersecurity Act)

77. Regulation (EU) 2016/679 of the European Parliament and of the Council of 27 April 2016 on the protection of natural persons with regard to the processing of personal data and on the free movement of such data, and repealing Directive 95/46/EC (General Data Protection Regulation)

78. Regulation (EU) No 513/2014 of the European Parliament and of the Council of 16 April 2014 establishing, as part of the Internal Security Fund, the instrument for financial support for police cooperation, preventing and combating crime, and crisis management and repealing Council Decision 2007/125/JHA

79. Regulation (EU) 2016/679 of the European Parliament and of the Council of 27 April 2016 on the protection of natural persons with regard to the processing of personal data and on the free movement of such data, and repealing Directive 95/46/EC (General Data Protection Regulation)

80. Salas, Eduardo., Rosen, Michael A., and DiazGranado, Deborah., (2010), Expertise-based Intuition and Decision Making in Organizations, Journal of Management, Vol.36, No.4

81. Siegel J. (2020), When The Internet of Things Flounders: Looking Into Gdpr-Esque Security Standards for Iot Devices in The United States From The Consumers' Perspective, Journal of High Technology Law, Vol. XX: No. 1, 2020

82. Tran Ngoc Huy, Dinh., (2010), A Set of Limited Asian Pacific Corporate Governance Standards After Financial Crisis, Corporate Scandals and Market Manipulation, Eurojournal, 2011

83. XiYing Zhang, Ivy., (2007),Economic consequences of the Sarbanes–Oxley Act of 2002, Journal of Accounting and Economics,

44 (2007) 74–115

84. OECD Corporate Governance Guidelines, OECD, 1999

85. The Emergency Economic Stabilization Act of 2008

86. Tricker, Bob., (2009), Corporate Governance: Principles, Policies and Practices, Oxford University Press, USA

87. Tapas Bala, Israt Jahan, Md. Al Amin, Mahmudul Haque Tanin, Md. Faridul slam, Md. Mahbubar Rahman, Tahira Khatun. (2021). Service Quality and Customer Satisfaction of Mobile Banking during COVID-19 Lockdown; Evidence from Rural Area of Bangladesh, Open Journal of Business and Management, 9(5)

88. The 2009 Principles of Corporate Governance for Listed Companies, Tokyo Stock Exchange, Inc.

89. 2009 White Paper on corporate Governance, Tokyo Stock Exchange

90. The Unofficial Corporate Governance Study Group Report, (2009), Ministry of Economy, Trade and Industry, Japan

91. Report on the Observance of Standards and Codes (ROSC)-The Philippines, World Bank, 2001

92. World Bank, World Development Report 2002:Building Institutions for Markets, 2001 (www.worldbank.org/ publications/); and Douglass C.North, Understanding the Process of Economic Change, 1999.

93. The Ministry of Finance, Circular No. 210 / TT-2009 / BTC guiding the application of international accounting standards on financial statement presentation and information disclosure for financial instruments, dated 6 / November 2009.

94. *The State Bank (2020), Circular No. 01/2020 / TT-NHNN dated 13/3/2020 regulating credit institutions, foreign bank branches to restructure the time limit for debt payment, exemption from , reducing interest and fees, keeping the debt group intact to support customers affected by COVID-19 translation;*

95. Thomsen, Steen., (2008), A Minimum Theory of Boards, Intl.

Journal of Corporate Governance, Vol.1, No.1

96. Tsai, C.-F., Huang, H.T., Jaw, Y.L., Chen, W.K.: Why on-line customers remain with a particular e-retailer: an integrative model and empirical evidence. Psychol. Market. 23(5), 447–464 (2008)

97. Trinh Thi Phan Lan, Financial risk management in Vietnamese enterprises, VNU Journal of Science: Economics and Business, Volume 32, No. 3 (2016) p51-59.

98. Vu Thi Hau, "Financial risks of industrial enterprises", Doctoral thesis, 2014.

99. Wang, Mo., and Shultz., Kenneth S., (2010), Employee Retirement: A Review and Recommendations for Future Investigation, Journal of Management, Vol.36, No.1

100.   Warren J., Marz N., 2016, Big Data. Best practices for building scalable real-time data systems, Warsaw.

101.   www.ecgi.org/codes

102.   http://www.corpgov.deloitte.com/site/ChinaEng/

103.   http://www.corpgov.deloitte.com/site/in/

104.   www.cfainstitute.org

105.   http://corporategovernanceoup.wordpress.com/

106.   http://info.worldbank.org/etools/docs/library/

107.   http://www.ifc.org/ifcext/corporategovernance.nsf/content/

108.   http://www.kpmg.com/aci/additional.htm

109.   www.thecorporatelibrary.com

110.   www.fic.wharton.upenn.edu

111.   http://www.eciia.eu/

112.   www.koreanlaw.com

113.   www.australian-corporate-governance.com.au/corp_gov_

codes.htm

114. www.iasplus.com

115. www.cbc.to

116. https://forbesvietnam.com.vn/tin-cap-nhat/wb-dieu-chinh-trien-vongtang- truong-gdp-viet-nam-nam-2020-down- the-49-10027. html.

117. Cục Thông tin khoa học và công nghệ Quốc gia, 2016, "Cuộc cách mạng công nghiệp lần thứ 4", truy cập tại website http://www. vista.gov.vn/LinkClick.aspx?fileticket=BDbI9Fg5FhY%3d&tabid= 152&language=vi-VN

118. Singh, Ankit, How is Marketing Management Related with Supply Chain Management? (September 26, 2013). Available at SSRN: https://ssrn.com/abstract=2394476 or http://dx.doi. org/10.2139/ssrn.2394476

Index

Appendix 1- Implementation form for Marketing activities in companies

Recommended Practices Form used in Organization

(Form Code: MM_01)

Name of Company:………………………….

Name of department:……………………………..

Name of position:…………………………………..

Name of person:………………………………………..

Date:………/………./………Revision:……….

I - BACKGROUND INFORMATION

- FACTORS AFFECT BUSINESS ENVIRONMENT AND MARKETING ACTIVITY IN FISCAL YEAR

- SWOT IN MARKETING IN FISCAL YEAR

II - KEY MARKETING INDICES IDENTIFICATION AND MEASURING MARKETING ACTIVITY

Analyzing and evaluating:………

III- RECOMMENDATIONs FOR MARKETING STRATEGY AND MARKETING PLANS

…………

Signed by Marketing officer (M.O)/ Approval by (CMO…….)

(Note: CMO or person in charge is responsible for implementing this practice)

Appendix 2- Implementation form for Competitor -Based Marketing in companies

Recommended Practices Form used in Organization

(Form Code: MM_02)

Name of Company:............................

Name of department:.....................................

Name of position:..

Name of person:...

Date:........./........./.........Revision:..........

I - OVERVIEW OF COMPETITION ENVIRONMENT

- ANALYSIS OF COMPETITORS , TARGETS, AND SUBSTITUTES

- ANALYSIS OF COMPETITORS BUSINESS AND MARKETING MIX STRATEGIES

II - ANALYSIS OF STRENGTHS AND WEAKNESSES OF COMPETITORS

- Market share, clients loyalty, revenue, sales, ROI, production, inventory, investment....

- Strengths and weaknesses, difference and similarities in products and marketing mix

- Discuss and comments:.........

III- RECOMMENDATIONs FOR OUR FIRM RESPONSES IN MARKETING STRATEGY

- Recommendations

- ....

-What market trends our firms can create...

Signed by Marketing officer (M.O)/ Approval by (CMO.......)

(Note: CMO or person in charge is responsible for implementing this practice)

Appendix 3 – Implementation Form of Twelve (12) Comparative Marketing Principles and Twenty Two (22) Marketing Standards

Recommended Practices Form used in Organization

(Form Code: MM_03)

Name of Company:………………………

Name of department:………………………..

Name of position:…………………………..

Name of person:……………………………..

Date:………/………/………Revision:……….

No.	Principle	Recommended Practices
1		
2		
3		
4		
5	………………………	
……12		
No.	Standard	Recommended Practices
1		
2		
3		
4		
…..22		

(Note: The CMO or person in charge is responsible for implementing this practice)

Appendix 4

User Manual

For Business people, the book serves as handbook and reference book.

Guides for Professors and Students, but not limited to:

Necessary tasks advised for students suggested as following:

- Read the case and case summary;

- Identify the problem(s);

- Summarize the information and relevant data;

- Prepare key issues for group meeting, if any;

- Group meeting;

- Select meeting secretariat;

- Analyze the information and data;

- Re-consider the problem(s);

- Answer the question quickly;

- Develop alternatives to deal with the problems(s);

- Assess and evaluate the advantages and disadvantages of each alternative;

- Recommend a proper alternative;

- Recommend a next implementation plan;

- Create a formal presentation of the whole process.

Appendix 5 - Integrated Framework for Customer-oriented Business Model Development (Source: Bernd W. Wirtz and Peter Daiser, 2018)

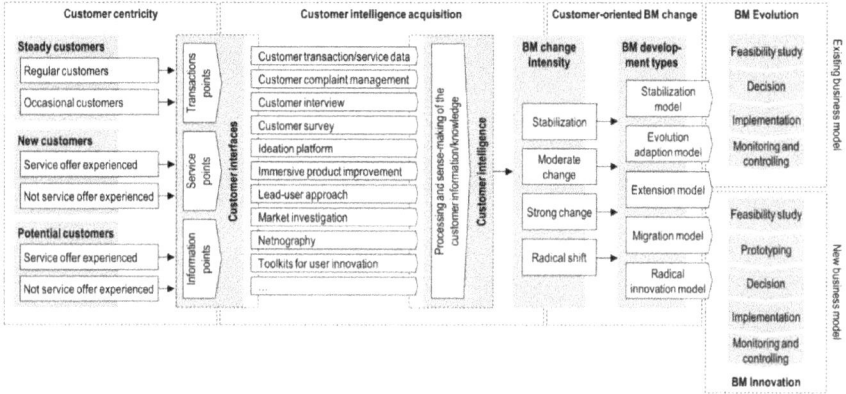

Appendix 6 - Corresponding Author

RESUME

Dinh Tran Ngoc Huy

Address: 616/23 Cach Mang Thang Tam street, Ward 11, Dist 3, Ho Chi Minh city, Viet Nam

Current address: 100 road 20 Binh Hung Hoa ward, Binh tan dist, HCM city Vietnam

Telephone:(848)39934160-CellPhone:(84)936410639-Email:dtnhuy2010@gmail.com

Date of Birth:16/Nov/1980-Place of Birth:Ho Chi Minh city -Citizenship: Viet Nam -Sex: Male-www.dinhslife.blogspot.com

EMPLOYMENT HISTORY

	From	To	Location	Company, Position	Research and Training
Work History	2002	2005	Ho Chi Minh city, VietNam	Bank for Investment and Development of VietNam (BIDV) *Financial analyst and Project Financing* - Financial statement analysis - Project financing for 20 SMEs -Advised and served 25 effective Vietnamese businesses, - Consulted 10 Businesses in opening L/C for importing machines - Offered presentations on granting loans for real estate & housing projects	- Applying auditing in Credit activities, BIDV - Modern banking, Banking University
	09/01/07	11/01/0 7	Ho Chi Minh city, VietNam	**Citibank** *Assistant Manager*	- Antimoney Laundering - Cash sales activities
	2008	2009	Ho Chi Minh city, VietNam	**1. SaiGon Commercial Bank** *Market risk dept. manager* *ISO project manager* - Manage the ISO 9001:2008 project team with 9 people - Implement ISO standards in the whole - System, esp. in International payment, Credit areas - Certificate: Lead Auditor QMS ISO	- Internal Audit ISO 9001, MC Co. - Lead Auditor, GIC Ltd., UK - SMEs management assessment, APO-Japan
				9000:2001 - Manage Market risk division with 4 team members - Analyze interest rate risk, credit risk, liquidity risk and banking market competition - Produce database forms **2. COFICO** *Finance manager*	
	2009	current	Ho Chi Minh city, VietNam	**University of Economics, Hung Vuong, Van Lang and IT Colleges** *Finance Lecturer* - Teach undergraduate students : Theories of Monetary and Fiscal Policy, Commercial banking and Credit Appraisal	- Certificate of Education methods in University

EDUCATION

	From	To	Location	Name
High School	1995	1998	Phan Thiet city, VietNam	**Tran Hung Dao high school**
University	1998	2002	HCM city, Viet Nam	**Banking University** - Bachelor of Economics (Major: Finance) - Thesis: "Project Appraisal from risk-management perspective at BIDV"
Graduate School	2005	2007	Niigata city, Japan	**International University of Japan** - MBA in International Management (Major: Finance with Management courses) - Thesis: "M&A: Corporate restructuring – NTT case" - Course committee: Macro Economics and Debt Securities Markets - Teaching Assistant of Corporate Finance & Strategic Management, Research Assistant for Corporate Finance Professor - Participant of a training program for freshmen at Itochu
	07/01/06	08/01/06	Arhus city, Denmark	**Arhus business school** - Taking Project management course by applying SimVision
	09/01/06	12/01/06	New Hampshire, USA	**Tuck school of business** - Taking MBA exchange with Finance and Management courses
Graduate School	08/2010	08/2014	Taiwan	**Chung Yuan Christian University** - PhD in Finance (full scholarship)

PROFESSIONAL QUALIFICATIONS

Certifications and Accreditations

MBA degree (Finance and Management electives)

Lead Auditor ISO 9001 (2008)

SMEs management assessment certificate (2008)

Best Scientist Award (2020)

AWARDS

IUJ's Chairman Compliment paper for IUJ Brandname enhancement and contribution to academic activity(07)

Asian Development Bank scholarship (full) for MBA study (2005-2007)

Banking University Director's yearly scholarship and compliment paper for contributions to the University and research activities (1999-2002)

SKT Telecom full scholarship for IT training (till 7/2010)

PhD (Finance) full scholarship (2010-2014)

PUBLICATIONS, WORKING PAPERS & CONFERENCES

"Thoughts of a training program of 300 Masters and Doctors", SGGP Newspaper, Viet Nam, 2005

Presentation at Urasa Conference, Japan (www.iuj.ac.jp/platform/pdf/s7-2.pdf), 2007

 "Corporate restructuring under holding company structure- NTT case", 2010. You can access my papers on the Social Science Research Network (SSRN) at http://ssrn.com/abstract=1723195 and posted at **Organizations & Markets: The Firm as a Nexus of Contracts (Boundaries of the Firm) eJournal**

"Should SA Tour use external financing to expand MICE business in China and Singapore markets", 2010. At : http://papers.ssrn.com/sol3/papers.cfm?abstract_id=1724615 , accepted at 1st Intl Business & Management Conference, Turkey (2011), see abstract at: http://www.icbmconference.net/ , and posted at **Cognitive Social Science eJournal**, 2010.

Other paper at: http://papers.ssrn.com/sol3/papers.cfm?abstract_id=1730278 and posted at IO: Firm Structure, Purpose, Organization & Contracting eJournal

 "A Set of Limited Asian Pacific Corporate Governance Standards After Financial Crisis", paper accepted at the 36th Economic and Historical Business Society Conference, Ohio, USA and posted at Corporate Finance: Governance, Corporate Control & Organization eJournal, 2011.

Published about 200 articles in international prestigous journals (ISI, Scopus and other...) + 15 books/book chapters (some books available via www.amazon.com)

TRAINING MATERIAL

Credit Appraisal in commercial bank, at Van Lang University, 2009

INTERESTS and COMPUTER SKILLS

Soccer, badminton, table-tennis, dancing, volleyball. Playing the organ and harmonica

Excel, Ms Office, Crystal ball, Spreadsheet modeling, Java, HTML, Javascript, Jquery, Bloomberg, DataStream Advanced, Macromedia, Solver, teaching, research, presentation, teamwork, Sim Vision, Visio

LANGUAGES

Vietnamese: Native ; English : Advanced (TOEFL 600); Japanese and Korean: Elementary.

Appendix 7 – Author Resume – Dinh Tran Ngoc Hien

CURRICULUM VITAE
ĐINH TRẦN NGỌC HIỂN

Email : ngochienbk01@yahoo.com

PERSONAL INFORMATION

Full name   : Đinh Trần Ngọc Hiển

Date of birth   : 17th March, 1986

Place of birth   : Binh Thuan

Material status   : Single

Home address   : 616/23 Cách Mạng Tháng 8 Street, Ward 11, District 3, HCMC

Mobile phone   : 0122 222 4061

Email address   : ngochienbk01@yahoo.com

SOCIAL & EXTRACURRICULAR ACTIVITIES

* Take part in Humanitarian Blood Donation

* Help students with College-entrance Examinations

* Join English Speaking Club, Youth Foreign Language School

* Computer skills

  • AutoCad (Grade of Certificate: Excellent)

  • Microsoft Project (Good)

  • Microsoft Word, Excel, Power Point (Good)

  • PSim, OrCad, MatLab (Moderate)

* Social or Life Skill
  * Presentation
  * Team work
  * Communication
  * Time management

PART TIME JOBS

* P&G Viet Nam, HCM city, HR department (2010)

HOBBIES

* Playing Electric Organ
* Listening to music
* Watching movie
* Traveling

Appendix 8 - Marketing library creating

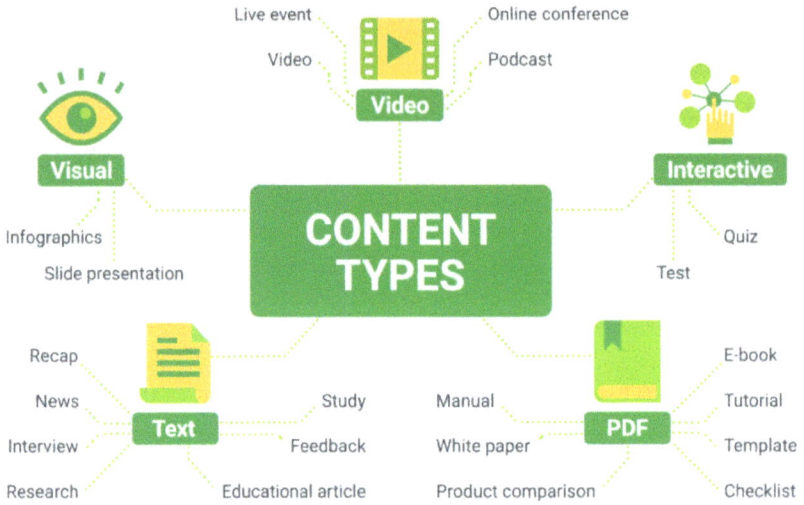

(Source: reliablesoft.net, access date 17/1/2022)

Appendix 9 - Smart RACE framework (source: Bsmartinsights.com/tag/race-planning-system/)

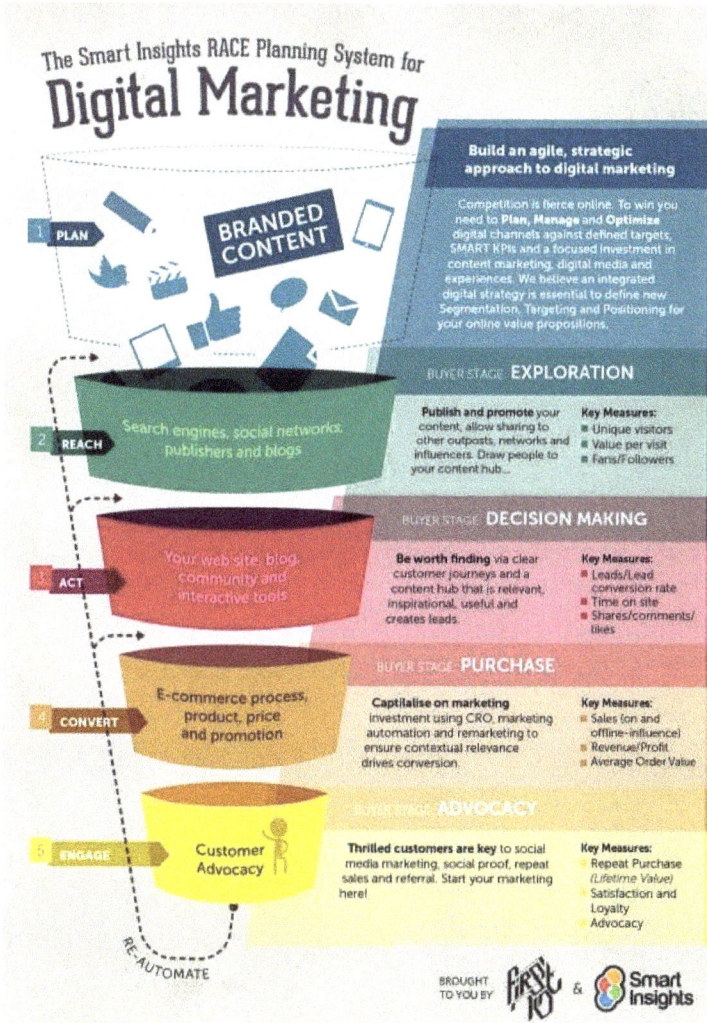

www.ingramcontent.com/pod-product-compliance
Lightning Source LLC
Chambersburg PA
CBHW040845210326
41597CB00029B/4729